The
Beginner's
Guide to
Collecting
Investing
and Starting
Your Own
Business

YOUR

1st

BOOK OF

Wealth

The
Beginner's
Guide to
Collecting
Investing
and Starting
Your Own
Business

YOUR

BOOK OF

1st
Wealth

A. David Silver

The Career Press
PO Box 34
Hawthorne, NJ 07507
1-800-CAREER-1
(In New Jersey: 201-427-0229)

Your First Book of Wealth, ISBN 0-934829-47-0, $10.95.

Figures 1, 2, & 9 copyright © 1987 A. David Silver, originally published in his book <u>Who's Who in Venture Capital</u>, John Wiley & Sons, Inc. Reprinted with permission.

The section on opening a brokerage account and stock or bond power in chapter 12 was adapted from <u>The Woman's Guide to the Stock Market</u> copyright © 1982 by Barbara Lee and used by permission of Harmony Books, a division of Crown Publishers, Inc.

Copies of this volume may be ordered by mail or phone directly from the publisher. To order by mail, please include price as noted above plus $1.00 shipping and handling for each book ordered. Send to: The Career Press Inc., 62 Beverly Rd., PO Box 34, Hawthorne, NJ 07507.

Or call Toll-Free 1-800-CAREER-1 (in New Jersey: 201-427-0229) to order using your VISA or Mastercard or for further information on all books published or distributed by The Career Press.

The
Beginner's
Guide to
Collecting
Investing
and Starting
Your Own
Business

YOUR

1st

BOOK OF

Wealth

Preface

How To Use This Book

Read everything—don't skip a chapter or even a page. Even if you are convinced your destiny is to be a stockbroker and aren't the least bit interested in collecting art or starting your own business, don't skip those chapters. You're too young to define your goals so narrowly and too inexperienced to be certain just what you may need to know in the future. (Many stockbrokers make enough money to consider investing in art or antiques!)

The best way to learn anything is to do it, so complete the individual exercises that appear at the end of each chapter. Some are intended to clarify concepts in the book or make sure you understand the basic formulas you need to know; others to introduce you to the "real world" of business and finance by suggesting trips, projects and research tasks. *(Teachers Please Note: There is a special list of suggested projects and field trips for a whole class in Appendix I. I hope these will help you formulate your own lesson plans using this book.)*

You will come across many new words in this book. Rather than interrupt the flow of each chapter with definitions and explanations, I have created a glossary—Appendix II—that you can consult. Every technical term from the fields of business, finance or economics—as well as any concepts I think may be new to you—has been underlined in the text the first time it appears and defined in this extensive glossary. Terms appear in the glossary even if rudimentarily defined in the text itself, often with more detailed explanations or more extensive examples.

If there's anything you still don't understand, feel free to write me a letter, in care of the publisher, with your questions. I will try to answer them all.

Now, let's get on with this exciting process of wealth creation.

Introduction

Do the rich *really* get richer while the poor stay poor?
Yep. They really do.

Which is why books on how to get richer are nice, but not
exactly needed. The rich always have options and opportunities to make more money, simply because they already have
their stake and *money makes more money.*

Trust me, getting rich*er* is not a difficult problem. (If it
were, that saying wouldn't be ages old.) Getting rich *in the
first place* is the tough part.

**Money makes
more money.**

This book will probably not make you truly rich—it isn't
intended to be a slap-dash "get-rich-quick" bible, especially
since most people *don't* get rich quick. It will, however, help
you understand the concept of wealth and how to create it.
By revealing the basic process of wealth creation and discussing the potential roads to travel, I hope to give you the head
start on a most exciting journey that, over time, *will* surely
lead to the riches you want.

Money Doesn't Know That All Men Are Created Equal

Even when I was just a boy, it was obvious to me that
while all men may be *created* equal, some of them seemed to
have a lot more money than others and, as a result, seemed
to lead very different lives than the rest of us. When I was
growing up, there were a number of families in my hometown, Knoxville, Tennessee, that had bigger houses, more
cars and/or bigger boats than others. They made larger
contributions to charities, took more interesting vacations
and entertained more. Their conversations seemed livelier,
their laughter louder, their smiles broader.

Especially during the Jewish High Holy Days, when

families took time from their busy lives to come to the synagogue, I was able to observe everyone in that sector of the community and to draw my first tentative conclusions about why some people were wealthy and others were not. I would make the same observations at school events to which parents were invited.

When I became a teenager and travelled to other cities in the South—Chattanooga, Memphis, Nashville, Birmingham, New Orleans—I saw examples of wealth unheard of in Knoxville—the great horse farms near Nashville, the campus of Vanderbilt University, the huge medical complex in Memphis, the Tulane University campus in New Orleans, and the huge homes on Lookout Mountain near Chattanooga.

I could observe, but since I hadn't a clue as to how wealth was created, I lacked the background to understand the concept of wealth on any level. It simply baffled me—there seemed to be no common visible traits or characteristics that distinguished wealthy people from non-wealthy people. Some were smarter, some weren't. Some handsomer, others not. Yet there *had* to be something different about them. What, besides their bank balance, was it?

None of my teachers could answer my simple question, "What is wealth?"

School Won't Teach You About Wealth

The high school that I attended provided a solid foundation in English, American history and mathematics, as well as all the sports and extracurricular activities I could ever want. However, none of my teachers could answer my simple question, "What is wealth?"

When I entered the University of Chicago, I quickly learned the names of abundantly wealthy families, because many of the buildings on campus were named for them. There was Rockefeller Chapel, one of many monuments to wealth created in the pioneering days of the young oil industry. Rosenwald Hall, named for Julius Rosenwald, an early investor in Sears, Roebuck & Co. The Field Museum of Natural History was nearby, named for the founder of a department store chain, Marshall Field & Co.

But none of my college professors could answer my questions about wealth.

After four years of college I entered the University of Chicago Graduate School of Business to study for a masters degree in finance. Surely, I thought, one of the professors at the Graduate School of *Business* could explain to me how wealth was created.

Wrong.

Business School students learned about accounting, banking, marketing and a variety of important tools young men and women needed to manage a business, but nothing about the creation of wealth.

I took several courses on <u>investments</u>, figuring that was as good a place as any to finally learn about wealth. These professors, supposedly, actually knew something about wealth...at least *their* definition of it—"the pile of cash" a person used to invest in the <u>stock market</u>. None of these professors, however, understood how to create that pile of cash in the first place.

Learning About Wealth By Creating It For Others

My formal education was ended, yet nearly two decades of schooling had added little to my specific quest for knowledge about wealth creation. It was obvious I would have to learn on my own why some people were wealthy and others were not. Only then could I begin to figure out how to go about creating my own wealth.

Chase Manhattan Bank hired me and trained me to be a loan officer. I began to meet a variety of businesspeople who wanted to borrow money from the <u>bank</u>. The more of them I met, the more I realized that the opinions formed as a boy in Knoxville were still pretty valid: People who had started their own companies were more enthusiastic about what they were doing. The employees of large <u>corporations</u> seemed far more concerned about avoiding mistakes than anything else.

The more exciting borrowers talked about their dreams, their plans, their ideas and their need for Chase Manhattan's money to help them realize these goals. The corporate employees were bright, well-prepared professionals and made good presentations, but they were uptight and boring p*eople*. Unfortunately, I saw more boring borrowers than exciting ones, so I left Chase Manhattan in search of the kind of people I wanted to be and work with.

An <u>investment bank</u> by the name of Kuhn, Loeb & Co. hired me. (An investment bank raises *serious* money—sometimes billions of dollars—to help companies expand their

People who had started their own companies were more enthusiastic about what they were doing.

operations or acquire other companies.) Kuhn, Loeb was a small company, only 150 employees, and was owned by 30 partners. After a brief training period, I began writing programs for Kuhn, Loeb's brand new IBM computer, having learned both Fortran and COBOL programming languages at Business School.

One of the partners decided that since I seemed to be adept at computers, maybe I could use them to locate some promising little companies for the company to invest in. Well, this accident finally put me in a position to find out how wealth was created—the partners were asking me to go out and create it for *them*. Since nobody had ever been able to explain to me how it was done, I supposed I could do it as well as anyone else.

My first recommendation was a small company called Automatic Data Processing Corp. (ADP) Corporate payroll checks had become more tedious to prepare because of all the deductions for Federal and state taxes, social security and insurance. A major firm with thousands or tens of thousands of employees had to spend an enormous amount of time and money just figuring all the deductions for each employee and preparing those checks. ADP had programmed formulas for these deductions into its computers, which permitted it to prepare large numbers of payroll checks more quickly and less expensively than the large corporations could themselves.

The need was there, and ADP filled it—a formula I soon would learn was a harbinger of success in almost any endeavor. And I liked the enthusiasm of ADP's managers and founders—Henry Taub, Joseph Taub and Frank Lautenberg—who had exciting ideas about expanding from a small New Jersey company to a nationwide operation.

The partners at Kuhn, Loeb followed my recommendation, investing in ADP and raising money from other investors as well. As ADP grew from $6 million in annual sales in 1966—when I first "discovered" it—to a major, highly-profitable corporation, the founders, managers and early investors in ADP created wealth. The first glimmer of an answer to my teenage question began to glow.

The Best Kind of Learning— Creating Wealth for Myself

I stayed with Kuhn, Loeb for a few more years. I learned a great deal from the founders of ADP about how a small business grows, and I applied this information in my search for other small companies. I got pretty good at spotting promising small companies for the partners to invest in.

Another company that I recommended was Chevway, which helped automobile dealers get into the automobile leasing business. The Kuhn, Loeb partners earned over $50 million on their investment in Chevway, and they rewarded me with a small investment in it as well. In a remarkably short time, my Chevway shares grew to $250,000, more than 25 times my annual salary. To me, *that* was wealth, and I had finally created it for myself. I was 26 years old.

My first thought about having some wealth of my own was that it was certainly a lot better than income, that weekly check everyone strived for. With wealth of my own, if I wanted to buy something expensive, I didn't have to wait for a raise or a bonus; I merely sold some stock and bought what I wanted. My wife and I took a trip to Europe and bought a car and a country house. And, of course, I kept trying to find other companies like ADP or Chevway for the partners to invest in, because I certainly liked the way they rewarded me.

Despite my seeming success as an "investment hunter," the partners wanted me to learn other investment banking tasks, such as doing studies for some of their larger corporate clients. This took time away from my major purpose— creating wealth, preferably for myself. It also meant that I had to deal with employees of big corporations and government agencies, not the lively, exciting founders of small companies whom I preferred to be with. I became dissatisfied with my job.

So in 1970, having just turned 29, I left Kuhn, Loeb and went into business for myself, hoping to help entrepreneurs raise money to start or expand their companies. At last I was working on a daily basis with exciting people who had big, ambitious plans, just the people I wanted to be with. And they lacked the money to realize those plans, money I hoped to provide.

Of course, I had to *find* that money first—I lacked both the personal wealth of Kuhn, Loeb's partners and a handy list of wealthy friends to tap for investments in the many small companies that came to me, so the first thing I did was start to find my own group of investors.

My travels were eye-opening. It finally became clear that whatever wealth was, it was *not* simply "a pile of cash." It was a process, a circle that widened and widened as it made more and more investments in small, promising companies.

Whatever wealth was, it was not simply "a pile of cash."

During my first couple of years in business, I helped nearly two dozen small companies raise <u>start-up money</u>. With every company, I learned more about the wealth creation process. I began to feel that I could even teach it to others.

Those Who Can Do And Teach, Write Books

I began to write books about the wealth creation process in 1975, and I have written one book per year since then. The books are used by founders of new businesses to help them do the right thing, by investors to help them select the best small companies to invest in and in universities to teach those students who want to start their own businesses after graduation.

This book is written for a much younger audience, those of you who are just as baffled about the whole concept of wealth as I was as a boy in Knoxville over 30 years ago. It will, I am sure, answer the many questions you have about wealth and its creation, answers it took me so long to find. (If you're over 18, please don't exclude yourself—if you know little or nothing about the world of finance, investing, collecting, etc., this book is certainly for you, too.)

I intend to give away thousands of copies of this book to hospitals, orphanages and agencies that take care of poor and underprivileged children. I would find it particularly satisfying to help the poorest children in America learn how to be wealthy.

Can this book help a poor child become a wealthy adult willing to share his or her wealth by returning it to the community? You bet it can. It's my dream. And if I can dream it, then it can happen.

Just like your dreams can.

Intro Individual Exercises & Projects

1. Visit your local library and research the biographies or autobiographies of a variety of highly successful men and women. How'd they do it? How many started their own companies? How many inherited a lot of money? How many worked for someone else? In other words, how did each of them create wealth? List the specific areas or industries in which they spent their careers. Do any stand out?

2. Visit your local bank and ask about the minimum amount required to open a checking or savings account. Then, if you haven't already done so and can afford to, open your own account(s). Before you do so, make sure you get literature from the bank on the different types of accounts available and list the merits and demerits of each.

3. Let's get even more familiar with your local bank—make a list of services they offer besides just holding your money. Do they make loans? To whom? For what? Do they offer their own versions of major credit cards? Talk with various bank personnel until you understand the services the bank offers and when and how you would use each in your own life.

4. Ask your mom or dad about how payroll deductions work. And, if they'll let you, ask to be involved at tax time when they fill out the various Federal and State tax forms.

5. Ask your parents if they'll let you be involved in the family budgeting. (Note: Not all parents will welcome their children's involvment in their personal finances. Don't be upset if yours don't!) Where does the family money go? Can you help your parents reduce expenses so they could redirect some of their income(s) to things you could all do together—a vacation, special trip, special purchase?

1

What Is Wealth?

In its simplest form, wealth means *maximizing your options*—having a sufficiently large pile of cash so that you have the option of doing anything you want whenever you want to do it. *If you **have** to work, you are not wealthy.* If you are free to do charity work full-time, tend your garden, manage your investments or simply do nothing at all without having to worry about how you're going to pay for food, clothing and shelter for yourself and your family, you *are* wealthy.

Or, as Mark Twain put it: "Work consists of whatever anybody is obliged to do. Play consists of whatever anybody is not obliged to do."

The Entrepreneurial Credo:
You've Got A Problem, I've Got A Solution

Another way to view the concept of wealth and its creation is as a problem-solving process.

In a free society such as ours, whenever a group of people have a <u>problem</u>, an entrepreneur will undoubtedly attempt to provide a <u>solution</u>. The *group* may be a company needing a new <u>product</u>, expertise or advice, a part of the population needing a particular service or product no one is currently offering or people requiring a *better* service or *better* product than is currently available.

The entrepreneurial *solution* may be providing the advice or <u>strategic planning</u> a company requires to expand its services or <u>product line</u> or founding a company to provide innovative products or services needed by a well-defined segment of the population.

Whichever problems an entrepreneur is prepared to solve, he or she must be assured that it is worth his or her effort. In a <u>free market</u>, if those with the problem believe that the entrepreneur's solution has value—*if it's worth its price*—and if it removes or lessens that problem—*if it does what it's supposed to do*—then they will pay the entrepreneur fair value for his or her solution. In time, these payments—<u>returns</u> on the entrepreneur's initial investment—will add up to wealth, both for the entrepreneur and for his or her investors.

The creation of wealth is an ever-widening circle of giving.

Some examples of successful entrepreneurs include: Dr. Edwin H. Land, whose polaroid camera and instant photography, when introduced in the 1950s, addressed the problem of having to wait several weeks to have photographs developed; Chester Carlson, whose Xerox copiers solved the problem of messy, time-consuming and difficult-to-correct mimeograph copiers; and Raymond A. Kroc, whose McDonald hamburger chain provided fast, quality meals in convenient suburban locations to busy two-income families.

The Land, Carlson and Kroc fortunes, now somewhat smaller because of charitable contributions, were at one time each in excess of $1 billion.

The Entrepreneur As Gift Giver

The entrepreneur's initial investment—the capital, concept, idea strategy, product and/or service that solve someone else's problem—is a <u>gift</u>, but *not* a selfless one. This gift is one offered with the *full expectation that equal value will be returned*.

This expectation of <u>reciprocity</u> impels the entrepreneur to develop the solution—a better camera, a more efficient office copier or a fast-food chain. If the entrepreneur believed that he would not recover the cost of creating and conveying a solution, plus a <u>profit</u> to enable him or her to expand and improve the solution, then he or she would never have attempted to solve the problem in the first place. In societies where people are not free—where the government employs virtually everyone and sets limits on rewards for problem solving—nobody solves problems; they have no incentive to do so. Have you used any Russian inventions lately? No. There haven't been many.

If a gift can be defined as the solution to a problem the entrepreneur expects will be reciprocated, wealth can be defined as that which is created in this gift-giving process.

It's a process with far-reaching benefits for everyone involved in it, including you and me, because we are all members of that great big <u>marketplace</u> called the economy. Even when an entrepreneur introduces a new product or service that solves a problem for one group of people, the rest of us still benefit from the increased choices we are thus afforded in the marketplace.

As the company's kinds of services or product line expands and improves and more people buy them, it will need more raw materials, more employees, more suppliers. The companies from which it buys these materials will need more employees. And as all these new employees move to the entrepreneur's town, *they'll* need more services—school teachers, plumbers, beauticians, policemen, etc. Jobs are created all down the line.

As the company continues to expand and create its own wealth, <u>foundations</u> are formed, community groups funded, charitable gifts extended...not to mention what the various levels of government do with the increased taxes paid by this now-thriving corporation.

The payments to the entrepreneur—the return of his gift—will enable his or her company to expand, too, creating even more jobs. Eventually, the entrepreneur and his or her investors will reinvest their wealth in the gift-giving ideas of the next generation of entrepreneurs, funding more companies that will create more needed products and services. And more wealth for more people. The Kroc family, for example, has given away more than $500 million to fund Ronald McDonald houses and cancer research, among other charities.

Thus, the entrepreneurial process creates wealth and distributes it throughout the community with practically every sector benefiting. This constant creation, investment and reinvestment of wealth is a process I call the ever-widening circle of giving. You may know it by its more mundane name—economic growth.

Those particularly suited to the entrepreneurial road to wealth creation, as opposed to those better suited to earning income, perceive things differently...especially their own actions. I walked up to a mason one day who was building an arch for a new church and asked him what he was making. He answered, "$20 an hour." The next day I visited the same church and asked another mason what he was making. He answered, "An arch." The third day I

By observing people at their work, you can frequently distinguish the gift-givers (entrepreneurs) from the problem-finders.

asked yet another mason what he was making. He answered, "A beautiful cathedral."

By observing people at their work, you can frequently distinguish the gift-givers (entrepreneurs) from the problem-finders.

Wealth Isn't Free; The Entrepreneur Must Be

It is impossible to create wealth in countries where the people are not free, since there is no circle of giving in such nations. It is a fact easily verified through your own experience that a person simply will not give a gift unless he or she believes that it will be reciprocated in some way. Whether that reciprocation is money, products in kind (barter) or simply the "good feeling" someone gets from making a charitable donation, *some*thing must be received back. This reciprocal act—payment in some form—creates the incentive for the first round of gift-giving. Where such incentives do not exist, the gift-giving process will never get started.

Freedom cannot exist without wealth.

The opposite is also true: Freedom cannot exist without wealth. America has always been free because it has always been entrepreneurial. And it has always been entrepreneurial because it has always been free. When politicians who do not understand the link between freedom and wealth make laws that diminish the rewards for being entrepreneurial, the country experiences a recession or depression. On the other hand, when entrepreneurs find the wealth creation process too simple, with rewards greatly exceeding costs, people start believing that everything is going up in value and the country experiences inflation. Neither recession, depression nor inflation are positive experiences, but they do concentrate the mind on becoming more moderate and rational. Free societies have a built-in mechanism for correcting the excesses of lawmakers and entrepreneurs—a mechanism known as the free market.

If people do not believe they have the opportunity to achieve wealth via the gift-giving process, they will simply choose whatever process is available, usually anti-social ones like force or theft. The greater the poverty and the less chance people perceive they have to achieve wealth via the gift-giving process, the more likely they will fall prey to a dictatorial leader ready to promise solutions to all their problems. In the short run, life under the dictator will seem to improve, particularly if his army invades other countries and robs them of *their* principal products. But eventually, the leader will build an ever-expanding bureaucracy (including, more than likely, a well-equipped army) to hold onto his or her power. To pay for these expenditures, the people will be taxed more than ever. The circle of poverty widens. Eventually, there's another revolution, another leader, another period of aggression, taxation and fascism.

To survive in such an oppressive society, people always seem to turn to the same solution—stealing from the government. Small quantities of factory parts start to find their way home with the workers, who, in the true spirit of wealth creation, assemble them into useful gifts they can sell to others. With the money earned, factory managers can be bribed to turn a blind eye to more extensive stealing. The ever-spiraling profits generated can then be used to pay bigger bribes to government officials for the purchase of products and services, travel visas, permits to own automobiles, permits to buy houses, etc. Thus is the <u>black market,</u> one completely outside the normal government-run economy, born. Notice that in their own way, these budding entrepreneurs are creating their own gift-giving process and finding ways to ensure reciprocity.

The very fact that the black market exists in such countries proves to me that the wealth-creation process is understood, perhaps instinctively, even by people who have never lived in a free country. I could even make a case that the poorer the person, the more oppressive their country of origin, the greater their chance of becoming wealth creators once they are given the opportunity. If you show a starving person how to become a gift-giver and the benefits that he or she can receive by solving problems for others, he tends to respond with abundant energy and enthusiasm. The same lesson taught to the heirs of a wealthy entrepreneur—children and grandchildren who grew up with the luxuries wealth can buy without having to learn about the process (or do anything to create it for themselves)—will tend to fall on bored-deaf ears.

Doing Things Right Vs. Doing The Right Thing

If you think about your experiences at school, on sports teams or in dating, I think you'll readily agree that you earn significantly bigger rewards for *doing the right thing* than

Wealth arises from doing the right thing, not from doing things right.

for *doing things right*. Doing the right thing is exercising good judgment, whether moral or entrepreneurial—for example, forming an after-school activity to help disadvantaged people in the community or acting responsibly and accountably to negotiate a serious dispute between two friends. Doing things right means carrying out a task skillfully—writing a good book report, hitting a grand slam, learning all the newest dance steps.

You can learn to do things right in a number of skill areas and the small rewards that you receive throughout your life—fees, commissions, salaries and bonuses, all of which are called income—may well be satisfaction enough for you. The average working person's income in the United States today is around $22,000 per year. Assuming that most people work 40 hours per week and 50 weeks a year, the average wage paid for doing things right is about $11 per hour.

Income rises dramatically for doing a *unique* thing right—anything requiring a skill that is in short supply and/or requires time to develop. The more unique your skill and the greater the audience for it, the greater your potential income. Actors such as Robert DeNiro and Tom Hanks receive salaries in the millions *plus* bonuses—a percentage of the profits earned by the movies in which they appear. Musicians like Guns n' Roses, U-2, Debbie Gibson and Bruce Springsteen receive income from record sales and concert tickets and bonuses, too—royalties every time their music is played on the radio. Such income may slightly exceed $11 an hour—Michael Jackson, for example, earned over $50 million from a single album, *Thriller*.

But most of us simply don't have the talents of a Tom Hanks or Michael Jackson. Our skills are not sufficiently unique nor their audience sufficiently large for our incomes to compare with such entertainers' (though a few corporate executives—like Chrysler chairman Lee Iacocca and his $20 million plus compensation in 1987—certainly qualify). For the vast majority of us, our incomes alone will never make us rich.

The form of payment for doing the right thing is wealth.

The form of payment for doing the right thing is wealth. If you do the right thing morally, the wealth that you create is spiritual—*you* feel good because you have made *others* feel good. If you do the right thing entrepreneurially, the wealth that you create is monetary. If you successfully solve a problem for a large enough group, you will sell a lot of your product or service. The price you are paid for the solution will exceed the cost of delivering it to them (at least, it will if you want to stay in business) and over time this difference—your profit—will multiply and produce wealth.

The key to creating wealth in the entrepreneurial arena, therefore, is judgment. Wealthy people *know* how to do the *right thing*. They *hire* people who know how to *do things right*. Learning a skill will feed and clothe you for a lifetime. Learning judgment will enable you to feed and clothe millions of people for many lifetimes...and make you very rich in the process. Entrepreneurs are very special people, indeed. Not everyone wants to become one. Not everyone is able to become one.

> **Wealthy people know how to do the right thing. They hire people who know how to do things right.**

Creating Wealth By Investing in Entrepreneurs

But there is a way to ride an idealistic entrepreneur's coattails without having to invest all of *your* time, energy or money into a business of your own. Entrepreneurs often must persuade others to invest in their fledgling companies so they have the capital to create, test and market their new products or services. Money invested in entrepreneurial ideas is known as <u>venture capital</u> because it is inherently more risky than simpler investments like <u>stocks,</u> <u>bonds</u> or real estate. The investor may be lucky to get his or her money back at all, let alone make a profit!

On the other hand, some <u>venture capitalists</u> become very wealthy indeed. Some, especially if they are asked to invest enormous amounts of cash, may even start out owning a larger portion of the company than the entrepreneur. And there have been many instances where an entrepreneur has understated his or her need for venture capital and had to return again and again to investors for more money. Each time, the investors ask for more and more <u>shares</u> of the company's <u>stock</u>. While greater stock ownership doesn't reduce these investors' risk, it does guarantee a much larger slice of any eventual payoff. If the entrepreneur's company succeeds, the investors usually wind up making more money than the entrepreneur. This is exactly what happened in the launch of Sears, Roebuck & Co., where the investor, Julius Rosenwald, wound up owning a larger slice of the company than Charles Sears, its founder. (Mr. Roebuck took early retirement.)

In some instances, the entrepreneur can wind up looking like his or her investors' poor relative. In order to build Federal Express, which had an enormous appetite for capital, founder Fred Smith wound up selling 95% of the company to investors. (Don't be too sympathetic—5% of a multi-billion dollar company is *not* chump change. And it's a lot better than owning 100% of a company that failed because it was <u>undercapitalized</u>.)

On the other hand, some of the wealthiest entrepreneurs in the country—multi-billionaires Sam Walton, founder of WalMart, and H. Ross Perot, founder of Electronic Data Systems, to name just two—launched entrepreneurial companies that did not require them to raise venture capital at all.

Investors who invest in entrepreneurial solutions achieve wealth in direct proportion to their ownership of successful entrepreneurial companies. If they invest in winning solutions that materially improve life on our planet, they will be generously rewarded for their gifts of capital to these entrepreneurs. It takes judgement to know which entrepreneurial ideas and which entrepreneurs to invest in; it also requires immense patience and constant monitoring of the investment. Investing in entrepreneurs, if done competently, can create wealth for an individual without requiring him or her to make the same full-time commitment as the entrepreneur and permit him or her to do other things—collect art, manage other investments, start another company, organize charitable events, etc.

Investing in entrepreneurs is one of the more active forms of investing, and it can take years before a new company takes off and you're able to recoup your investment. Like owning your own company, it is not an idea particularly well-suited to people who seek faster and more mellow roads to wealth, let alone those with a natural fear of losing all their money!

Creating Wealth By Investing

Most people—and certainly most *young* people—do not go out and start their own businesses. Nor do they have the money or expertise to invest in someone else's new company. The road to wealth for the vast majority of us is via investments in <u>financial instruments</u> (stocks and bonds, <u>limited partnerships</u>, etc.), real estate (our own house and, if we're lucky, perhaps a vacation home) or <u>collectibles</u> (from art and antiques to stamps and coins to baseball cards and Elvis memorabilia). Compared to the <u>active</u> involvement of an entrepreneur and his or her investors in a new company, all of these other investments are relatively <u>passive</u>—requiring, for the most part, less time, less energy and certainly less money to get involved in. Section II—Investing & Collecting—discusses all of these potential roads to wealth in greater detail, as well as some less travelled roads like commodities, options, etc.

The road to wealth for the vast majority of us is via investments.

Let's discuss just one example—buying and selling stocks—to begin to understand what's so different about such investments and starting your own company (or supplying venture capital for someone else's).

First, investing in financial instruments like stocks and bonds is, for the most part, an intellectual pursuit that requires little of the hands-on, chaotic, frenetic pace of venture capital investing, let alone your own business. You can pretty much decide how little or much time you want to devote to it and be as active or passive as you want—buying and selling stocks every day, every week, every year or every decade.

Second, it requires far less money to get started—you could buy your first share of stock for less than $100, your first <u>savings bond</u> for even less. Again, the stock market is completely flexible—you can invest as much or as little as you want.

Third, it's relatively easy to obtain the information you need to get started. There is an incredible array of companies in which to invest—over 25,000 U.S. companies, over 10,000 foreign ones. And an equally tremendous amount of literature available—from on-line sources that provide up-to-the-minute data and daily radio and television shows and financial newspapers like the *Wall Street Journal* to weekly and bi-weekly magazines, newsletters, books, seminars and audio tapes. Stock market investors are avid readers, and they absorb this enormous amount of data like sponges, storing the most minute financial data in their memories for long periods of time.

You could buy your first share of stock for less than $100, your first savings bond for even less.

Finally, more than 25 million people in the U. S. currently invest in the stock market, roughly one out of every three households.

How Much For Mickey Mantle?

There is a thin line that separates the investor from the collector.

One important distinction is that it usually takes much longer to create wealth via collecting, because it takes time for a sufficient number of people to agree that a specific collectible—baseball card, duck decoy, painting, sculpture, etc.—has a greater value than what it cost to produce.

Another is that many collectors didn't start collecting paintings or stamps or baseball cards simply because they expected to make money (as opposed to stockholders, few of whom bought their first share because they liked the designs on the stock certificates). They collected because they liked the beautiful objects they bought and/or the memories they evoked. This was obvious at a baseball card exposition in White Plains, New York, that I recently attended. There were 430 dealers buying, trading and selling baseball cards, plus some 5,000 collectors, ranging in age from six to 60. Sure, there was a lot of business going on, a lot of money changing hands, but everyone seemed to be having *fun*, too, whether it was a youngster adding a 1988 card to his newly-started collection or an oldster with tears in his eyes as he gazed at a 1941 Lou Gehrig, remembering the day he actually saw Gehrig and Ruth and other legends at Yankee Stadium.

Which is why I personally find collecting so fantastic! While the entrepreneur may eventually be able to pose proudly next to his or her tomato-picking machine and the successful stock market investor feel satisfaction when he or she makes just the right moves at the right time, somehow neither experience can be compared to the joy of owning a beautiful painting or antique or a memory-laden baseball card, old record, rare book or classic movie poster. While such beautiful memories and the experience of the object is all most people could ask for, a canny collector can certainly create wealth, sometimes substantial wealth, especially if he or she discovers a collectible item before everybody else does.

When I began collecting baseball cards in 1952, a 1951 Topps Mickey Mantle card was worth a penny. For nearly 30 years, this card grew steadily but slowly, until the almost sudden perception that this small "painting" was valuable pushed its price up hundreds of thousands of times. Seven years ago, its price was still under $1,000. One year ago it was worth $6,000. It's now worth $9,000. ("But my mother threw out all my old baseball cards," you lament. Don't blame her. Applaud her. If she and thousands of other mothers hadn't shrunk the supply of old cards, they wouldn't be anywhere near as valuable today. Fastidious mothers made the baseball cards some of us collect very valuable indeed!)

How can you tell when you are entering a particular collectible market early enough? For one thing, the price of the objects—even the scarcest ones—should be very low. For another, there should be practically no information available about the objects—no newsletter, no big trade show, not even a paragraph in the antiques magazines.

If you enter such a market early enough, you will be in a position to create substantial wealth as soon as enough other people come to agree with you and start bidding up the prices of the objects you've collected.

Of course, you always face the possibility that no one else will appreciate the inherent value of the objects you've been collecting so ardently, in which case you will, at least, still have a collection you can appreciate for its esthetic value. Even if your chosen object never becomes a collectible at all.

For example, old fashioned eyewash cups—tiny, colorful glass or metal cups used to wash dirt out of eyes—are actively collected by a handful of people throughout the country. There is even a monthly, four-page, mimeographed newsletter devoted just to eyewash cups. Nevertheless, the eyewash cup has not exactly attracted a thundering herd of collectors. Because of the low demand for this specialized collectible, prices have been relatively flat for the last ten years—a good eyewash cup from the 1940s would only cost you about $5.00 today.

Why does a local baseball card show attract thousands of people at prices that might fetch a new car while still inexpensive eyewash cups are appreciated by only a handful of collectors? A few obvious comparisons: Baseball is fun. Washing dirt out of your eye isn't. Old baseball cards are small, skillfully-produced paintings. Eyewash cups are machine-made objects that required little craft to produce. Baseball evokes happy memories of hot dogs, banners and an outing with your family. Eyewash cups evoke few (if any) memories, none of them particularly joyful. There's lots of data printed on a baseball card, none on an eyewash cup. Such a comparison should enable you to draw some conclusions about what makes one product a collector's joy and the other an event still waiting to happen.

What if you aren't particularly fond of baseball? Well, just as an example, there's enough of a relationship between baseball cards and rock 'n' roll memorabilia—records, posters, sheet music, etc.—for me to recommend that you consider saving the products of singers or groups you think are destined for stardom. Like the cards of once-rookie baseball players that have since ascended to stardom, a rock singer's or group's earliest singles (45s) showcase raw talent, attract fierce loyalties and evoke pleasant memories.

You might be able to begin a poster, figurine, T-shirt and/or record collection of emerging musical groups for less than $100. If the singer or group achieves Elvis- or Beatles-like status, any objects from their "early days" will be worth a king's ransom. (A pair of basketball shoes once worn by Elvis, for example, were sold at Sotheby's, one of America's largest auction firms, for $2725 in July, 1988.)

What will a perfect sample of the first Apple computer be worth in the year 2000?

A second idea for the more technically inclined among you: How about collecting "vintage" computers and/or software? There have been hundreds of personal computer manufacturers and thousands of software producers that have come and gone since the microchip was invented in 1968. What will a perfect sample of the first Apple computer be worth in the year 2000, 30 years after Steve Wozniak built it in Steven Jobs' garage? How about a vintage floppy disc of "Temple of Apshai," one of the first games made for the personal computer?

Creating wealth via collecting is as much a gift-giving process as investing or starting your own company because it involves the active trading, bartering, exchanging, buying and selling that keeps the free market active, fresh and exciting. Anyone, regardless of their economic or social position, can enter or leave the collector's market at any time. It is completely free, requiring only a little bit of cash and an intense interest in and love for whatever you've decided to collect.

In the following pages, we will discuss all of these roads to wealth in much greater detail. Whatever your current thoughts about the road that's right for you, study them all before you decide on your next step, then choose the one (or two or three) that matches your particular interests, goals and talents...and your savings account balance.

1   Individual Exercises & Projects

1. Look around your own community and find a local entrepreneur to talk to. He or she doesn't have to be a multi-million dollar success story; it could be the person or couple that owns the local drive-in, video store or fast-food franchise. Ask him or her about their business, how it was started, etc.

2. Read at least one biography or autobiography of one of the success stories cited in this chapter—Dr. Land, Ray Kroc, etc. (and, if you want, prepare a book report for school).

3. Research each of the following topics, either for your own knowledge or as part of a school project: Inflation, recession, the Great Depression. Can you explain their relationship?

4. Do you understand the concept of a free market? Can you explain how tariffs, protectionism, farm price supports and other examples of government intervention affect markets? Are such markets free?

5. Explain the black market. What goods in the U.S. are sold on the black market?

6. List five major U.S. companies started primarily with the help of venture capital. Can you cite any examples of such firms in which the founder actually wound up owning less of his or her company than the investors? What happened to the founder?

Section One

Entrepreneurship

2

The Concept of Entrepreneurship

Entrepreneurship is *not* an exclusively American concept, but it does express an art of creation that *is* profoundly American.

Founding your own company, being your own boss, going where you want, doing what you want. Yes, it sounds grand. But the reality is not so enticing, certainly not at the beginning. Many successful entrepreneurs begin with nothing and are undoubtedly unprepared for the difficulties they must endure along the way. But many of them *do* endure and, in the process of making something out of nothing, probably learn more about themselves than they ever thought possible. In fact, it's often during the periods of their greatest suffering, in the face of disbelief and discouragement from established authorities and experts, that they learn their greatest lessons.

> It's often during the periods of their greatest suffering that entrepreneurs learn their greatest lessons.

They learn that they are unique individuals who are truly alive only when they *must* face such suffering, precisely when everybody else is telling them they're crazy. They learn that what is in their hearts and minds cannot be taken away from them. That their insight, their dream, is so true and elegant that they must follow it, even if they fail.

Apple Pie, Motherhood And A Business To Call Your Own

Do you believe in the "American Dream," that old-fashioned, chest-thumping platitude that America is the one place in the world where *any*one, no matter how humble, can rise to the top? Today's entrepreneurs not only believe it, they live it. And there are certainly enough successful examples around to show that such optimism is not misguided.

Entrepreneurs are a different breed of human being, one seemingly capable of walking through fire and emerging cool and happy on the other side.

Jack Tramiel, a short, stout, ravaged-faced survivor of Auschwitz, took Commodore Business Machines to the summit of the home computer market, selling more than 1,000,000 machines in just three years. In the process, he almost single-handedly laid waste to the plans and investments of Texas Instruments, Warner Communications, Timex, Coleco and the Japanese consumer electronics industry.

Kemmons Wilson dropped out of school in the eighth grade because his hard-working mother, so tiny she was known as "doll," became too ill to work. Thrust into entrepreneurship as a teenager, he started by purchasing peanut vending machines, convincing their former owner to accept a series of post-dated checks as payment.

To make good on the checks, young Kemmons ran around to all of his peanut machines every day to empty the pennies and run them over to the bank. Whatever the hardships of this day-to-day entrepreneurial existence, it was inestimably superior to watching his mother's demise and starving in the process. And it taught him the kind of hard work necessary to make his future ventures successful. The successful venture most of you know Kemmons for was called Holiday Inns.

Jack R. Simplot ran away from the father he feared when he was just fourteen. To survive on his own, he hatched an ingenious plot. He discovered that if a sheep gave birth to more lambs than she could take care of, the farmer killed the "extras." Jack collected forty of these lambs over a period of several months, raised them to a point where they could be sold back to the farmers and cleared a $140 profit, a princely sum for an Idaho teenager in 1922.

Jack never stopped entrepreneuring. Ever the <u>contrarian</u>, he was the first to freeze-dry potatoes. His patented french-fried potato became a key element in the success of a hamburger chain called McDonald's—people swear their french fries are simply better than any other fast-food chain's. As a venture capitalist, Jack provided most of the $20 million needed to launch Micron Technology Corp., a Boise semiconductor manufacturer that grew to half a billion dollars in sales by 1983. According to semiconductor industry experts, that initial investment was barely one-fifth of the minimum capital required to launch such a firm.

We could certainly cite hundreds of other examples, but let these few suffice to prove our point: Entrepreneurs *are* a different breed of human being, one seemingly capable of walking through fire and emerging cool and happy on the other side. It isn't supernatural or luck. It's because they learned early in their lives that they would have to work hard merely to survive, harder still to succeed, harder than anyone to excel.

Whether fleeing oppression in a foreign land, economic oppression at home or the pain inflicted on them because they just seemed "different" than everybody else, entrepreneurs learn how to turn that pain into a superhuman drive to succeed against often incalculable odds. They are realists, sometimes to a fault—in their own afflicted lives, they quickly discover that goals will never come easily, that all of human life is a hard predicament, but that the failure to achieve their "dream" can't ever be as brutal as the oppression, deprivation or affliction they're fighting to escape.

Entrepreneurship As A Religious Experience

Entrepreneurs begin with an idea or an insight, usually a surprisingly simple one. This "quiet," formative phase of the entrepreneurial process offers no obvious flash of inspiration, no comic-bubble lightbulb suddenly lit. But once they've developed that idea and prepared to follow it to its end, these quiet thinkers are suddenly transformed into fanatical dream chasers.

The entrepreneurial sacrifice is a near-religious experience. Entrepreneurs give wholly of themselves, sacrificing everything—time, marriage, assets, friends and, most certainly, sleep—for their private, tenacious belief in an idea only they may initially appreciate. Without a moment's self-doubt, with savings dwindling, family neglected and friends forgotten, they prepare and follow their plan to launch their new company. And continue fighting for its existence long after everyone else has given up.

> Entrepreneurs give wholly of themselves, sacrificing everything—time, marriage, assets, friends and, most certainly, sleep.

Every day, sometimes every *hour*, is a struggle to keep that dream alive. Like a trapped miner, the entrepreneur spends each day tunneling up from the bottom of a deep shaft—making a little headway here and there, slipping back two feet to avoid a falling boulder, moving forward three feet as soft gravel gives way, even going sideways to see if the tunnelling appears easier. Day after day, night after night—sometimes sleeping next to their <u>prototypes</u>, in basements, rented lofts, abandoned storefronts—entrepreneurs keep digging.

The smallest of victories, the tiniest progress out of the darkness, is an occasion for celebration—holding off a <u>creditor</u> one more week, <u>debugging</u> a tricky software package, convincing a customer to pay in advance, getting the bank to cover Friday's <u>overdraft</u> with Monday's expected deposit. Each tiny bit of progress gives the entrepreneur the courage to go yet another week without salary.

Amazingly enough, miracles often happen. Against all odds, beyond all calculation and usually in the face of stubborn production obstacles and bankers that bounce the most important of their checks, these entrepreneurs begin to ascend out of the darkness.

After digging and clawing for months, a tiny speck of light appears at the far end of the tunnel. It is miles away, but clearly visible. The entrepreneur can see his idea confirmed, his strategy validated. The light provides a shot of adrenalin that speeds the entrepreneur up through the tunnel.

The entrepreneur emerges from his "tunnel" with the clear and exquisite knowledge that his idea is correct, demonstrable and proveable, that his journey down that frightening mineshaft to find it, work with it, shape it and test it was worth the effort. Though his desk is still full of unpaid bills and he must still deal with the worried looks of family and friends, as born-again Christians say, "he has found his strength in an ideal." This is the first stage of the process of entrepreneurship. It is no more or less critical, no more or less difficult, than any of the others to come.

Entrepreneurship is a solitary, lonely, often fiendishly difficult road, one many people should never travel.

The Expanding Process Of Entrepreneurship

Entrepreneurship is a solitary, lonely, often fiendishly difficult road, one many people should never travel. Some of the anxiety and uncertainty of entrepreneurship can be reduced by an understanding of the whole process. But don't kid yourselves—to understand the process is *not* in any way comparable to actually going through it.

Does this seem like an unnecessarily harsh and maudlin description of the supposedly wonderful concept of owning your own business? It's not. For the most part, it is the common experience of entrepreneurs everywhere. But remember: Entrepreneurs are not masochists, putting themselves through all this for $11 an hour. They are betting that the payoff down the road is so substantial that it's *worth* all the hard work. And that's all we're really talking about here—hard work—though, granted, probably harder work than most people contemplate ever doing.

So this whole description is *not* meant to scare you off or encourage you not to follow your dream (and if you're a real entrepreneur, you probably wouldn't be so easily discouraged anyway). It *is* meant to give you a more realistic picture of the single-minded focus and dedication that is absolutely necessary. You might have no choice about becoming an entrepreneur—circumstances or your own psyche might force you into your own business. You might as well know upfront that it's not going to be easy.

Though everyone can't—and shouldn't—be an entrepreneur, everyone *can* participate in the entrepreneurial process as a manager, helpful spouse or active investor. So even if you never anticipate starting your own business, all of you should seek to at least gain some understanding of the process now. Perhaps a retelling of the Entrepreneur's Legend will help.

Legend Has It That...

Far back among the mists of time, a family prepared a feast for some important visitors from another tribe. In doing so, they unknowlingly created <u>productivity</u>, employment and <u>innovation</u>. And started the first business.

The family hunted and killed many birds, harvested vegetables, and picked fruit and coconuts to feed their guests. They persuaded a friend to cut down a tree and build them a table and benches for the guests' comfort. They asked others to clear an area from the jungle in which the feast could be held. Still others were asked to cook, serve and clear away the meal. All told, a dozen people worked on the feast, and the family promised each of them a reward when the feast was over.

The feast was lavish and beautifully prepared. It tasted better than any meal the visitors had ever eaten. They promised to reciprocate and, a week later, sent the host family a fine goat as a thank-you present. The family gave goat's milk to all of the people who had helped them prepare the feast. The workers were so pleased with the way the law

The Concept Of Entrepreneurship

of reciprocity worked that they eagerly volunteered to help prepare another feast, and another, and yet another.

The feast business flourished and was soon transformed into the first large-scale restaurant operation. All too soon, however, some of the workers grew bored with performing the same tasks day after day. One of them, the table maker, left the first entrepreneur's team and built himself a floating table, which he called a boat. He planned to purchase food from the feast-giver, load it into his boat, transport it to nearby islands and sell it to the tribes who lived there. The family of restaurant owners saw this enterprise as a second source of <u>revenue</u>, so they invested in the table maker's new food exporting business.

Life is random, however, and rewards are uncertain. When the <u>exporter</u> arrived on the nearby island with his cargo of food, the tribe welcomed him with cries of joy and offered him a thousand coconuts as his reward. But it was not the food that they wanted. They had plenty of that. They wanted his boat.

Like many an entrepreneur in the centuries to follow, this food exporter found that he had to make a major change in his plans. There was no food shortage problem for him to solve; there was, however, a serious need for boats. Because good entrepreneurs are flexible, the food exporter quickly transformed himself into a boat manufacturer.

Months later, one of the boat maker's cleverest workers achieved a high-technology breakthrough—he invented the wheel. Which left him with a very unique, large solution for which he had to find a problem or, preferably, several problems. Eventually, he decided to use his invention to solve the widespread problem of waste removal. He and his family began to produce wheelbarrows which could be used to cart the waste to the shore, where the second entrepreneur's boats waited to float it away. After firmly establishing his wheelbarrow business, he continued to expand, setting up a waste hauling enterprise, a wheel manufacturing business and dozens of other related operations.

As the years passed, many other entrepreneurs were spun off from the original three. The circle of problem solving kept widening to include more and more solutions and more and more receivers of those solutions. Service organizations were established, and the manufacture of components became an important industry.

The tribal people came to understand that their profits

would exceed their costs by a significant margin as long as three circumstances prevailed:

1. The solutions had to solve large problems for their receivers.
2. The solutions had to be unique or presented in a unique, nonduplicable manner.
3. The law of reciprocity had to be obeyed to the letter.

> **If a tribal entrepreneur gives a feast for the rest of the tribe, it creates in each of them a liability— a feeling of obligation on the part of the guests—for receipt of the asset (the feast). Since the giver lived nearby the receiver, he could repay with barter (a goat for a meal). When trade between more distant tribes began, forms of money were created as a means of extinguishing liabilities. As giving expands, therefore, so does the supply of money.**

Many inventor-entrepreneurs (like the one who invented the wheel) develop <u>elegant</u> solutions first and then find suitable problems for them. Note that the formulation of a problem is crucial, however, for no matter how elegant and unique the solution may be, it is of little value—or no value—if it is not needed to solve a serious problem. Contrary to Ralph Waldo Emerson's claim, people will not beat a path to your door if you develop a better mousetrap, which is a solution lacking a serious problem.

Are Entrepreneurs Born To Suffer?

Some people will tell you that entrepreneurs are born and not made. That entrepreneurship is an art rather than a science. I do not believe this.

One of the reasons that nobody could explain wealth to me when I was growing up, in college or in graduate school, was that *they* never understood the relationship of wealth to entrepreneurship. Economists, for the most part, still believe that entrepreneurship is an art. That it is not a discipline. That it cannot be taught.

Poppycock. Entrepreneurship *is* a discipline. And it *can* be taught. It is, in fact, a *game* (or science) with rules, fundamentals and strategies. I have collected these rules of entrepreneurship—which I refer to as **Silver's Three Rules of Entrepreneurship**—in the following chapter. Together with a discussion of the DEJ Factors (Chapter 4), Solution Delivery Methods (Chapters 5 & 6) and the development of a Stragetic Plan (Chapter 7), their study will enable you to have a much better idea of just what entrepreneurship is all about and how one succeeds. Hopefully, this understanding of the process will encourage you to experience it yourself.

> ## You've Got To Love The Chase
>
> **There is a myth that entrepreneurs are born, not made. It is simply not true. Entrepreneurship is a game. Like any game, it has rules, fundamentals and strategies that can be learned. It also has winners and losers.**

IMPORTANT NOTE: There is a detailed business plan for and discussion of the creation of the Hot Dog Dance Club—a business you could start yourself right now—in Chapter 8. However, with the exception of this chapter, the rest of the chapters in this section talk to you as if you were going out tomorrow to raise a million dollars (or more) to start a major company. They are written in the same manner as if this were a book intended for professionals...because any budding entrepreneur must learn the same rules and lessons, whatever your age, whatever your starting capital, whatever your dream.

That is, there is no fundamental difference whatsover between starting the Hot Dog Dance Club and founding the next IBM as far as entrepreneurial concepts, rules and requirements. There are only differences of degree—more or less time, money, etc.

And trying to "simplify" any of these lessons doesn't work...it just distorts them. Wherever possible (and I've tried to help in the Exercise section at the end of each chapter), try to relate the rules and lessons to your own life and experience.

A nice result of this approach is that when *ever* you start planning a new business and no matter how old you are when you start, these same chapters are absolutely pertinent. So don't throw this book away just because you're not planning on starting the next IBM tomorrow!

2 Individual Exercises & Projects

1. List the qualities of the "perfect" entrepreneur. Which of those qualities do you think are essential?

2. Based on (1) and on your understanding of entrepreneurship, can you list qualities that, while not seemingly negative, would *not* be helpful for an entrepreneur to have (those that would, in fact, make it more difficult to succeed)?

3. Identify one service or product the students in your school really need. Do you think it could be developed by an entrepreneur? What problems would have to be overcome?

3

Silver's 3 Rules Of Entrepreneurship

Rule One: W = P x S x E

Non-mathematicians, don't be scared! This is not a hard rule to understand once you know what these letters stand for, what they mean and what concept the equation purports to show:

W = Wealth! (Yes, after all this time, I was able to discover the secret formula. This is it.)

P = The size of the *Problem* that the entrepreneur has identified.

S = The elegance of the entrepreneur's *Solution.* In the case of a product, this is a combination of its proprietary nature and its appropriateness to the market. In terms of a service, the uniqueness of the marketing systems is the biggest factor.

E = Quality of the *Entrepreneurial Team*—the experience, competence and degree of cooperation of and between the members of the company's initial management group.

In other words, the amount of wealth created is determined by multiplying the size of the problem, the elegance (uniqueness and effectiveness) of the solution and the competence of the people executing the solution.

There are two important things to notice about any such equation. The greater the values of P, S and E—the bigger the problem, better the solution, more competent the team—the greater amount of wealth (W) created in the shortest period of time. On the other hand, any time any *one* of those three values (P, S or E) is zero, so is W—because multiplying any number, no matter *how* large, by zero still equals zero.

In the mid-1970s, John Z. DeLorean created a solution—the DeLorean automobile—that was not unique and did not have a non-duplicable delivery system. Thus, the "S" factor of DeLorean Motor Co. was zero. What's more, it was a solution for a problem that didn't exist—there were already many sports cars in the marketplace. So the "P" factor was also zero. Multiplying any value of "E" by one zero would already give a zero value for "W." Two zeros didn't make it any worse, but certainly didn't change the outcome. As a result, the investors in DeLorean Motor Co. lost their money—nearly $125 million—in a very short period of time and Delorean found himself spending the next three years in court (where he was acquitted of both fraud and narcotics charges).

On the other hand, Intel Corp. produced a large amount of wealth for its entrepreneurial team (Robert L. Noyce, Andrew Grove and Gordon Moore) in less than ten years. In 1968, they identified the Problem: The high cost and large size of core memory used in mainframe computers made such large computers useful to a very small number of people. Their solution was the development of metal oxide semiconductor memories placed on silicon chips, which reduced both the cost and size of core memory. The Intel founders—the Entrepreneurial team—had worked together in similar positions at Fairchild Semiconductor Corp. and knew what they were doing. The entrepreneurs and their principal backer, Arthur Rock, invested approximately $2 million in Intel in 1968. Ten years later, the company's valuation (W) in the stock market was nearly $2 billion. Not incidentally, Intel's solution turned out to be the key to the development of personal computers, arguably the most important and far-reaching technological development of the last two decades.

Remember the story of the first entrepreneur who served a feast and thereby created a gift-giving process that included the gift itself, productivity in the community, innovation and change, wealth and a spin-out of new entrepreneurs? The same thing occurred in the community south of San Francisco known as Silicon Valley (so nicknamed because the properties of silicon were discovered there). Over fifteen chip manufacturers were spun out of Fairchild and Intel, and many of them have widened the circle begun by Noyce,

Moore and Grove still further: Rheem became Raytheon Semiconductor (via acquisition); Jean Hoerni founded Amelco, which became Teledyne Semiconductor; Jerry Sanders formed Advanced Micro Devices; Charles Sporck founded National Semiconductor; and the Parkinson Brothers, backed by Jack Simplot, founded Micron Technology.

These chipmakers supplied the components to personal computer entrepreneurs, who in turn spawned software entrepreneurs, among them William Gates, whose company Microsoft Corp. became publicly-held in 1986 and made him a *billion*aire before his 30th birthday.

These entrepreneurs needed information (the Problem) and Patrick J. McGovern, founder of International Data Group, Inc., provided them with *Computerworld* (the Solution) in 1967 and 61 additional computer magazines since then.

The computer industry also needed a trade show (Problem), and Sheldon Adelson provided them with the COMDEX trade show (Solution) in 1971. Currently 200,000 computer dealers and customers attend COMDEX each year. And so the circle of giving widens.

It's very easy, now that you know the secret formula, to study the service businesses and products you know and figure out why they were successful. Let's look at a few more examples that you'll all be familiar with:

In 1961, Ray Kroc noticed that more and more people were moving to the suburbs. So did a lot of other people. But Kroc identified one key thing such a population shift meant: lots of families who would want a clean restaurant that would process their orders quickly. The drive-in forerunners to today's abundance of fast-food restaurants were filthy, noisy places frequented mainly by loud teenagers in loud cars. By providing a solution to an anticipated problem—and by doing it competently and quickly—Kroc created a company called McDonald's.

In a 1971 college term paper, Philip H. Knight described another shift occuring in America, one toward health care and physical fitness. He predicted one important trend—the great increase in America's interest in "getting in shape"—and came to an equally important conclusion—that such people would want to know and emulate the kinds of clothing and equipment professional athletes were wearing or using. Knight believed that if he could create a high-quality, low-cost shoe for professional athletes, then get those athletes to endorse his shoes in television commericals, he would sell a lot of running shoes.

He was right. By 1987, Nike Corp. was worth more than $500 million.

Remember when just about the only telephone your family could use was one manufactured by a subsidiary of AT&T? Thanks to the unflagging determination of Thomas L. Kelly, Jr., no one has to rent telephones from AT&T for $25 per month anymore; we can now buy one at a retail store for as little as $10. Kelly correctly perceived AT&T as a leasing company trying desperately to protect its monopoly position. He didn't think they could.

After the Supreme Court's Carterphone decision in 1965, which permitted other manufacturers to interconnect their telephones to AT&T's lines, Kelly was ready. He designed telephones superior to Ma Bell's, had them made very inexpensively in Japan and began battling AT&T in the marketplace and in the courts.

Kelly won. The value of TIE/communications' common stock in 1987 was approximately $600 million.

You may have noticed the appearance of little billboards affixed to the shopping carts in your supermarket, reminding shoppers of products they can purchase in the store. They were the creation of Bruce Failing, Jr., then 27, and his father, who believed that a product's sales would increase dramatically if the advertisement appeared at the point-of-sale. With consumer studies in hand, they convinced many advertisers of their findings and agreed to pay the supermarkets 17% of ActMedia's ad revenues for renting space that the supermarkets were not using. Everyone became a winner, including the Failing family, whose shares of ActMedia are now worth over $250 million.

Garbage collection is a peculiar line of work for an accountant, but Tom Fatjo, Jr., age 27, simply got upset about the way the city of Houston collected his garbage. Convinced he could do it better—and make some money in the bargain—he bought a truck and went into business. It soon became clear that he *was* more efficient and cheaper than the City. His business flourished.

Not long after, he noticed that many owners of garbage collection companies around the country wanted to sell their businesses and retire. No buyers existed. He began buying these companies—hundreds of them—with stock and notes. He combined them into Browning-Ferris and created a

Successful entrepreneurship begins by formulating problems.

company worth over $1.2 billion in 15 years.

Finding Problems—Where the Process All Begins

Successful entrepreneurship begins by formulating problems. This means seeing problems as opportunities and asking some basic questions:

1. Does the problem affect a large number of people?
2. Does it affect them in pretty much the same way?
3. Are they aware that they have the Problem or would they first have to be convinced of that?
4. Are there barriers that could prevent someone delivering a Solution to them?
5. What is the current cost to the people who have the Problem and will my Solution be less expensive?

Measuring the size of the Problem (P) is the first step in seizing an entrepreneurial opportunity. I started a small business when I was a trainee at Chase Manhattan Bank that helped moped and motorcycle drivers avoid tickets. It's a classic case of finding an elegant solution to a small problem.

Successful entrepreneurs see problems as opportunities.

When my wife and I moved to New York City in 1964 we bought a Honda moped. I dropped her off at the school were she taught, drove to the Wall Street area where I worked and parked the moped vertically between two parked cars. Every day I got a $5.00 ticket for vertical parking, and so did everyone else in New York City who parked vertically.

But when I looked up the law, I discovered that vertical parking in New York City was perfectly legal! (How else could trucks make furniture deliveries except by backing into driveways of tall buildings?) I beat 150 tickets in court, but that didn't stop the policemen, who just kept issuing new tickets every day. I found a Solution: I typed the law onto an index card, made 500 photocopies, embossed them and drilled two little screw holes in the bottom of the cards so that they could be easily affixed to a moped's or motorcycle's license plate. Then I sold the cards to every moped and motorcycle dealer in the city for a dollar apiece.

Wealth is a function of the size of the Problem.

This venture satisfied four of the five questions posed above: 1. Everyone knew they had the problem—they got ticketed everyday. 2. The market was homogenous. Everyone with the problem was affected by it in the same way—they got a ticket. 3. Since the cost of a ticket—$5.00—was five times the cost of the plaque—$1.00—my Solution (S) was much less expensive than the Problem (P). And 4. There were no barriers to entry (competition, licensing requirements, etc.).

Unfortunately, the relative size of the popluation affected by the Problem was small; as a result, so were the profits—I only generated $500 in total revenues, netting perhaps $300. I had identified a small problem. Entrepreneurial fortunes are not made of small problems.

Which brings me to Silver's Second Rule of Entrepreneurship—the Law of the Big P:

Rule Two: W = (f) P

Meaning: Wealth is a function of the size of the Problem.

This is, to an extent, a logical outgrowth of the first rule (and a common-sense conclusion to which a study of the previous examples should lead you). Rule One defines wealth and tells you how to create it: You find a problem and put together a competent entrepreneurial team to create and market a unique solution.

Rule Two tells you how to create the *most* wealth: With everything else being equal, the larger the problem that the entrepreneur attempts to solve, the greater his or her potential wealth. Let's look at some examples.

Ex-commercial banker Robert A. Swanson, 29 years of age, met Herbert W. Boyer, one of the first scientists to synthesize life, and, over a beer in a San Francisco pub, each man agreed to invest $500 to try to develop commercial products via genetic engineering technology (hence the name "Gen-en-tech"). Swanson and Boyer raised over $300 million in seed capital, joint-ventures with large pharmaceutical companies, public offerings of Genentech's common stock, and research and development limited partnerships. The company went public in 1981 and the stock market bid its valuation up to $800 million *five full years before Genentech even had a product to sell.* In 1987 Genentech's valuation in the stock market approached $2 billion. It still had only a handful of products in the marketplace. But it was involved with the "Big Problems" of health, disease, curing and caring, problems that were so huge they overshadowed (and made up for) the slow development of the Solutions.

John H. Foster saw such a "Big P" opportunity in the speech therapy market. People who have had strokes must work long and hard with a competent therapist to regain

Rule One defines wealth and tells you how to create it; Rule Two tells you how to create the most wealth.

their speech ability. While speech therapy was certainly not new, Foster's way of doing business was unique to his market—he began "acquiring" speech therapists for common stock and introduced standardized therapies and management efficiencies to make each therapist more profitable than they would have ever been alone. Then, with 30 therapists under one roof (who owned, because of Foster's unique deals with them, 40% of the company), In-Speech went public at a valuation of $150 million. That's <u>$2 million for each therapist</u> and $90 million for Foster. Ask the speech therapist in your community if he or she would like to add $2 million to his pile of cash and still have the income from his or her practice.

The list of "Big P companies" (those who tackle the big problems) goes on. And it is often the same as anybody's list of the fastest-growing companies. I believe so strongly in this Rule and that potential entrepreneurs should enter the fields of caring and curing that I launched a newsletter in 1987 called *The Silver Prescription* to service entrepreneurs who enter the field. The newsletter monitors 25 <u>publicly-held</u> Big-P companies whose missions are solving major, monumental problems like hunger, disease, illiteracy and mental illness. The average <u>p/e (price/earnings) ratio</u> of the companies in the Big-P Index in mid-1987 was 45, nearly four times the average p/e ratio of the stock market as a whole. In other words, a company in a different field with the same <u>earnings</u> as a comparable Big P company was valued only a quarter as much. This means the public agreed that there was a greater potential for tremendous earnings in the future, even if current earnings didn't show it.

A thorough understanding of the Law of the Big P is vital on a personal as well as an economic level. As we've discussed, entrepreneurship is an arduous process that requires at least five years of great personal sacrifice—eighty-hour work weeks, a severely-reduced social life, sometimes the endangerment of close relationships or even a marriage. It seems foolish to risk all of this in order to establish a "small P" company producing a me-too product or service that no one really needs. Why not make the sacrifice worthwhile by addressing one of the many large social or medical problems that exist in the world today? The personal rewards you will gain—from reducing the risk of heart attacks, for example, or from improving the lives of old people—will make your hard work worthwhile. Big dreams, after all, are the stuff of which

American heroes are made.

Bear in mind that accidents and luck are definitely factors in the life of many entrepreneurs. In 1965, John Schlatter, a scientist researching ulcer therapies, discovered aspartame when he licked his fingers to turn a page. Aspartame is a non-carcinogenic sweetener that the makers of numerous products have used to replace saccharine. You probably know it by its brand name—Nutrasweet.

And in 1886 John Styth Pemberton, an Atlanta pharmacist, created what he thought was a headache syrup from caffeine, extract of cola nut and other oils. Turned out people liked drinking it even when they didn't have headaches. They called it Coca Cola.

Rule Three: Be Risk Averse

Most entrepreneurs (certainly most successful ones!) are *not* gun-slinging risk takers who hit the beach firing in every direction and then run toward whatever target falls down. Competent entrepreneurs are careful planners who consider all of the possible "what-ifs," then plan for the worst that can happen. Successful entrepreneurs devise a "<u>worst-case scenario</u>" for each major step they take and plan an escape route in the event the worst does indeed happen.

Five Stages in the Life of a Company

1. **Research and development**
2. **Manufacturing start-up**
3. **Marketing**
4. **Management**
5. **Growth**

Timothy A. G. Hay, president of Security Pacific Capital Corporation and one of the most successful venture capital investors in America, calls this <u>downside planning</u>—being prepared for the worst that could possibly happen.

"The most competent entrepreneurs always hear footsteps coming up behind them," Hay asserts. "They are continually planning how they will deal with the footsteps, how they will avert risk."

All the while, of course, entrepreneurs must maintain and project an optimistic, "can-do" attitude in order to persuade customers, <u>vendors</u>, employers, lenders and investors that the most optimistic scenario will occur and that they are a vital part of the dream. This kind of optimism is vital to the success of the entrepreneurial process.

Optimism is vital to the success of the entrepreneurial process.

Just remember: The image of a bold, swashbuckling entrepreneur must be presented to the public from time to time, but the winning entrepreneurial formula is based on careful planning and systematic risk aversion.

To better understand why you should try to avoid risks and ways to do so, let's look at each of the five stages in the life of a new company:

1. Research and development
2. Manufacturing start-up
3. Marketing
4. Management
5. Growth

Competent entrepreneurs typically assume risk in the first two phases, but "hand off" the risks of the other three stages to others. Let's get a better understanding of these five stages and then examine how the better entrepreneurs avoid risk in each.

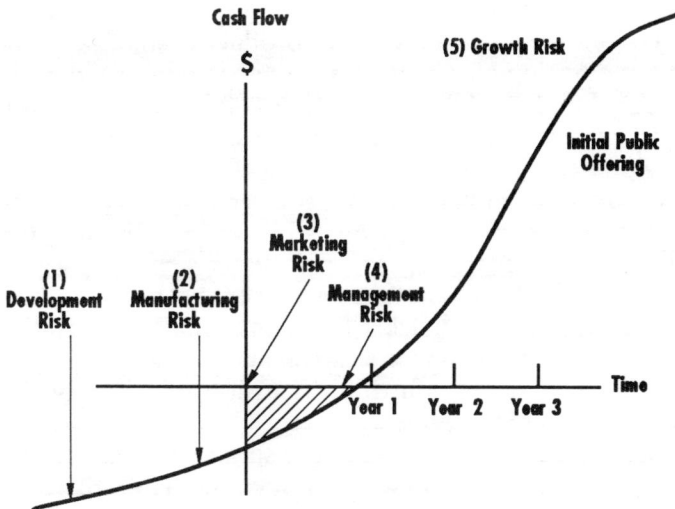

Figure 1. Five Risks in a Start-Up Company

Stage 1: Research & Development (R&D)

Think of *research* as problem formulation and *development* as creating the solution. Depending on the nature of the problem—industrial, social, recreational or medical—the formulation of a suitable solution may require weeks, months or years. The entrepreneur must identify how many people have the problem, find out if the receivers are homogenous, determine if they realize they have a problem and estimate the price they would pay for an effective solution. Problem formulation is the most important step in entrepreneurship, and it is ongoing throughout the life of the new company. Without a continuous emphasis on understanding your customers and their needs, your solutions may eventually fail to satisfy.

Creating the solution also can require weeks, months or years, depending on the nature of the solution and its delivery method (see Chapters 5 & 6). In establishing a company of any kind, however, you will have to assume some risk during the R&D phase. The amount of risk you face will depend in large part on the type of company you choose to establish.

In <u>high-technology</u>, <u>capital equipment</u> and <u>consumer product companies</u>, the uniqueness of the solution is of critical importance, and several years of product design, development and testing are required. Remember that the first wheelbarrow could not be produced until the wheel was invented. Similarly, several years of product design, development and testing may be necessary before *your* product can be offered to the public. In companies of this sort, then, you as the entrepreneur must assume most of the risk in the R&D phase.

Other kinds of companies, however, may pose less risk for the entrepreneur during this stage. In <u>facilities management</u>, <u>franchising</u> and newsletter-seminar packaging, for example, a solution can often be designed and developed reasonably quickly, often on the customer's facilities and with the customer's capital and assets. (Again, see Chapters 5 & 6 for a further discussion of a number of solution delivery methods.)

In most kinds of companies, you should be able to begin the R&D phase while still working at your old job. Exhausting as this may turn out to be, it ensures that nothing will be at risk except time—you will not be risking the loss of your livelihood as well. Also keep in mind that if the Problem is sufficiently large, potential customers and others can be persuaded to finance the research and development stage. You can <u>leverage</u> a Big P. Thus you will need to assume only part of the R&D risk.

Stage 2: Manufacturing

During this stage, the emphasis shifts to producing a commodity that your potential market(s)—the receivers of your solution—need and will value highly. Here all of the responsibility for risk falls on your shoulders—you must test, debug and retest your product, put it into the hands of potential consumers for more testing, then package it effectively.

During this stage, you will probably have less money than you need, perhaps far less, which will mean getting it wherever you can—customers, suppliers, employees (by having them work overtime), family, friends, lenders and investors. As time passes, the amount of risk you face will be more closely related to the value of your product. If the receivers—your potential customers—consistently value your company's solutions more highly than you must pay to produce it, most of the company's continuing need for capital will be financed up front by customers, and the amount of risk you must bear will be reduced accordingly.

Stage 3: Marketing

Once you move into the marketing phase, your company will begin to grow rapidly and will incur large <u>cash flow deficits</u>. At this point, however, a competent entrepreneur will know that it is time to start sharing the risk—hiring managers to oversee many of the company's functions and attracting an experienced board of directors to advise the managers. Also during this phase, various segments of the company will be subdivided in order to ensure appropriate attention to detail by those managers. The marketing area, for example, may be subdivided into such departments as sales, advertising, public relations, telemarketing, after-sale support, customer service and administrative support. Production, finance and the other critical functional areas will go through a similar stratification. The cash flow deficit will be reduced by getting all interested parties—customers, employees, etc.—to share the risk. If money is still tight, you may consider selling <u>equity</u> interests to venture capitalists, thus, again, reducing your risk.

Stage 4: Management

Your new company has demonstrated that its solution satisfies the needs of many receivers. The enterprise is profitable and growing rapidly. By now you have stepped aside, and the managers are making most of the day-to-day operating decisions. It may be time to enter a new phase and they may well start to consider options like a <u>merger</u> with a similar or complementary company or an initial <u>public offering</u> to diversify the entrepreneurial team's wealth into other assets and raise <u>ancillary capital</u> to develop additional and complementary products ("<u>models</u>").

Stage 5: Growth

During the growth stage, your new company usually has all of its functional areas overseen by experienced managers, and its products have solved long ago the problems they were designed for. The problems, in fact, may have been long forgotten, and by now the public may mention your solution reverently, as in "Do you remember what life was like before Federal Express?" Or even identify your solution as the only solution—people blow their noses in Kleenex, not in facial tissues, even if the brand they're using isn't Kleenex. And of course, you xerox, even on a Savin copier, not "photocopy." If so, you will indeed have become a giver, and your gifts will have become basic components of daily life.

It is during the growth stage, however, that many companies lose their most important managers. If the value of their <u>stock options</u> provides these key people with enough capital, they often decide to sail the entrepreneurial waters themselves. If too many of your company's most energetic and innovative employees leave to do other things, your company's solutions will begin to lose their value, and your <u>sales curve</u> will start to flatten.

Like any set of rules, Silver's Three Rules of Entrepreneurship are a basic formulation of how to *play* the game of entrepreneurship, which, after reading them, virtually anybody can do. What follows in the next four chapters is a discussion of the Fundamentals of Entrepreneurship: what you need to know to *win* the game.

> ## Silver's Three Rules of Entrepreneurship:
> **Rule No. One:** $W = P \times S \times E$
> **Rule No. Two:** $W = (f)P$
> **Rule No. Three:** **Be Risk Averse**

3   INDIVIDUAL EXERCISES & PROJECTS

1. List five examples of elegant and non-elegant solutions. Make sure you understand the difference!

2. Make two lists, one of small problems, the other of big ones...whether or not anyone is currently providing solutions for them.

3. What are the fastest-growing industries in the U. S.? What are the slowest growing? Can you find anything in common among the industries on each list?

4. Find a successful small business in your community or city. Can you identify the problem it set out to solve, how it delivered its solution and measure the quality of the entrepreneurial team? Can you find a similar company that failed and figure out why it failed?

5. What did the companies you searched out in question 4 do to avert risk. Did the unsuccessful company follow Silver's Third Rule?

6. Certain brand names, like Kleenex and Xerox, have become generic, i.e., people have replaced the the actual name of the product (facial tissues) or service (photocopy) with a particular brand name. Can you list other such products or services? Can you explain how the companies who have accomplished this did so (or what their competitors didn't do)? Why don't you blow your nose in a Marcal or "Savin" a copy?

4

Winning The Entrepreneurial Game

In the last chapter, we learned the rules for playing the entrepreneurial game. In the next four, we will learn what to do to make sure you win the game: predicting success before you begin by analyzing **Demonstrable Economic Justification ("DEJ") Factors** (this chapter); choosing the correct way to set up your company to deliver the product or service you've created (Chapters 5 & 6); and developing a workable strategic plan to start, fund and grow your business (Chapter 7). I've even applied all of the lessons from this first section into a hypothetical start-up—Hot Dog Dance Club— whose business plan is discussed in Chapter 8.

Why Hasn't Anyone Ever ...?

As we've seen previously, entrepreneurs don't really see different things than the rest of us; they just see things differently. Whether you are still a student, out in the work force or home taking care of a family, you confront obstacles every day that an entrepreneur would immediately identify as opportunities. These "gaps" in life that no one has ever filled may be relatively simple to identify and solve—an attachment that would make it easier for students to carry books and other supplies with them on their bikes, discovering the need for a day care center in your neighborhood because of your own inability to find competent help, my vertical parking plaque—or complicated problems requiring innovative and expensive solutions—a pizza chain that delivers hot pizza in less than 30 minutes, an entirely new high technol-

> Entrepreneurs don't really see different things than the rest of us; they just see things differently.

ogy product no one's ever thought of, a delivery service that fills a niche left open by the Postal Service (United Parcel Service, Federal Express).

With no solution in sight, such insights, when expressed, usually conclude with "What this country needs is..." or "I wonder why no one ever thought of..." If you are a budding entrepreneur, you may well be inspired to start a new company to develop your insight into a real solution—a new product or service that people who have the problem will purchase.

Should you actually bite the bullet and do so? Is your insight a valid one? Does the problem really exist? Is your solution really the right one?

In other words, are there fundamental questions or tests that you can apply to your ideas that will indicate which entrepreneurial opportunities will succeed or fail, which should be pursued and which passed over?

The answer is yes. Potential entrepreneurs *can* predict the eventual success or failure of their inspirations by counting the number of "DEJ" factors their new business idea possesses. DEJ stands for "Demonstrable Economic Justification." It's a mouthful, but it really means simply eight questions that will prove or disprove the validity of your idea. (I prefer using "DEJ"—pronounced "*dedge*"—because fundamental concepts should be new words that serve a single, original and unique purpose and cannot be misunderstood or misapplied.)

The Eight DEJ Factors

1. **Existence of Qualified Buyers**
2. **Large Number of Buyers**
3. **Homogeneity of Buyers**
4. **Existence of Competent Sellers**
5. **Lack of Institutional Barriers to Entry**
6. **Easy Promotability By Word-of-Mouth**
7. **Invisibility of the Inside of the Company**
8. **Optimum Price/Cost Relationship**

The beauty of the Eight DEJ Factors is their absolute infallibility—A new company is either *"Super DEJ"* (possessing all eight DEJ Factors); *"Majority DEJ"* (seven out of eight); *"Marginal DEJ"* (six out of eight); or *"Minority DEJ"* (five or less).

WHAT TO DO IF YOUR PROPOSED COMPANY IS...

SUPER DEJ—Run, don't walk, to launch the new company; it is virtually guaranteed to be successful.

MAJORITY DEJ—Vigorously pursue your idea; it has a very high probability of success.

MARGINAL DEJ—Consider carefully before launching; it is likely to be only marginally successful.

MINORITY DEJ—Forget the idea; it will waste your time and trash everyone's cash.

If a potential entrepreneur can be confident that his or her insight or idea possesses all eight DEJ Factors, he or she should run, not walk, to launch the new company. Such Super DEJ Companies practically assure the entrepreneur of solving a problem for a large number of people and becoming very wealthy in the process. Moreover, Super DEJ Companies do not require very much initial capital—less than $500,000 (which really is a pittance if you're planning to start the next Fortune 500 corporation!), possibly as little as a few thousand dollars. The problem is usually so large and the solution and/or its delivery system so unique that the new company can be launched largely with <u>customer financing</u>. With few investors with whom to share ownership, Super DEJ entrepreneurs become enormously wealthy in a short period of time.

With seven of the eight DEJ Factors—a Majority DEJ situation—the idea for a new company should be vigorously pursued because it has a very high probability of success. However, it will require a considerable amount of venture capital, perhaps ten times that ($5,000,000 or more) required by a Super DEJ company. The rate of return on a Majority DEJ company will be less than for a Super DEJ and not merely the return on capital, but the return on the entrepreneur's time and labor as well.

An insight or idea that possesses six of the eight DEJ Factors is a Marginal DEJ Company and, as the name implies, is likely to be only marginally successful. It should be very carefully considered before it is launched because it will require two to three times the venture capital of a Majority DEJ company ($10-15,000,000) without a comparably high probability of success.

If the potential entrepreneur can count five or fewer DEJ Factors—a Minority DEJ Company—the idea should be forgotten. It will waste the entrepreneur's time and trash everyone's cash.

Let's examine these DEJ Factors and see what it is that makes them the fundamental predictors of entrepreneurial success:

Existence of Qualified Buyers

The persons to whom the product must be sold know that they require the product. They don't have to be educated (told they have a problem to which your product or service is the solution). They know they must pay for a solution and are willing and able to do so if the solution really solves their problem.

Large Number of Buyers

The number of potential buyers sharing essentially the same problem is very large. One way to quickly test whether you satisfy this criteria is to multiply the number of potential buyers (sometimes referred to as the universe of selling sites) times the price they would be willing to pay for the solution (your product or service) to their problem. If the number exceeds $1 billion, the business plan should be undertaken.

Homogeneity of Buyers

The problem that the entrepreneurial company solves is essentially the same for all buyers, with only minor differences in degree or severity. The solution does *not* have to be customized for each buyer.

Existence of Competent Sellers

The solution does not require a nobel laureate in physics to explain it; rather, it can be marketed by merely competent salespeople. (The root word of competent, *competere*, is the same as the root word of competitive. To be competent in marketing is to be competitive.) The longer it takes a potential customer to consider buying your product, the more capital you will require.

Lack of Institutional Barriers to Entry

The buyers are not organized—they do not belong to an association and there is no regulatory body to which they are responsible for their activities (such as the American Medical Association or Federal Aviation Administration). Scaling institutional barriers to entry can be as difficult as seeking Federal Drug Administration approval for a new drug—a $56 million proposition, on average—or as simple as obtaining a state license to sell a product or service.

Easy Promotability by Word-of-Mouth

The solution is easily passed along from buyer to buyer by word-of-mouth advertising. Not only is this the cheapest form of advertising—it costs nothing—it is also the most effective. Any solution passed along from buyer to buyer has far greater credibility than one that must be advertised in order to attract buyers. This will allow invariably scarce capital to be spent on the product itself, not on advertising.

Invisibility of the Inside of the Company

If a company does not heavily advertise or promote itself, it minimizes the risk that larger and/or better-funded competitors will become curious about this new little innovator in their marketplace. Curiosity could lead to early competition. When a company goes public very early in its life, for example, it risks allowing potential competitors to gain information about its business plan and financial statements. Exposing a business plan to a large number of venture capitalists can also sacrifice one's invisibility and lead to earlier than expected (or wanted) competition.

Optimum Cost/Price Relationship

The price of the solution must be equal to or lower than the current cost of the problem.

Let's presume, for example, that for lack of any alternative, you are forced to ride your bike five miles round trip to school every day. It costs you $15 a month in *direct* costs to do so—the cost of the bike and parts, maintenance, repairs, etc.—plus the *hidden costs* you must pay—the time and energy you spend peddling, the inconvenience of riding in rain and snow, etc., which you estimate are worth another $15 a month. Your problem is that you really aren't crazy about riding to school every day, but you can't afford any other currently available solution (buying a car, taking a taxi, etc.) because they cost more than $15 a month in *direct* costs, perhaps more than the $30 in total costs.

If someone created a student commutation service that charged you $10 a month or less to pick you up, bring you to school and bring you home every day, allowing you to leave later, arrive earlier and travel in comfort (albeit with a dozen other students), wouldn't you be willing, even eager, to change modes of transportation? You bet you would. The service is a bargain.

The eight DEJ Factors represent the fundamentals of entrepreneurship. They are not used *during* the entrepreneurial game; they are meant to help you decide whether to play in the first place:

If you enter the game with five or fewer DEJ Factors, the company will almost certainly fail.

If your venture has six DEJ Factors, it will require several million dollars of venture capital and will have a low probability of success.

With seven DEJ Factors the probability of success is high and the need for venture capital relatively small.

Possession of all eight DEJ Factors could mean starting with a few thousand dollars and creating wealth of more than $100 million. More than 100 entrepreneurs have done just that in the last 15 years. Possession of all eight DEJ Factors virtually ensures your company's success *without* having to raise start-up capital from venture capitalists, unless, of course, you fail to carry through the launch in a competent manner. (The launch includes building a skilled management team, designing an intelligent business plan and remaining <u>market driven</u> and innovative as the company starts to grow.) Nothing is completely guaranteed—there have been instances in which entrepreneurial teams have screwed up Super or Majority DEJ Companies. But they are too few to count.

If you have identified a problem in your community that you think cries out for an entrepreneurial solution, use the DEJ Factor Test to measure its probability of success *before you begin*. If the opportunity has all eight DEJ Factors, you will not need more than a few thousand dollars to begin, because your company will be customer-financed (like Kemmons Wilson's peanut vending machines in Chapter 2). This will be covered in the next section—Solution Delivery Methods—where you will learn that many successful entrepreneurial solutions are customer financed and require very little venture capital.

How can the lack of just a single DEJ factor spell defeat or make it extremely difficult to even get into the game? Let's take the example of Factor #5. An entrepreneur facing institutional barriers to entry—that is, missing only one DEJ Factor—may need to spend a million or more dollars to knock down (or go around) that barrier. Barriers may include: Federal, state and local government laws and regulations; the "not-invented here" syndrome (corporations will frequently block an entrepreneurial solution if they didn't think of it themselves); trade journals that support the big guys who buy their advertising space and make it difficult for the little guys to gain <u>market share</u>; and plain old lethargy.

Let's look at an example: The commutation problem in big cities like New York, Boston and Los Angeles is horrendous. Traffic gets worse by the day. People are beginning to shoot at one another on the highways. This Big Problem could be mitigated by the hovercraft—an inexpensive, large boat that floats a foot or two above the water and is pushed forward by fans. Hong Kong and other port cities move millions of people per day via hovercraft.

In the mid-1970s, I tried to help a hovercraft entrepreneur begin operations in New York City, but we found a huge barrier to entry. New York City would not give us docking rights. The people who controlled the docks had friends in high places, and they simply prevented this elegant solution from happening.

All of the DEJ Factors are just as important. So don't find a way to convince yourself that missing "just" one or two isn't a problem. It is.

But used correctly, the DEJ Factors will help you de-cide—long before you or your friends or family spend a dime—whether your brilliant idea is really so brilliant after all.

4 Individual Exercises & Projects

1. Identify areas in your own life or community you think may be entrepreneurial opportunities. In other words, what problems exist that no one else is solving or not solving well?

2. From the financial pages of a major newspaper, find two or three companies going public ("new issues"). Contact a local brokerage firm and get those companies' current annual report (if one exists) and/or the prospectus for the stock issue. Then figure out how each company does on the DEJ Test. Which of the companies would *you* want to invest in?

3. Name at least one product and one service that, while solving a problem, would require educating the people who have the problem (DEJ #1).

4. List at least three products that satisfy DEJ #2 and three that don't.

5. List at least three products that satisfy DEJ #3 and three that don't.

6. List two products and two services that satisfy all but DEJ #5 (institutional barriers to entry).

7. What makes a product or service easily promotable by word of mouth? What makes it difficult?

8. Find at least one start-up company—in your community or from your library research—that has failed in the last six months. Analyze its DEJ Factors. Could you have predicted its failure?

5

Delivering Your Elegant Solution, Part 1

You've used the DEJ Factor Test in the previous chapter to evaluate your idea and, *eureka!,* it's an idea whose time has come. The next step in the entrepreneurial game is to select one or more Solution Delivery Methods ("<u>SDMs</u>")—the marketing method by which you intend to convey your Solution (product, service) to your market and, not incidentally, generate some up-front cash. To provide their solution to the greatest number of people, competent entrepreneurs generally select one primary Solution Delivery Method and then develop several ancillary ones (or <u>SDM sub-sets</u>) to generate additional cash. (I'll talk more about the latter in Chapter 6.)

The twelve Solution Delivery Methods—the overall ways by which solutions to problems are delivered to the people that need them—are:

1. Franchising
2. Leveraging with OPM (Other People's Money)
3. Prepaid Subscriptions
4. Party Plan
5. Newsletter/Seminar
6. Facilities Management
7. The Cookie Cutter
8. Consumer Product Start-Up
9. Celebrity-Endorsed Consumer Product
10. High Technology Start-Up
11. Capital Equipment
12. Highway Tollgate

We'll discuss the first six, which generally require the smallest start-up capital, in this chapter. The latter six, which may require significant amounts of initial capital, are covered in chapter 6.

Franchising

Franchising began in 1851 when the I. W. Singer Company, manufacturer of the first sewing machine, was financially strapped and unable to fill the demand for its product. A hotshot salesman in Ohio was taking orders for sewing machines faster than Singer could supply them and was earning $8,000 a year, a princely sum in those days. Salesmen in Illinois and Michigan were doing almost as well. In order to raise cash to produce the machines, Singer started charging its salesmen a fee for the right to sell its sewing machines in designated territories, effectively transforming its sales employees into independent dealers.

Today franchising accounts for a significant portion of U.S. retail sales. According to the United States Department of Commerce, total retail sales of franchised companies were approximately $750 billion, or roughly one-third of all retail sales, in 1986. In that same year, <u>franchisees</u> contributed 20% of the nation's <u>Gross National Product (GNP)</u>, and over 12 million people were employed by franchised companies. The growth rate of franchising in just the last 15 years has been remarkable—total retail sales of franchised companies were a mere $168 million in 1973. Well-known national chains like McDonald's, Kentucky Fried Chicken, Burger King, Century 21 and a myriad of fast-food, cleaning service, auto care and other franchised companies promise to maintain its popularity well into the future.

Creating a franchising plan often requires very little up-front cash—as little as $25,000 to $50,000 may be needed to open a prototype store, test the concept and see what products or services the customers like best and what they're willing to pay for them. Having "fine-tuned" his or her product, the <u>franchisor</u> can then, subject to applicable laws, sell the right to open and operate identical stores in a variety of different regions to franchisees.

Why are franchised businesses suddenly so successful?

From the franchisee's standpoint, buying a franchise of an already established (or, at least, already-tested) business is an attractive alternative for someone with an entrepreneurial

Although an excellent SDM that generates cash quickly, franchising is first and foremost a financing strategy.

bent who lacks his or her own "Big Idea."

The franchisor has already done all the work—formulating and evaluating the entrepreneurial opportunity, creating the elegant solution, working out all the details. Every solution, no matter how elegant, requires some trial and error to work out the many details. Entrepreneurs with great ideas sometimes run out of cash before they've managed to answer the thousand and one questions that must be answered before they can even get started. Franchisors have already worked out the smallest details and prepared detailed instructional material for franchisees. They know that <u>Murphy's Law</u>— "Everything that *can* go wrong *will* go wrong"—operates in virtually every franchise situation. Providing answers to franchisees' questions, no matter how minute, is, after formulating the idea in the first place, their primary function. So not only are the big questions—What's the problem? What's the solution? How do we do it?—already researched and answered, so are the littlest ones.

Franchisees, in other words, virtually get to own their own already-proven businesses without having to "test out" the idea themselves, giving them, in some sense, the best of all possible entrepreneurial worlds—maximum freedom, minimum risk.

There's also a great reason franchising is attractive to the franchisor—it is, first and foremost, a means of raising cash, since franchisees usually pay an up-front fee plus a share of the franchisee's sales or profits (a <u>royalty</u>) in order to sign on. And these up-front fees can be considerable—buying a new franchise location from a well-known company like McDonald's could cost $1 million or more! In addition to paying for the franchise itself, the up-front fee usually requires the franchisor to provide management advice, national advertising and other services common to all franchisees for the life of the franchise.

Within two to three years after its launch, well-managed franchisors normally go public and, with part of the proceeds from their sale of stock, attempt to buy out their most profitable franchisees (those whose profits are larger than their monthly royalties). This is an added incentive to all franchisees—not only can they do very well running their own franchises for a while, but the more successful they are, the more likely they will be able to sell themselves back to the franchisor down the road and become really wealthy. (There is a danger here, though—many franchising companies have

Franchising offers some the best of all possible entrepreneurial worlds—maximum freedom, minimum risk.

fallen apart when the franchisor went public and its founders became visibly wealthy but failed to share that wealth with its most profitable franchisees.)

Although an excellent SDM that generates cash quickly, franchising is first and foremost a financing strategy.

Leveraging With OPM (Other People's Money)

Why invest in capital equipment or bricks and mortar to start a new business when you can obtain leverage with OPM—Other People's Money?

ActMedia was started in 1976 by the Bruce Failing family as an in-store media company. The Failings convinced large consumer products companies of the potency of placing their ads at the point of purchase. The entrepreneurs Beta-tested the idea in several large supermarkets and calculated the results—product sales increased dramatically in stores where shopping carts had advertisements. Armed with such black-and-white data, ActMedia was able to convince a number of advertisers to pay up-front fees to join their plan. ActMedia's market value exceeded $250 million less than ten years after it was started...on an initial investment of $3 million. The supermarkets paid for the stores and the carts, and the food companies paid for the advertising. ActMedia simply leveraged these assets.

Another version of leveraging with other people's money is buying businesses by borrowing on their own assets, then repaying the loans out of their cash flow. This form of acquisition, known as a leveraged buy-out (LBO), is extremely popular among Wall Street raiders. But while it may create substantial wealth for *them,* it does nothing to increase innovation or employment or create solutions to major problems. So it is not discussed further in this book. If LBOs interest you, get a copy of Up-Front Financing: Revised (1988, John Wiley & Sons).

> The prepaid subscription method requires very little start-up capital but has one of the highest probabilities of success.

Prepaid Subscriptions

The prepaid subscription method (also known as *membership merchandising)* requires very little start-up capital but has one of the highest probabilities of success.

The father of membership merchandising is Sol Price, who, in 1975, created The Price Club, a chain of 20 large warehouses selling non-durable merchandise at substantial discounts to members only. It costs individuals or businesses $25 a year to become members of the Club. For an additional $10 per person, a member may designate two additional buyers. Price launched his business in the West by signing up 170,000 $25 members and 800,000 $10 members—that represents $13.5 million in annual prepaid membership fees, or $600,000 per store. A successful entrepreneur can leverage $13.5 million in up-front cash into a fair amount of warehouse and inventory financing to grow his business, and Sol Price has done just that.

You're probably more familiar with some other companies that use prepaid subscriptions as a Solution Delivery Method, such as the Franklin Mint, Book-of-the-Month Club, Harry & David (Fruit-of-the-Month Club) and the Columbia Record Club. Even very specialized products can be delivered via this method: Commerce Clearing House, for example, uses it to sell its daily compilation of court decisions to lawyers. And, of course, there are two entire industries founded on this SDM—magazine publishing and insurance, both of which obtain your money before they have to deliver a thing.

The newest group of entrepreneurs to use this extraordinary SDM are Health Maintenance Organizations ("HMOs"). These are the newest alternatives to medical insurance (Blue Cross/Blue Shield, etc.); and, since they pay 100% of your medical bills, not the 80% you usually get from insurance, they are a very attractive alternative.

To join an HMO, you pay a monthly fee, after which the HMO is responsible for providing you with all of the health care services you may need—from doctor's bills and lab fees to medication and hospital expenses—as long as you are a member (with the possible exception of a token fee per office visit or prescription, usually $5.00 or less).

The HMOs use the subscribers' prepayments as their initial operating capital, which reduces the need for venture capital. They then contract for the services of doctors, hospitals and other health care providers, paying (in advance) so much per person per year, rather than paying for each service or procedure as required.

The Party Plan

This SDM (sometimes called *in-home marketing*) has

been under-utilized, but for those who have adopted it—Tupperware, Mary Kay Cosmetics, Discovery Toys, Shaklee, Amway, Transart Industries and others—it has been a <u>cash cow</u>.

Mary Kay Ash, the founder of Mary Kay Cosmetics, now a $300 million cosmetics company, is proud to say that more women earn over $100,000 working for her than for all other companies in the world combined. She's right.

Mary Kay used her entire life savings—$5,000—to found her company in 1963. Her goal was to create a company in which being a woman would not hinder either advancement or financial rewards. Her particular entrepreneurial insight was in creating a unique motivational system that would attract, train, encourage, keep and reward an all-woman marketing organization. The product these women would sell—her elegant solution to a large problem—was not part of her initial formulation at all.

Ash finally chose a cosmetic that she had been using for years, a skin-care line based on a formula developed by a hide tanner. She rented a store and pulled her 20-year-old son Richard out of college to assist her. Ash immediately began hiring and training "beauty consultants" to begin home demonstrations. (Another nice marketing touch. Wouldn't a woman rather be called this than a saleswoman?)

Her sales system was unique and simple: Each beauty consultant bought a sales territory (and the exclusive right to sell the Mary Kay line of cosmetics in that territory) from the company. She was taught the merits and uses of the cosmetics and how to market them most effectively. She also received training in selling, managing other salespeople and developing communication skills. As the beauty consultant got more successful, she was encouraged to sell regions of her territory to other women ("regional directors"), who were, in turn, encouraged to sell portions of their regions to still others.

The advantages of party-plan selling are the low overhead and immediate cash flow.

This army of salespeople—the number now exceeds 250,000—called on housewives and asked them to arrange "parties" in their homes for eight or ten other women, a comfortable environment in which the beauty consultant could leisurely demonstrate her cosmetics for the hostess and her friends.

A lucrative commission structure ensured that everyone—from the consultant and hostess to the many layers of local, district and regional saleswomen—earned something on each sale: The hostess and consultant each received a commission of 15%; the district manager and the person who trained and supervised her received a smaller commission. The regional manager received an <u>override</u> on the sale, as well. (There is very little product advertising in the party plan SDM, thus permitting these hefty commission structures.)

Ash keeps her beauty consultants fired up at conventions that rival the fire-and-brimstone oratory of revivalist tent meetings. "I created this company for you," she tells her consultants. "If you are here today, you're too smart to go home and scrub floors." Mary Kay has helped more women earn more than $100,000 per year than all other United States corporations combined. Her SDM must be working.

The advantages of party-plan selling are the low <u>overhead</u> and the immediate cash flow. Since all of the selling is done in others' homes and the consultants pay their own expenses, a huge office setup is not required. Secondly, the cost of the products can be entirely customer financed: The salesperson writes invoices for each customer, promising shipment within three weeks, but receives payment in full *at the time of sale*. In fact, the orders are usually telephoned into the company's warehouse from the hostess' home, as is the information on those paying by credit card. Checks and cash are deposited the next day. Thus the party-plan company has the use of the customer's cash for three weeks. This "<u>float</u>" means that when money is especially tight—like when the company is just starting—the virtually immediate sales income can pay for any needed products up-front.

How do you know whether a product or product line is particularly suited for party-plan selling? First, the products should not be available in stores. Otherwise, why would people bother attending a party to buy them?

Second, they should be the kinds of products that require touching, feeling, moving around and playing with for the customer to really appreciate, things you don't mind doing at home but wouldn't care to do in a store or showroom.

Last, the price must be low enough to convince buyers of the product's "good value" but high enough to pay for itself (<u>cost of goods sold</u>), the various layers of commissions, all other expenses (overhead) and a reasonable profit for the entrepreneur. As a rule of thumb, party plan companies usually figure commissions at 40% and overhead at 20%. That leaves 40% for the cost of the product and the entrepreneur's profit. Based on others' experience, there's a simple way to work all this out: To adopt the party-plan SDM, your company's product should be marked up in price at least ten-fold over cost of goods sold.

Products Suitable For Party Plan Selling:

1. Should not be available in stores.
2. Should require a lot of touching and feeling to appreciate.
3. Must be able to sell at ten times cost of goods sold.

For example, a Transart framed print that will sell for $60.00 in the home should cost the company no more than $6.00 to produce. Assuming that commissions to all management and sales levels add up to 40% and that the $2.00 freight charge is also borne by the customer, a typical transaction on one item might break down as follows:

Retail Price	$60.00	
Shipping	2.00	
Total Receipts		$62.00
Commissions:		
Hostess (15%)	$ 9.00	
Salesperson (15%)	9.00	
District Manager (10%)	6.00	
Regional Manager (5%)	3.00	
Total Commissions	27.00	
Cost of Goods Sold	6.00	
Freight	2.00	
Total Expense		$35.00
Gross profit per item sold		$27.00
Minus overhead (20%)	-12.00	
Net profit per item sold		$15.00

Newsletter/Seminar

The newsletter/seminar launch is used *when the solution has not been developed and when the people with the problem need more information about it before they will pay for its solution.* It can be used in any marketplace in which buyers and sellers need to come together several times a year to gain information about both the problem, as others like themselves see it, and the solution, as problem-solvers believe they can deliver it.

As a means of identifying the people interested in potential solutions to particular problems and providing them with information about those problems before the solutions are in sight, the budding seminar (or trade show) sponsor may choose to generate awareness of his or her knowledge by publishing a newsletter.

Virtually any industry of any size has at least one newsletter; some, like the computer industry, have many. Want to start a newsletter about antique eyewash cups? You're too late. The eyewash cup collector's newsletter has been around for years. The trick, obviously, is to *identify a problem no one else has noticed.* Or, at least, not one they've started a newsletter about.

Not incidentally, the prepaid subscriptions to the newsletter can provide the cash flow to launch the seminar business. (And if the problem is sufficiently large, advertisers who wish to address the same group of people will buy space in the newsletter, thus creating a second source of revenues. *Ms.* magazine, for example, was launched in this manner.)

The newsletter-seminar launch also leads into other revenue generating areas, such as consulting and facilities management. It can be seen as a pyramid (one that begins at the bottom and works towards the top).

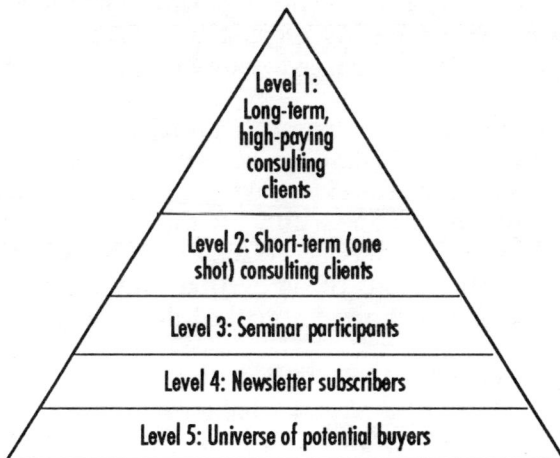

Level 1:
Long-term,
high-paying
consulting
clients

Level 2: Short-term (one shot) consulting clients

Level 3: Seminar participants

Level 4: Newsletter subscribers

Level 5: Universe of potential buyers

Here's how it works: Having identified a particular problem and the group of people who might be interested in its solution, you create a newsletter to offer the information and mail subscription offers to the entire group (Level 5).

A percent of those mailed respond to the newsletter offer and subscribe (Level 4).

After you have a reasonable number of subscribers, you announce a seminar (in the newsletter, of course) to discuss the various issues in which this group is interested (Level 3).

A percentage of the seminar participants, convinced that the problem exists and willing to pay for a solution, hire you to consult with their companies on a short-term basis (Level 2).

A percentage of these one-shot clients, convinced that a long-term solution is in their best interests, hire you on an on-going basis to actually begin implementing solutions. Let's look at a detailed example of such a launch.

Michelle was, until quite recently, the human resources (personnel) director of a large corporation. During her five years on the job, she wound up spending a lot of time dealing with the stress that her corporation's frequent relocation policy caused middle managers and their families. Moving nearly every year or two, sometimes across the country and back again, took its toll on everyone, it seemed. Wives complained that they could not sustain meaningful friendships. Some children's school work slipped badly. Some of the managers and/or their spouses turned to alcohol or drugs to handle the changes.

Michelle realized that such a problem could eventually tear the company apart, sacrificing many of its valuable employees in the process. As a first step, she suggested to her employer that families receive counseling before they were relocated.

Tackling the problem head-on, Michelle began reading everything she could find on relocation stress. She soon became somewhat of an expert in the field and began making senior management more sensitive to this issue, even prompting them to revise their policy to allow more managers to stay put for longer periods of time. After only a few months, Michelle's studies showed a marked decrease in problems relating to relocation.

Unfortunately, when Michelle's boss left the corporation one year later, a Neanderthal took his place. Her new boss was convinced that if an employee refused to be relocated, he simply wasn't a team player and should be canned. And any problems he or she had with the move weren't the company's concern. Michelle's activities were stopped.

Michelle's reading and counseling activities within her own organization had clearly illustrated the size of the problem. Her experience with her new boss and conversations with human resource officers at other companies soon showed her the lack of a clear-cut solution. She decided to create and market one.

She began by announcing a relocation stress newsletter that she offered on a subscription basis (ten issues for $120) to the human resources officers at the 2,000 biggest U.S. corporations. Because of their highly specialized nature, newsletters traditionally charge far more per issue than the consumer magazines you're probably used to. At $12 an issue, Michelle's was relatively expensive.

Yet look at the numbers Michelle was contemplating—if she could sign up 20% of her initial target market, just 400 people, she would have raised $48,000 before she even published her first issue.

Michelle had definitely identified a problem others were also concerned about—she reached her subscription goal within three months and began publishing her newsletter, reporting on the subject from every imaginable angle.

After six months, believing that many of her now-650 subscribers were ready to meet in person to discuss the relocation stress problem, she announced a seminar...in her newsletter, of course. For $500, she offered her subscribers two days of panel discussions and lectures by psychologists and psychiatrists. Checks were received from 75 human resources officers—$37,500 in revenues.

Michelle actually spent only $10,000 on a first-class seminar—good lunches, good speakers and a comfortable hotel in which to hold the meetings (the guests paid for their lodging). This left her an initial profit of $27,500. But then she announced the availability of tapes of each of the seminar meetings. Through the next two issues of her newsletter, she sold over 200 tapes to non-attendees (@ $75), effectively recouping the cost of producing all the tapes plus the $10,000 she actually spent on the seminar.

In other words, every penny generated from the seminar was profit!

Each of the 75 seminar attendees represented corporations that were beginning to take relocation stress seriously. In a separate mailing, she suggested to each of them a chance to buy her expertise—$1,000 for one day's analysis. Twenty corporations signed up over the next three months—$20,000 more...for 20 days consulting. At this point, Michelle resigned her job.

Out of 20 consulting assignments, two corporations emerged that were ready to tackle their relocation stress problems on a long-term basis. Michelle was awarded performance contracts worth $25,000 each (plus expenses) for one year, requiring her to counsel all of the families that had been asked to relocate and recommend to the corporation whether they could handle the stress or simply should not be moved.

In its first twelve months of operation, Michelle's business, therefore, generated a total of more than $170,000 in revenues. Note that with the exception of her initial small investment to identify her prospects and print and mail a newsletter announcement, Michelle never had to invest a dime in her business. The customers paid for each step before Michelle even had to pay for it herself! Given such economies, such a newsletter-seminar business is one idea that can be launched even by full-time students.

Remember the marketing pyramid that appeared at the start of this section? Here's how Michelle's pyramid evolved:

2
Long-Term
Clients
20 One-Shot
Contracts
200 Seminar Candidates
400 Newsletter Subscribers
2,000 Human Resource Officers

Facilities Management

In this SDM the entrepreneur agrees to manage a certain facility for a corporation or government agency at a price equal to (or less than) the corporation or agency is currently paying (its <u>budget</u>). The entrepreneur assumes full responsibility for the direct expenses and overhead of the facility. If he or she is able to deliver the solution efficiently, the difference between what he or she charges and what he or she spends—the profit—is the reward.

Jack Massey, the 82-year old co-founder of Kentucky Fried Chicken, for example, recently bid to manage Tennessee's state prison system, firmly believing his Corrections Corporation of America could run it for less than the $170 million per year the state was spending to do it itself. It's a "can't lose" proposition for the state—under Massey's proposal, the cost to them *cannot exceed* the $170 million they're already paying. And, of course, if Massey is right—if he can significantly reduce the budget—he stands to make millions.

The founder of the facilities management SDM was H. Ross Perot. Perot used customer financing as the principal source of up-front cash to found Electronic Data Systems Corporation (EDS) in 1964, investing only $24,000 of his own money. EDS sells facilities management contracts to data processing departments of large corporations and government agencies. Because no outside equity capital was required, Perot owned most of EDS's common stock and became a billionaire within ten years after start-up. Ten years later, EDS was worth $2.5 billion.

H. Ross Perot used only $24,000 of his own money to found Electronic Data Systems Corporation (EDS) in 1964 and became a billionaire within ten years after start-up.

The problem that EDS addressed was, at the time, very large. Although this partially explains the enormous wealth created, it's important to note that EDS possessed all eight DEJ Factors. EDS should be regarded as the perfect facilities management company—if you're planning to use this SDM, you should study its organization, structure, marketing plan, history, etc. You couldn't find a better model.

Government agencies have recently become exposed to the concept of facilities management contracts, though the facilities they seem most willing to spin off to entrepreneurs are the less attractive ones, such as waste removal and prisons. But as the entrepreneurial revolution builds up a head of steam and more and more people select entrepreneurship as a career, governments will probably start "selling off" many more agencies to them. Even the pork barrel agencies in which cousins of campaign workers are given do-nothing jobs and paid exorbitant salaries—those overseeing highway construction, schools, bridges, libraries, hospitals, and more—will sooner or later be spun off to entrepreneurs.

Don't be too quick to dismiss this SDM as impractical; utilizing it does not require taking over a prison or hospital system. Just remember: The key element is providing a service *at someone else's facility,* one that the company itself would normally have to oversee. Joan Barnes's Gymboree Corp., for example, provides pre-school centers at factories or offices, allowing working mothers to bring their toddlers to work with them, even visit them for lunch. Gymboree is an elegant solution to *two* big problems: While more and more corporations are realizing the importance (in some cases, the necessity) of providing quality, trustworthy day care centers for their employees, few want (or are able) to do so on their own.

5   Individual Exercises & Projects

1. List three local companies and three national corporations utilizing each of the six SDMs in this chapter. Do not include any of the companies already cited in the text.

2. Can you explain the factors that would make one product or service franchisable and another not?

3. What makes a product or service a cash cow? What's the opposite of a cash cow?

4. Go to your local library and find a couple of newsletters in fields that interest you. Can you find a field that seems to lack a newsletter?

5. In the newsletters you found, how many SDM sub-sets can you find that the publishers have used?

6. Can you identify companies, products or services using one SDM that you think should be using another? Or multiple SDMs? (For example, a unique restaurant that should consider franchising or a retail product that should consider party plan selling.)

6

Delivering Your Elegant Solution, Part 2

Alas, there are several SDMs that require venture capital in order to get off the ground. A <u>capital-intensive</u> product, for example, must be produced, demonstrated to customers, tested, debugged, re-manufactured, re-demonstrated and finally sold. Salespeople must be trained to understand the product, which ties up more capital. The six SDMs discussed in this chapter generally require more time, effort and cash than those covered in the previous chapter.

The 12 Solution Delivery Methods

1. Franchising	7. The Cookie Cutter
2. Leveraging with OPM (Other People's Money)	8. Consumer Product Start-Up
3. Prepaid Subscriptions	9. Celebrity-Endorsed Consumer Product
4. Party Plan	10. High Technology
5. Newsletter/Seminar	11. Capital Equipment
6. Facilities Management	12. Highway Tollgate

The Cookie Cutter

"You can't franchise quality," the axiom says. If you have a solution that is best marketed through multiple retail locations, your initial thought may be to sell franchises. After all, it has that most attractive benefit—up-front cash from the customer. However, if the product is relatively difficult to produce or assemble, if extensive training is required to use or market it or if the customer must be serviced after the sale, you will probably have to consider owning and operating your own retail outlets.

When he was 27, Sam Moore Walton left J. C. Penneys, where he had started as a trainee a few years previously, to found his own retail operation, opening his first Ben Franklin store in Newport, Arkansas. It folded in 1950. Just months later, he opened another Ben Franklin five-and-dime in Bentonville, Arkansas. It didn't fold. In fact, by 1962, Walton had sixteen Ben Franklins. His brother, James, gave Walton the idea for discount stores, and the Ben Franklins were converted to form the base for what has become one of the greatest family fortunes in America. (The principal source of funding for the early Wal-Marts were government guaranteed loans, which are available to entrepreneurs who create jobs in small-town America.)

What did Sam Walton figure out 26 years ago that others overlooked?

For one, Walton tends to locate his stores outside large metropolitan areas and in the small towns he's familiar and comfortable with.

Second, he is a hands-on manager who cares about his people and listens to them. To this day, he flies from small town to small town in his Piper Aztec, often visiting four stores a day, spending a couple of hours with each store manager, the associates who run the various departments and the customers. As he explained to *Forbes*: "We like to let folks know we're interested in them and that they're vital to us. 'Cause they are. Those department heads are the only ones who really know what's going on out there in the field, and we've got to get them to tell us." Walton knows thousands of employees *by name,* and he has earned and kept their loyalty.

True to the Cookie Cutter approach, Walton carries an idea that's worked in one town to others. But he doesn't arbitrarily implement even those solutions. First he asks the manager if *he or she* thinks the idea will work in that store, taking the time to discuss its pros and cons. An idea doesn't get adopted unless the manager goes along.

Wal-Mart's boundaries are set by one-day truck routes from six warehouses; 80% of the goods Walton's stores sell pass through these huge company distribution complexes for trans-shipment. Volume discounts and Wal-Mart's own trucking system save 2-5% on cost, no small matter to a company with only a 7% pretax margin.

Success for Wal-Mart is also the result of caring for its customers. The stores are big and attractive and they say to the customers, "You may be small town people, but you have big town taste!" Walton pays his customers a compliment; they've paid him back many times in return—Walton owns 39% of the corporation currently valued at $5.7 billion.

Claude and Donna Jeanloz were tossed out of an African country in 1974 by a dictator who hated the United States and its Peace Corps. They returned to their home in Massachusetts and, for lack of anything better to do, began restoring their colonial house in Northfield. Like many do-it-yourselfers before them, the Jeanlozes soon discovered that many of the authentic fixtures they were looking for were just not made any longer. And when items *were* available, getting them took infinite patience and dogged pursuit. Sheer desperation finally drove them to manufacturers' directories, from which they painstakingly hunted down sources for the items no one else could supply.

Four years later, the couple had completely restored their house in Massachusetts and another in Canada. In the process, they had answered dozens of inquiries from people confronting the same supply problem they had. Where had they ever discovered so many impossible-to-find items?

Claude and Donna recognized an opportunity when it stared them in the face, so they started a mail order catalog featuring exactly the kinds of electrical and plumbing fixtures, hardware and ornaments that so many other house restorers needed but couldn't find themselves. Their main catalog offered necessities for fixing up old houses of any period or region. Later supplementary catalogs offered specialty products to add finishing touches, nostalgia and whimsy.

As the business grew, the Jeanlozes moved it into an old garage (which, of course, they restored), later still to a large factory down the street (which also went through a complete renovation). Sales grew from $34,000 in 1978 to $12 million in 1983. The introduction of a computer early on to collect subscriber names and inquiries and store product information was critical to the company's rapid growth. To generate additional revenues, the Jeanlozes permitted manufacturers to advertise in their catalog.

Stunning cash flow permitted the couple to rapidly diversify into a chain of retail stores called Renovator's Supply. The first was opened in Flemington, New Jersey, a historic town with a restored old town section; the other thirteen stores are primarily situated in New England.

In some ways, their approach was similar to a newsletter/ seminar launch. First they started a catalog, a relatively inexpensive tool that gave them up-front cash and generated a long list of interested buyers. When they had figured out the size and location of their market, they opened retail outlets to complement their catalog, using the catalog's continuing cash flow to fund initial operating expenses for the retail operation.

Consumer Product Start-up

A large number of consumer products are launched every week. The success rate is quite low, however, because the entrepreneurs (or new products divisions of consumer-oriented corporations) fail to evaluate the product's DEJ Factors. If the DEJ Factors are not observed and followed, the new product or company will probably fail (unless it's a "trend-catcher" like the pet rock or hula hoop, which tends to fall outside the DEJ Factor Test).

The most frequently-absent DEJ Factor in new consumer product companies is a large problem in search of a solution. VisiCalc, the first spreadsheet software package for the Apple Personal Computer, solved large problems for its users. Most of the other five thousand software packages launched into the marketplace in 1983 with excessive amounts of venture capital did not. Those companies have failed. VisiCalc (and Apple) has prospered.

In addition to measuring a new company against its DEJ Factors, the launch process for a new consumer product must be carefully executed. Here are the steps:

1. Market research indicates the need for a consumer product solution.
2. A design and development team with demonstrable experience in successfully creating the appropriate consumer product is formed.
3. Prospective <u>marketing channels</u> (direct mail, catalog, retail, franchising, etc.) for this type of product are evaluated and decided upon.
4. The events in the launch are <u>Pert charted</u> **(see page 99)**

5. A business plan is prepared, assigning cost values to the events and establishing revenue projections
6. The strategic plan for the company is developed.
7. A prototype of the product is produced and <u>focus groups</u> of potential purchasers are formed to determine their reactions to the product's packaging, price, etc.
8. The prototype is revised and the business plan modified according to the focus groups' responses.
9. A "corporate achiever"—a marketing-experienced person with a record of achievement in a related industry—is hired to manage the company.
10. The start-up capital called for in the modified business plan is raised.
11. The strategic plan is implemented, launching the product based on the initial marketing decisions.

Elisabeth Claiborne Ortenberg, 52, has distinguished herself as one of the best entrepreneurs in America in an industry that has taken the toll of more businesses and had more grown men crying in their pillows than any other. In New York it's called the "rag business"—its function is to design, produce and deliver to merchants throughout the country the clothing that we wear.

Many apparel companies are here today, gone tomorrow, lasting a season or less, primarily because they concentrated solely on a short-term trend and didn't attempt to solve a real problem. Liz Claiborne, Inc., is different—it solved a problem. The company was launched with $250,000.

While professional women do not have the time to shop for apparel or stay up-to-date with styles, they cannot afford to look *out* of style. Liz Claiborne's solution to this need was a line of apparel—somewhere between classic and avant-garde—designed exclusively for young female executives. This was the elegant solution to the big problem.

But Claiborne took her business one step further, developing a unique marketing plan: She would sell her line of clothes like a service, not like a product. While she recognized the necessity of training salespeople in how to sell her line, especially given her unique concept, she didn't want to go to the expense of opening and operating her own stores. Instead, she created a merchandising aid—"Claiboards"—and provided them free to the retailers who stocked the line.

As Irene Davis wrote in *Women's Wear Daily:* "Claiboards [are] a trademarked concept using sketches, photos and printed explanations showing how merchandise should be displayed in groups." Claiboards explained to retailers how to mix and match Liz Claiborne apparel to maximize each customer's appearance, telling them, in effect, "Here's how to service your customers so they'll keep coming back to your store."

Claiborne's line, while different, was still off-the-rack clothing, not a particularly unique product. But she gave the retailers a reason to stock her line rather than someone else's, an absolute necessity in a highly competitive marketplace where just getting into the stores is half the battle. And she gave customers what they wanted—not just quality and stylish clothing, but service, too. There are at least thirty computer manufacturers, many of them no longer in business, who could have learned a valuable lesson from this example. They may have been able to obtain a larger portion of scarce shelf space in computer dealer stores had they created Claiboards or their equivalent.

Celebrity-Endorsed Consumer Product

Virtually all of the steps necessary to launch any consumer product must also be followed in this SDM. What differentiates them is more a marketing/public relations strategy than any major differences in the way the solution is delivered to customers.

In the celebrity-endorsed SDM, a well-known figure proclaims the virtues of a product or service, and he or she is marketed as a testimonial to its value. While the celebrity is usually not active in the business, his or her likeness may become so closely associated with the product or service that most consumers don't realize that. Arthur Murray Dance Studios and Charles Goren's highly successful bridge tour and book business are prime examples. Neither's death has deterred the revenue growth or profitability of the businesses they endorsed.

One of the most successful celebrity-endorsed consumer product companies was the Park-Hines Corporation, launched in 1955 by a young advertising executive, Roy C. Park. Park convinced restaurant critic Duncan Hines to represent his product line and do personal appearances. Park and Hines would visit a city and have the mayor declare it "Duncan Hines Day," gaining thousands of dollars of free publicity and selling a lot of cake mix along the way. While

Hines never had anything to do with the business itself, his is the product name we still know. Not too many people know Roy Park's name. Park-Hines Corporation was subsequently acquired by Proctor & Gamble for a substantial sum.

And don't underestimate how important a celebrity tie-in can be for raising much-needed up-front cash. Independent movie producers are the masters of generating up-front cash to turn out a product. Beginning often with only a <u>bankable</u> star (the "celebrity"), maybe even a script, they regularly raise $5 million to $10 million to produce their movies, money that's relatively easy to obtain almost solely because of the star's participation.

Thinking strategically in this manner, like an independent movie producer, is good practice for an entrepreneur at any stage of a consumer product launch. How might the skills of an independent movie producer transfer to other entrepreneurial opportunities? You might use a celebrity to co-author software packages or videocassettes that help teenagers avoid drugs or alcohol. Or license a celebrity who is a hero among poor inner-city children to endorse a program that encourages and trains these youths to become productive. A self-defense training system for women might be more successful if endorsed by a female athlete noted for her strength. The list is endless.

High Technology Start-up

For entrepreneurs seeking to solve some of the world's major problems—those involved with health, food supply, the environment, etc.—knowledge of the high technology start-up method, coupled with an understanding of the DEJ Factors, is critical. This SDM has been successfully used by a number of biotechnology companies, the best-known of which is probably Genentech (which we originally discussed in Chapter 3).

Genentech's founders—Robert A. Swanson, 39, and Herbert W. Boyer, 50—have formed the most potent entrepreneurial team in bio-technology, one equally and simultaneously acceptable to investors, the scientific community and the large pharmaceutical companies. In the chase to conquer life-threatening diseases, the ingredients for a successful company are significant capital, great scientists and the participation of outstanding marketing companies (like Eli Lilly). Genentech has won the hearts, minds and pocket-

Genentech's initial strategic plan violated several implicit rules of high-tech entrepreneurship as promulgated in Silicon Valley during the 1970s.

books of all three. It raised over $300 million and licensed Eli Lilly, Hewlett-Packard Company, Boehringer Mannheim Corporation, Miles Laboratories and others to market its products or co-develop new ones. How did Swanson, who left Kleiner & Perkins at 28, and Boyer, a scientist, pull off this miracle where so many others have failed?

A chemical engineering major, Swanson completed his undergraduate work at MIT in three years. He then convinced the Sloan School of Management to let him begin graduate school early. Later Citicorp Venture Capital hired him and, though he was just 25, sent him to San Francisco to open an office for them. A year later Kleiner & Perkins hired him. It was a rapid rise most <u>fasttrackers</u> would have envied, but Swanson was an entrepreneur, not a venture capitalist. He needed to find a problem that he could be happy solving.

After learning about Cetus Corporation, a very successful 1971 biotechnology start-up, Swanson focused his investigations at the local library on the infant science of bioengineering. He compiled lists of authors and started telephoning scientists one by one for their opinions on commercializing gene splicing. Each call would give Swanson more data, but none of the scientists believed that recombinant DNA could be bottled and sold as a remedy. Then Swanson called Boyer. Boyer replied that it could. Genentech, the new company in which each of them invested only $500, was born.

Their initial strategic plan violated several implicit rules of high-tech entrepreneurship as promulgated in Silicon Valley during the 1970s.

Instead of selling stock to raise millions of dollars to plow into huge expenditures for plant, equipment and employees, Swanson and Boyer contracted out their early research to university labs. Rather than attempting to bring a product to market immediately (which is, after all, the goal of any new company), they opted simply to demonstrate that the technology would actually work—that through genetic engineering a microorganism could be made to produce a substance that it ordinarily *didn't* produce.

In previous experiments by Boyer, an artificially-created gene had simply been replicated (or cloned). Now they were trying not only to create and clone a gene in a laboratory, but also to place it inside bacteria and cause the bacteria in turn to manufacture a useful protein. This had never before been accomplished. This certification of the technology, the two believed, would generate the excitement and money necessary to finance a continuing operation.

For their experiments, Boyer selected somatostatin, a hormone found in the brain. While there was no commercial market for synthesized somatostatin, Boyer chose it because he felt certain, given its relatively simple structure, that it *could* be synthesized. He planned to synthesize the DNA fragments, recombine the DNA and insert it in a bacterium (in this case *E. coli*, a fast-reproducing bacterium found in the human intestine), then try to detect somatostatin in the "molecular soup" that developed.

The first experiment took seven months and was unsuccessful. They couldn't find any somatostatin in the resulting "soup." Swanson was worried. Then one of the scientists thought of protecting somatostatin from some proteins in E. coli that might be attacking it. Good idea. Somatostatin had been there all along. The technology worked.

Knowing that, it was time for Swanson and Boyer to choose a product to synthesize that *would* be marketable— they chose human insulin. In order to complete this task in less than a century, they couldn't keep farming out their labwork—they needed to raise capital and recruit scientists *right now*. Swanson went after the best molecular biologists, protein chemists and fermentation experts he could find. And he found many of them, compressing at least ten years of new product development at a major pharmaceutical company into months.

Swanson also decided on a unique strategy for raising up-front cash. Immediately after the somatostatin synthesis, he informed Eli Lilly & Company, the $3 billion pharmaceutical giant, of their plan to manufacture and market synthetic insulin. Eli Lilly had begun marketing insulin in 1923; by 1979, it held 80% of the American insulin market. Swanson knew that the mere existence of synthetic human insulin would seem a threat to the giant. And that it would be futile, perhaps suicidal, to challenge Lilly's advanced sales and marketing staff.

But Swanson never had any intention of competing with Lilly. Instead, he offered them the chance to market Genentech's synthetic insulin as soon as it was available. The up-front licensing fee he charged Lilly for this privilege was all the capital Genentech needed to start work on their first product.

Though years of government paperwork would pass before any of its products would reach the marketplace, Genentech now had the credibility to attract major financing and find more scientists to join it. The future of entrepreneurship as a mechanism for solving major social problems owes a large debt to the initiative of Swanson and Boyer.

The initial steps in the launch of any high technology start-up company are similar to those in a consumer product company launch:

1. Identify a large problem in search of a solution.
2. Determine that the solution is a technological one.
3. Determine that the eight DEJ Factors are in existence. (Frequently one of them—institutional barriers to entry, such as the Food & Drug Administration's approval logjam—will be missing. This will increase the need for venture capital.)
4. Locate a scientific team with demonstrable achievement in the appropriate field to design and develop the solution.
5. PERT chart the events needed to launch the company and plot them against time.
6. Prepare a business plan.
7. Produce a prototype of the solution.
8. Beta-test the solution with a prospective initial user and protect it with __patents__.
9. Debug the solution according to the results of the Beta test and modify the business plan.
10. Hire a corporate achiever from a related industry to manage the company.
11. Raise venture capital to fund the start-up deficits.
12. Begin production and marketing.

Additional steps that are particularly useful in high technology start-ups:

1. Form a scientific advisory board to assure high standards of quality in production.
2. Encourage the formation of users' groups to gain continuous marketplace feedback.
3. Form a board of directors which can advise a strong management team while opening industry doors.

In a high technology SDM, you will have to raise significant amounts of venture capital—tens of millions of dollars. But the.pay-off is frequently proportionately higher than in other consumer product companies—Genentech's current market value exceeds $1.2 billion.

Capital Equipment

"This device will allow you to save 30% of your departmental costs, operate 30% faster than your current methods and be 30% more efficient," the salesman says to the industrial customer. "How can I say no to that?" responds the customer. Because the microprocessor seems to reduce the cost, increase the speed and enhance the efficiency of practically every device it's used in, the so-called "Rule of 30-30-30" (a 30% improvement in cost, speed and efficiency) has become the norm among capital equipment start-ups.

If a capital equipment company cannot promise improvements of at least that magnitude when its product is installed in the user's plant or office, the sale will very likely not be made. The reason is that the user must uproot and replace old systems, routines and equipment at a significant cost in dollars and time. The new equipment must justify the cost of changing the way the user has been doing business.

In a capital equipment start-up, the entrepreneur must be particularly cognizant of the DEJ Factors, because such start-ups typically require venture capital, which dilutes the entrepreneur's ownership from the beginning. If he lacks one or two of the DEJ Factors, the need for venture capital will increase significantly.

If the product does not solve problems for a large, homogeneous, qualified number of buyers, then the company is likely to be unsuccessful or require several rounds of venture capital, thus diluting the entrepreneur's ownership even further.

Among the most successful capital equipment start-ups of the last twenty-five years was Rolm Corporation—launched with $1 million of venture capital in 1976...and acquired by IBM Corporation for $1.9 billion in 1985.

> Rolm Corporation—launched with $1 million of venture capital in 1976...and acquired by IBM Corporation for $1.9 billion in 1985.

Eugene Richeson, M. Kenneth Oshman, Walter Lowenstern, and Robert R. Maxfield (the first letters of their last names spell Rolm) conceived their billion-dollar baby at a monthly poker game in 1968. Lowenstern eventually talked the others into setting up their own shop in a prune-drying shed in Santa Clara in 1969. Oshman was named president because he had always dreamed of having his own company. Lowenstern and Maxfield preferred engineering. Richeson became the marketer because he was comfortable selling Rolm's initial product—fail-safe computers for the military.

Five years later, when sales hit $3 million, Oshman convinced the team to spend $1 million to diversify into the microprocessor-based <u>PBX</u> business. The Intel 8080 chip, far superior to previous microchips, had arrived on the scene and Oshman wanted to be the first to utilize it in a telecommunications product. This decision put the company squarely into the office automation business.

Rolm Corporation's bread-and-butter product, the Rolm CBX, is a PBX designed for business with 16 to 10,000 telephone extensions. Its microprocessor-based telephone sets interface with the PBX unit, integrating voice and data signals. Messages can be sent, received and answered electronically through a video terminal connected to one of Rolm Corporation's telephones.

Each year Rolm Corporation seems to come out with new features that are 30% better, 30% faster, and 30% cheaper than competitive systems. In 1983, for instance, the company introduced Phone Mail, a PBX enhancement that combines telephone answering, message notification, and voice storing-and-forwarding features with a new digital feature. It's clear why they continue to be leaders in their market.

Oshman built Rolm Corporation to be a "great place to work." One Halloween three of the founders—who are in their mid-forties—came to work dressed as three of the Seven Dwarfs. Their fortunes are anything but dwarf-like.

Highway Tollgate

The most lucrative companies in America are those that extract a fee from anyone who wants to enter their market. Numerous state governments, for example, use tollgates to prevent people from entering a highway without first paying a fee. This proves that the government knows a good deal when it sees one. Other governmental "tollgates" include a variety of licenses (drivers, pilots, etc.), certification tests for licenses (in medicine, law, teaching, etc.) and regulatory agencies (the Food & Drug Administration, Federal Aviation Board, etc.). All require consumers or businesses to pay fees in order to be allowed to do whatever it is they want to do—drive a car, practice medicine, market a new drug, etc.

Likewise, the object of a highway tollgate launch is to

create a justification that will enable the entrepreneur to extract a fee from people who wish to enter a market, entrance to which he controls. A careful reading or viewing of Mario Puzo's The Godfather as a business book will point out how protection became the justification for the tollgate put in place in many markets by one group of immigrant entrepreneurs.

> **The most lucrative companies in America are those that extract a fee from anyone who wants to enter their market.**

Exclusivity (snob appeal) is frequently as useful a justification as protection. Real estate companies selling high-priced, high-security condominiums have effectively combined them, offering the exclusivity high prices almost automatically confer and the protection of a 24-hour guard service, TV cameras, are high walls.

As both these examples demonstrate, fear can be a potent justification, indeed.

Highway tollgate businesses, however are usually built on information. While frequently free if unorganized, an entrepreneur who packages information in an efficient and usable format can then charge customers for access to it. Remember what the scorecard salespeople shout out over and over again as you enter a baseball or football stadium: "You can't tell the players without a scorecard." Well, you can if you take the time before the game to hunt up the information. But why should you? Just buy a program for two bucks.

In a rapidly changing world, the need for *current* information increases daily; the price of that information—packaged in a usable format—increases accordingly. The advent of the personal computer has resulted in a number of highway tollgate companies, such as CompuServe, Inc., as it enables entrepreneurs to package information rapidly and accurately and offer interactive options that a book listing the same information can't. Can you think of old forms of delivering information that can be changed using computer networks? Printed directories of wines, pharmaceuticals, actors and actresses available for movies or commercials, electronic parts, legal services and the like are all available as computer software...or will be soon.

Creating Additional Sources of Revenue— SDM Sub-Sets

Extraordinarily creative (or merely desperate) entrepreneurs have demonstrated how to develop numerous sub-sets of SDMs that create additional <u>channels of distribution</u> to consumers and an equal number of sources of revenue to the entrepreneur. Publishing entrepreneurs seem to be exceptionally good at conceiving them. In addition to the magazine itself—which has two primary revenue sources—subscriptions and advertisements—built in, the following revenue-generating sub-sets frequently are created:

> Rental of subscribers' names (<u>list rental</u>)
> Seminars, symposiums
> <u>Joint venture,</u> <u>direct response</u> marketing sales
> Sales of feature articles to small town newspapers to use as Sunday features
> Audio cassettes of important articles
> Video cassettes of interesting features
> Books composed of several series
> Sale of articles in foreign markets
> Diaries
> Pre-paid membership clubs (such as travel)
> T-shirts, sweatshirts
> Consulting services
> Endorsement fees (e.g., the *Good Housekeeping Seal of Approval*)
> Trade shows
> Reprints of popular articles

Fifteen sources of cash. Fifteen additional methods of providing solutions to needs.

And there are always entrepreneurs able to find more. Two now-successful entrepreneurs from Knoxville, Tennessee, Phillip Moffitt and Christopher Whittle, did something quite unique in magazine publishing, generating a substantial amount of cash while solving major problems for consumer product advertisers. Moffitt and Whittle formed 13-30 Corporation in 1969 to solve the dual need of helping magazine advertisers reach specific audiences and providing those audiences with valuable information in a reliable format.

While still students themselves, they persuaded Moffitt's economics professor to guarantee bank loans for them and began publishing informative magazines for college students. Bank debt reached $1 million before 13-30 Corporation became profitable, but revenues in 1986 were approximately $125 million and earnings were estimated at more than $10 million.

13-30's unique marketing concept was *target publishing*. Moffitt and Whittle, for example, contacted the marketing managers at Kimberly-Clark Corporation, a major manufacturer of paper hygiene products. 13-30 offered to design a publication that would reach one of the company's key markets—female high school seniors. Moffitt and Whittle would provide articles and stories of interest to this audience; Kimberly-Clark would be the sole advertiser. The company enthusiastically bought the idea, and the <u>progress payments</u> they made as the magazine was put together meant 13-30 didn't have to raise any venture capital.

Moffitt and Whittle next approached Johnson & Johnson Corporation (makers of baby powder, baby shampoo and related products) about a publication for new parents, as natural an idea for them as the first magazine had been for Kimberly-Clark. The magazine that 13-30 created for Johnson & Johnson—*New Parent.*—is now read by 1.9 million new parents a year. With two successful sales under their belts, Moffitt and Whittle rolled up their sleeves and launched fifteen additional target publications in rapid succession, including *Tables*, a publication for waiters (funded by Seagram Company Ltd.) and *On Your Own*, a publication for high school seniors (funded by the U. S. Army).

13-30 purchased *Esquire* magazine in 1979, when its revenues were a couple of million dollars per year. By turning it into a modified target publication—selling only a single *category* of advertisers in each issue, depending on the editorial theme of that issue—they expanded its revenues to over $35 million. *Esquire* was eventually sold to the Hearst Corporation in 1987 for nearly $100 million (not long after Moffitt and Whittle's partnership broke up).

Does their targeted publishing concept sound like a simple idea? Like a "Now, why didn't *I* think of that?" plan? Like so many entrepreneurs before them, 13-30 Corporation simply took a simple idea and executed it with elegance. Bear this example in mind as you review the twelve Solution Delivery Methods.

You have now learned the fundamentals of delivering your solution to the problem (entrepreneurial opportunity, if you prefer) that you have identified. Go through them all again until you understand not just how each works, but when each should be utilized.

And don't underestimate how important it is to choose

the right Solution Delivery Method. Many entrepreneurial companies have failed because they selected the wrong SDM. Just look at the graveyard of computer software companies that ignored potentially effective SDMs like catalog marketing (*prepaid subscriptions*), a *celebrity-endorsed* launch or licensing the name of an educational publisher *(leveraging with OPM)*, plunging pigheadedly ahead with a consumer product SDM, trying to buy market share. And the many fast-food retailers that failed to make the cut because they ignored the franchising SDM. There are probably several abandoned locations in your hometown.

6

Individual Exercises & Projects

1. Make a list of three local companies and three national corporations for each of the six SDMs in this chapter. Do not include any of the companies already cited in the text.

2. Make a list of at least six products or services you feel would benefit from using the celebrity endorsement SDM. What celebrities would you select as spokespeople for these products/services? Why?

3. Pick any local or national company utilizing any SDM. Can you identify the SDM sub-sets they're currently using? Can you find others they should consider?

4. Review all twelve SDMs. Can you find examples of otherwise good products or services that you think are utilizing the wrong SDM? What SDM (or multiple SDM) do *you* think they should be using?

7

Planning For Success

Once you know the rules of the game (chapter 3), have decided whether to play at all (chapter 4) and, if so, what game to play (chapters 5 & 6), you must develop your game plan—the step-by-step strategy to successfully develop and market your idea. *This step must be taken before you start raising capital and implementing any solutions.*

While such a planning stage should be obvious, you'd be surprised how many entrepreneurs fail simply because they leap from identifying a problem right to raising capital. If they manage to raise the money they (think they) need, it just has to sit there while they go back and do the intervening steps—creating the solution, testing it, developing marketing and sales goals, etc.

In order to launch your entrepreneurial company in the most effective way, you should follow an orderly progression of events, which we will call the launch (or strategic) plan Here are the twelve steps in such a plan:

1. Formulate the problem;
2. Develop the solution to the problem;
3. Select the solution delivery method;
4. Create a PERT chart;
5. Write a business plan;
6. Create a prototype of your solution and protect it with a patent or copyright, if necessary;
7. Beta-test your solution;
8. Debug the solution and modify your business plan;
9. Begin production in small quantities;
10. Hire a corporate achiever;
11. Raise the necessary start-up capital;
12. Begin full production and marketing.

> You'd be surprised how many entrepreneurs fail simply because they leap from identifying a problem right to raising capital.

Don't try to burst into the market-place by brute force.

To avoid losing time, wasting capital and compromising your credibility, you should follow these twelve steps *in order*. Otherwise you will likely end up with a scrambled (and unsuccessful) launch. Take your time—don't try to burst into the marketplace by brute force. That doesn't work either.

In this chapter, I'll take you through these twelve crucial steps one at a time, explaining each move and giving examples to clarify certain points. Many of the initial steps have already been covered in previous chapters. That's okay; this chapter will serve to summarize them and help you see how all the steps work together. As you plow ahead with your own entrepreneurial launch, return to this chapter as often as necessary to ensure you're staying on the safe path to entrepreneurial success.

Formulate the Problem

This is the most creative aspect of the entrepreneurial launch, requiring you to analyze the problem that you have chosen to solve, studying it from every possible angle. You can accomplish this most effectively by asking yourself some of the questions posed in previous chapters:

Are people aware of the problem?

Do they know what the problem currently costs them?

Is the problem equally severe and costly to all of them? Most of them? None of them?

Is the problem common to a widespread geographic area?

Is the problem discussed in a newsletter or trade journal, in newspapers or on television?

Do people who have the problem attend seminars or industry-wide conferences where solutions and new ideas are discussed? Or do they wait for solutions to come to them?

Where do people who have the problem customarily buy solutions? From entrepreneurs? Consultants? Large companies?

Is there a trade association or any other institutional barrier that may restrict the flow of new ideas into this marketplace?

Will this product (your solution) need to be accompanied by an instruction manual? Will it require servicing after the sale?

The answers to these questions will both help you complete the DEJ Test and decide which SDMs should be considered.

Develop the Solution to the Problem

What you do at this stage of the launch will depend in part on the sort of problem and SDM you have chosen. If you are working on a high-tech start-up, for example, you will now seek and hire a scientific team to help you develop your product. If you have chosen a consumer product or capital equipment solution, now is the time either to assemble a product development group or to license the right to produce and market a product someone else has developed.

Whatever solution you have chosen, attempt to standardize it.

Whatever solution you have chosen, you should now attempt to standardize it—that is, find the common factors that will make it useful to the largest possible number of people. Also, if your product is to contain a component that must occasionally be replaced—like the blade in a razor or the ribbon in a typewriter—spend some time right now developing (or researching where to buy) replacement parts that are efficient, reasonably priced and easy to install.

Keep going over the DEJ factors. Analyze your solution from every possible angle, always remembering that it will be successful only if it has as many DEJ factors as possible, preferably all eight.

Select Your Solution Delivery Method

Review chapters 5 & 6. Study the twelve SDMs until you are certain which one will be right for your solution. (You may decide to combine *several* SDMs into one business plan, especially if you are an information or franchise entrepreneur. Newsletters are often marketed by prepaid subscription; franchising chains occasionally use celebrity endorsements.)

Create a PERT Chart

The word "PERT" is an acronym for "Program Evaluation and Review Tool." Using the sample PERT chart (Figure 2) on page 99 as your model, diagram all of the steps in your business launch, plotting each move in your strategic plan against time and keeping the tasks organized into

Consider the worst-case scenario for each step.

categories such as finances, facilities and equipment, product, etc. Assign a cost to each activity, and include all twelve launch steps in your PERT chart.

Schedule each move carefully, taking time to consider the worst-case scenario for each step. Remember that if one event—say, developing the prototype—takes two months longer than you planned, your company will need additional capital to cover rent, salaries and other expenses during those extra eight weeks.

PERT charting will encourage you to temper your optimism with downside planning, an ongoing exercise in which you continually ask yourself, "Now, if this move backfires, what can I do to repair the damage or cover the shortfall?"

Write a Business Plan

Your objective here is to take the skeleton of your PERT chart and start adding some flesh to it by appending descriptive material, especially detailed financial information, since each of those events you've plotted will cost a certain amount of money. Projections of revenues and cost of goods sold will need to be figured. The result will be a cash flow projection of 36-60 months (3-5 years). Figure 3 shows you how to diagram this flow numerically and graphically.

Do your business plan projections by hand. Do not use a software package.

Do your business plan projections by hand. Do not use a software package. This old-fashioned method will result in a more thorough understanding of the business plan. When it is finished, ask your board of advisors or directors to evaluate it.

The key elements necessary to construct any business plan are:

1. The components of revenue
2. The components of variable costs
3. The components of fixed costs

These components are a function of the events of the launch process that you have developed up to this point.

Keep in mind that your revenue projections must be based on valid, meaningful assumptions; otherwise your cash flow projections will lack credibility. If that happens, sophisticated investors will not back your business, and good managers will not join your company.

Variable cost components include production-, sales- and marketing-related expenses.

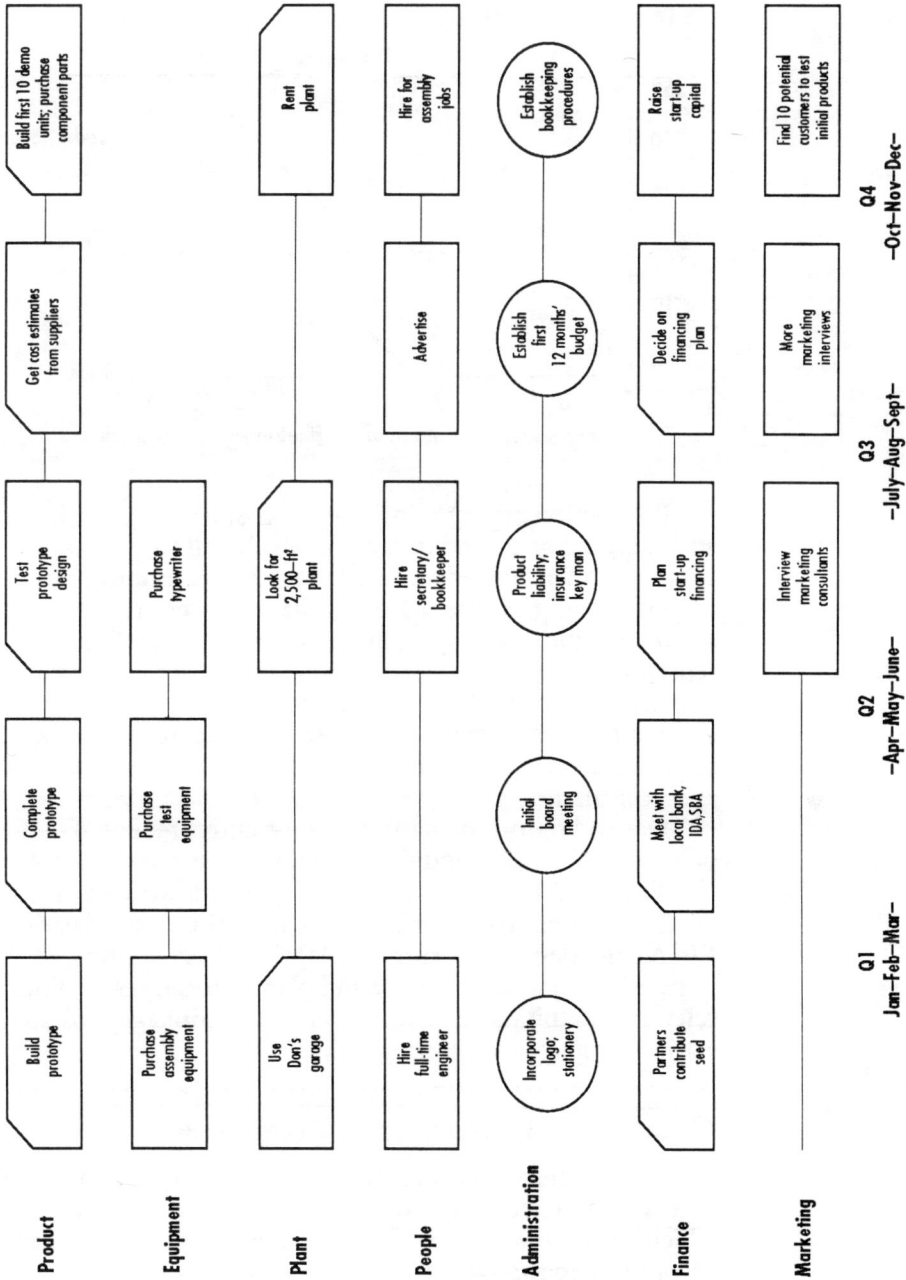

Product — Build prototype → Complete prototype → Test prototype design → Get cost estimates from suppliers → Build first 10 demo units; purchase component parts

Equipment — Purchase assembly equipment → Purchase test equipment → Purchase typewriter

Plant — Use Don's garage → Look for 2,500-ft² plant → Rent plant

People — Hire full-time engineer → Hire secretary/bookkeeper → Advertise → Hire for assembly jobs

Administration — Incorporate logo; stationery → Initial board meeting → Product liability; insurance key man → Establish first 12 months' budget → Establish bookkeeping procedures

Finance — Partners contribute seed → Meet with local bank, IDA,SBA → Plan start-up financing → Decide on financing plan → Raise start-up capital

Marketing — Interview marketing consultants → More marketing interviews → Find 10 potential customers to test initial products

Q1 — Jan–Feb–Mar– Q2 — Apr–May–June– Q3 — July–Aug–Sept– Q4 — Oct–Nov–Dec–

Figure 3. Developing Cash Flow Projections

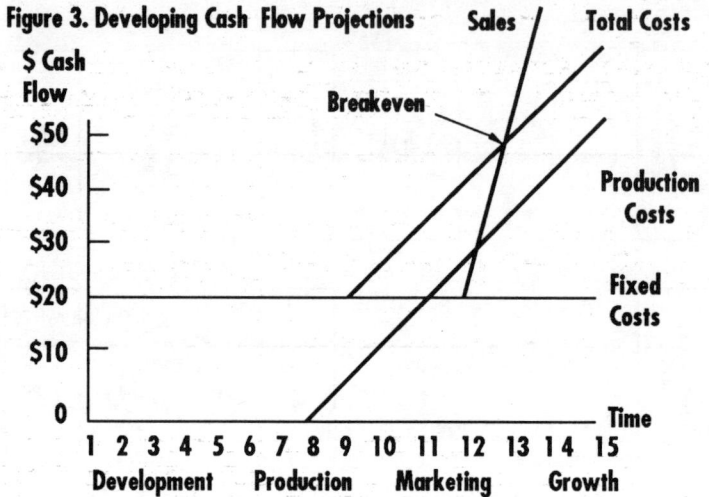

Production expenses include the cost of materials, labor and shipping and handling, all of which will vary according to the number of products made each week, month or year.

Depending on the SDM you have chosen, the costs of selling will include support and commissions for direct sales representatives, marketing representatives, dealers, franchisees and/or party-plan representatives.

Your variable marketing costs will be spread among advertising (print, broadcast and/or direct), public relations and consultants.

Depending on the nature of your entrepreneurial company, you may have additional variable cost components.

The fixed cost components of your business will most likely include: management and administrator's salaries, FICA and benefits; insurance; legal and accounting fees; rent; office equipment; office and plant furnishings; utilities; telephone; sanitation; factory overhead; shrinkage; postage; stationery and other consumables.

Create and Protect Your Prototype

If your solution is a product, you must now design, build and assemble your prototype—the original model from which all copies will be fashioned. As soon as you have accomplished this (and even before you test it and debug it), you should patent your product. A patent attorney can help you file the necessary materials with the U. S. Patent Office.

A patent is absolutely vital if you wish to prevent others from infringing on your right to the exclusive use of your idea. (For this reason, you may even wish to introduce some complications into your patent application to make your device particularly difficult for others to copy.) *Do not go public with your product until you have filed it (and any improvements you make in the testing/debugging phases) with the Patent Office.*

If your solution is a service, you will have to describe it in complete detail in a manual. (Again, you may wish to confuse some important details a bit so as to make it difficult for imitators to copy.) When you are satisfied with your description, file for a copyright with the U.S. Copyright Office. Again, the services of an attorney will be useful here.

If your solution is information, it should be described in elaborate detail in a manual and then copyrighted like the service solution.

Beta Test Your Solution

When you have created your product or service, you should test it thoroughly in your plant or office to see if: (1) it works; and (2) it is innovative. These are known as <u>alpha tests</u>.

Beta tests are conducted outside your plant or office, putting your solution into the hands of potential consumers and letting them use it. The most common type of beta test is probably the focus group. For this test, you simply assemble a group of potential customers in a conference room or in someone's home, put the product into their hands, show them how to use it and then watch and listen. This will help you discover what they think of various important aspects of your product—its name, price, usefulness, packaging and general appearance; how it feels in their hands; how easily it can be operated; whether (and how well) it does what it's supposed to do; the directions that come with the product; and its color, size and ease of use.

Decide ahead of time what you want to learn through your beta tests, then choose your focus groups and meeting places so you're sure to get the information you need. And consider offering your beta testers a discount on future purchases in return for their help.

> A patent is absolutely vital to prevent others from infringing on your right to the exclusive use of your idea.

> Is your product innovative? Does it work?

Debug Your Solution and Modify Your Business Plan

Business plans are not written in stone; they may need to be modified many times.

Chances are the beta tests will turn up one or more weaknesses in your solution. If so, your next step is to debug your product or service—in other words, correct any weaknesses and rebuild or rewrite the solution so as to incorporate these necessary changes. Once you've done that, you'll need to run a second wave of beta tests on your newly-debugged product.

When you finally get your solution into working condition, you'll need to modify your business plan to reflect all of the changes, cost differences and delays. The modified business plan—which, by the way, might have to be revised many *more* times—will become your company's strategy. You'll use it to hire key managers, and you'll show it to banks and other sources of capital.

Begin Production in Small Volume

At this stage, you need to put your production system into operation, not so much to turn out goods to sell as to gain necessary information about the production process before you roll out your product. Here are just a few things you'll be looking for at this stage:

What problems, if any, are likely to crop up in the mass production process?
How good is the production team?
Are they adequately trained?
Do they work well together?
How good are the suppliers?
How many alternative suppliers are available?
Will the production process be slowed down because of delayed delivery of supplies?
Are raw materials in abundant supply?
How many alternative sources are available?
What kind of quality-control mechanism works best for this particular production team?

Depending on the nature of your solution, you may have to add to or subtract from this list. Compile a detailed list of things *you* want to learn from your small-volume production process. During this stage, make whatever adjustments seem necessary to achieve the most efficient and satisfactory production operation.

Hire a Corporate Achiever

At this point you're ready to hire a corporate achiever to manage your company and/or to bring in a business partner. If you're hiring a corporate achiever, he or she must already have demonstrated a high level of ability in the corporate world, preferably in a field related to the one your new company is about to enter. And he or she should possess skills that complement, not duplicate, your own—if you're a highly creative, high-energy person, for example, the corporate achiever should be thorough and meticulous.

Don't make the mistake of hiring someone who is less capable than you are or lacks the strength of character to stand up to you when he or she believes you are wrong. Try to find someone who is as courageous, intelligent and capable as you are.

In most instances, corporate achievers are older and more conservative than entrepreneurs. They usually have greater personal assets to protect, and they may be more meticulous in dress, speech and demeanor. Their reasons for joining an entrepreneurial company should include a desire to build something, to become a member of a problem-solving organization and to regain their sense of purpose. The glue that binds them to the entrepreneur is equity—a piece of the action.

Try to find someone who is as courageous, intelligent and capable as you are.

Raise the Necessary Start-Up Capital

It is possible, though unlikely, that this step will not apply to your entrepreneurial company. There are, after all, a good many businesses that don't require start-up capital or need an amount so small that it can be raised through family and friends. In the case of a multiple-SDM company, you may be able to get started with customer financing only. If you're one of the lucky entrepreneurs who can do without outside investors, feel free to breeze right on past this step.

If you need to raise capital, however, get it without delay. You will need it to fill the deficit that will inevitably show up when you prepare your marketing cash flow sheet. Keep a sharp eye out for changes in your need for capital. You may have to adjust the total amount needed each time you run into a delay or make a change in your production schedule.

If you need to raise capital, get it without delay.

Begin Full Production and Marketing

At this point you are ready to roll out your product or service, to give your entrepreneurial gift to the audience whose problem you have set out to solve. If you have taken care to complete every step in the entrepreneurial process to the best of your considerable ability, your launch will be a success.

Read The Next Chapter

Have seven chapters of charts and graphs and figures and statistics completely worn you down? Don't dismay! It's an awful lot of information to absorb in a single sitting. Some concepts, no matter how well-explained, no matter how many examples are cited, may still be just beyond your grasp.

Since I believe that the best way to understand any concept is to actually apply it in a real-life situation, Chapter 8 gives you an opportunity to do just that—to see how everything covered so far would actually work as you plan your own start-up company, the Hot Dog Dance Club.

7 Individual Exercises & Projects

1. Find a problem you feel cries out for solution and answer the questions on page **96**.

2. How would you solve this problem?

3. What SDM would you use?

4. Is this a business that should actually be undertaken by someone? (Hint: Apply the DEJ Test) If so, how would *you* proceed?

5. How much money would you need to start and operate such a business? Where would you start looking for it?

8

The Hot Dog Dance Club

It's time to see how everything we've covered in the first seven chapters of this book could be applied to an actual business, one, as a matter of fact, you could go out and start tomorrow. I've assumed you've been a very industrious young man or lady—you have worked after school, on weekends and in the summer and put your disposable income into a savings account at the highest yield offered in your community. Your liquid net worth is now $7,000.

Let's Pretend...

...that one day you take a different way home from school and notice an obviously-abandoned restaurant. You never really noticed it before—apparently no one else did either—but now the a weed-covered lot in the center of an otherwise busy block appears to you as a golden entrepreneurial opportunity.

You know your friends and other teenagers in your community are bored—there's no cool place to hang out. Movies and quick service restaurants are the only inexpensive options. What about a dance club just for teens?

Ok. Good idea. But maybe too trendy, especially since young people leave one fad and jump on another faster than any other market segment. Your dance club will need another revenue source, something stable but with a high gross <u>profit margin</u>. How about a hot dog stand?

You begin to observe, to formulate, to inquire, to research. The property is near your high school, has a kitchen and about 1,500 square feet of useable space if all the seats and tables are pulled out. Your idea for this abandoned restaurant begins to take shape. It is a dual use concept: hot dogs, french fries and soft drinks for the high school students' lunches and for the general public four nights a week (Monday through Thursday). On Fridays and Saturdays, it becomes a teen dance club with a soft drink bar. Although you've discovered that the location has failed three times before...twice as a restaurant...you believe focusing on a market you know—the teenagers who attend the nearby high school—will be the secret of your success.

Now Let's Go To Work

You decide the dance club is the key concept and plan to test market the idea on the students. Once they get into the habit of using the facility as a dance club, you reason, they will come by for a hot dog, fries and a soft drink for lunch. In the summer, the dance club can operate six nights a week, and you can broaden your marketing effort to include hotels, travel agents, church groups, youth groups and the like. On some nights, the dance club can be rented out to private parties.

The initial tasks necessary to transform the abandoned location into a hot dog stand and teen dance club are to make the parking lot neat, bright and safe (which means adding spotlights) and to put a sign out front and on the building.

You begin to find ways of reducing expenses right from the start. You plan to find a soft drink or hot dog producer to supply your out-front sign for free. The cost of readying the parking lot, excluding your labor and friends' and siblings' labor, is around $650. Once you start working on this idea, you quickly find a junk dealer willing to pay you $650 for the tables and chairs left by the previous owners. So your initial capital needs are taken care of. Now, let's see what kind of cash flow the Hot Dog Dance Club (my choice for a name) generates. That will tell you how much you can pay the seller, the bank or the lender who, you hope, will provide the financing to help you buy the property.

Push The French Fries!

Let's look at the restaurant operation first. Before you can figure out how much it can earn you (or, for that matter, even how much to charge your customers), you need to know the gross profit margins of the three products that you are planning to sell: hot dogs, french fries and soft drinks. You call various suppliers and talk with other retailers to find these answers:

Hot dogs	30%
French fries	80%
Soft drinks	60%

These numbers should already be teaching you something. Clearly, you want your counter help to push french fries and soft drinks because they offer the best profit margins. In fact, given the huge disparity between the costs of these three items, you realize you can even offer specials on hot dogs—at or near your cost—in order to generate greater traffic, customers to whom you plan to sell *lots* of fries and soft drinks.

Once you start getting a handle on your costs, you will need to estimate sales. You do this by projecting the number of customers you expect to attract to the restaurant and, separately, to the dance club.

Projecting revenues is a tricky business. You can only *estimate* how many customers you will have (at least, until you have some actual operations experience to go by), and to do that you have to make assumptions, some of which may well turn out to be wrong. There are times when you will think there is a plague on your business because nobody comes by (which always seems to happen immediately after an advertising program has consumed a big chunk of your very precious capital). The weather can be a factor, as days of rain slow traffic to a trickle. A competitor could lower its prices or offer an attractive special that lures more customers away from you. The utility company could dig up the street in front of your driveway to fix some pipes or wires, making it impossible for customers to even get through the front door

Projecting revenues is a tricky business.

What can you do about these unexpected bolts from the blue? Nothing at all, except be aware that Murphy's Law—"Anything that could go wrong will go wrong"—is always in operation. To give yourself solace, remember that it doesn't discriminate. All new companies must go through the same period of estimating, planning, worrying, and, inevitably, dealing with the unexpected.

So be ready to revise your projections downward when the unexpected occurs—because it will—so that you are always prepared for a worst-case scenario. Leave some slack, perhaps 20%, in your cash flow projections to take care of any sudden, inexplicable, sustained and uncomfortable fall off of revenues.

Anyway, back to projecting. Let's start with our (hopefully realistic and reasonable) assumptions: Your high school has 500 students. After doing some initial advertising (putting up some posters on school bulletin boards) and conducting market research (talking to all of your friends and all of *their* friends), you estimate that 50 students (10% of your potential audience) will drop in for lunch in the first month and 10 more each month until 100 students per month come five days per week. In addition, you project that 30 non-students will come by for lunch and 30 for dinner, and that the number of non-students at lunch will increase by 10 per month until the number reaches 70 for lunch and 50 for dinner four nights per week. The customer head count for the first year is shown in Figure 4.

Figure 4 Projected Traffic Count (Total Customers per Day) —Hot Dog Stand							
Month 1	50	+	30	+	30	=	110
Month 2	60	+	40	+	40	=	140
Month 3	70	+	50	+	50	=	170
Month 4	80	+	60	+	50	=	190
Month 5	90	+	70	+	50	=	210
Month 6	100	+	70	+	50	=	220
Month 7	100	+	70	+	50	=	220
Month 8	100	+	70	+	50	=	220
Month 9	100	+	70	+	50	=	220
Month 10	100	+	70	+	50	=	220
Month 11	100	+	70	+	50	=	220
Month 12	100	+	70	+	50	=	220

We're going to further assume that each customer, on average, orders one hot dog, one order of fries and a medium soft drink at the following prices and unit gross profits:

Figure 4a. Gross Profit Projections (1)				
	Price	Unit Cost	Gross Profit Margin	Gross Profit
Hot Dog	$1.95	$1.37	30%	$.59
Small French Fries	.60	.12	80%	.48
Medium Soft Drink	1.00	.40	60%	.60
Total	$3.55	$1.89		$1.67

On a $3.55 sale, you will make $1.67 or 47%. One way of increasing your gross profit margin would be to lower the price of a hot dog to $1.75 (your cost is $1.37 per unit) to customers who buy a larger order of fries, for which you'll charge $.85 per bag. Here's what your unit gross profit would look like then:

Figure 4b. Gross Profit Projections (2)				
	Price	Unit Cost	Gross Profit Margin	Gross Profit
Hot Dog	$1.75	$1.37	22%	$.38
Small French Fries	.85	.14	84%	.71
Medium Soft Drink	1.00	.40	60%	.60
Total	$3.60	$1.91		$1.69

Once again, you cannot predict the orders that your customers will place. Some may come in for only a soft drink, hogging a prime parking place or tying up the drive-up window. Some may come in, ask to use the bathroom and order nothing. But you have to make some assumptions, and a single hot dog, order of fries and a soft drink is not an outrageous one. Trying to guess right is part of the fun of being your own boss.

As to operating costs, you will need at least two full-time employees (of which one will be you in the summer). Let's assume they will cost $1,200 per month (including all benefits and taxes). You will also have to pay for utilities, consumables (paper products) a telephone and insurance, which we will estimate at $1,500 per month.

Let's Eat The Hot Dogs And Dance

Estimating the traffic to your dance club is probably more difficult, because it is a service rather than a product, and there are numerous alternatives on a weekend night to dancing. Your service must be exactly what the market wants and needs at that moment in time, or people will spread negative information about the club.

There are a total of 159 available "dance nights" per annum (nine per month during the school year, 26 per month for the three summer months). Let's assume that you open the club in May, as students are preparing for finals. This projected traffic count is shown in Figure 5:

Figure 5 Projected Traffic Count—Dance Club			
	Nights	Patrons Per Night	Total Patrons
May	9	150	1,350
June	26	100	2,600
July	26	90	2,340
August	26	80	2,080
September	9	90	810
October	9	100	900
November	9	150	1,350
December	9	200	1,800
January	9	175	1,575
February	9	150	1,350
March	9	150	1,350
April	9	150	1,350

In the above projections, note the seasonality of your dance club business. It declines in the summer as people take vacations, go to camp, go on out-of-town trips and do other things in the evenings, frequently outdoors. It picks back up in the Fall and peaks around Christmas when everyone is joyous and festive. But then, you've taken seasonality into account in your projections, haven't you?

How much can you charge for a night of dancing? Teenagers do not have a whole lot of disposable income so the dance club will be <u>price</u> <u>sensitive</u>—that is, you will lose 20% or so of the people you attract at your "optimum price" for each 20% increase in price. You do more testing of your idea to the students at the local high school to determine the price that will draw the optimum number of people—let's say an average of 150 per evening. It appears that $2.50 per person will do. (For evenings on which you feature a live band, you might charge $4.00, with the majority of the extra $1.50 going to the band.) You can also assume that each patron will purchase, on average, one soft drink per evening ($1.00 more in per person revenue). So you should be able to project your expected monthly and yearly revenues from the dance club by multiplying the average revenue per person ($3.50) times the number of people projected per month or year (from Figure 5).

You know the soft drink costs, but what are the equipment and operating costs of the dance club? The operating costs include security (a guard to keep out the rowdies), insurance (in case someone is injured on the premises), music replenishment, utilities (air conditioning, electricity, heating) and janitorial services (have you ever seen a teenage dance club after a single night?). As for capital costs, you will need to buy a compact disc or stereo player (which we'll assume you'll buy for $3,000 but finance over 36 months at $116.66 per month). The costs of the dance club each month as shown in Figure 6.

Figure 6 Projecting Dance Club Monthly Operating Costs		
	Weekends Only	Six Nights Per Week
Security ($15/hr, 4 hrs/night)	$ 540.00	$1,560.00
Insurance	750.00	750.00
Utilities	150.00	250.00
Janitorial ($6/hr, 1 hr/night)	54.00	234.00
Music Replenishment	150.00	250.00
Equipment Financing	116.66	116.66
Total	$1,760.66	$3,160.00

Break-Even Analysis:

You've already done your projections of the number of people you *expect* to attract to your club. To determine how many patrons you *need* to attract per evening to break-even—that is, cover all operating costs—you use a standard formula: divide your gross profit margin on the product you are selling (variable cost) into fixed costs. In this case, a soft drink is your only variable cost and you figure the gross profit margin on each sale by dividing unit revenue into unit cost— $3.50 unit revenue/$0.40 unit cost = 88.6%. So your break-even point is $1,760.66 (fixed costs from Figure 5)/.886 = $1,987.20. Since each patron represents $3.50 in revenues, you need 567 patrons per month ($1,987.20 fixed costs/ $3.50 revenue per person) or 63 per evening (567 total patrons/9 available nights) during the school year. Every night you draw more than 63 people to your dance club represents profit to you. Every night you draw less represents a deficit.

During the summer months, when the dance club is open 26 nights per month, your break-even point will be $3,160.66/.886 = $3,567.34, which means that you need 1,019 patrons per month ($3,567.34/$3.50) in the summer or 39 patrons per evening (1,019 total patrons/26 available nights) to break even. Your profits increase handsomely in the summer because most of your operating costs are fixed. You can afford to have bands on Saturday nights in the summer without charging more than a $1.50 premium ($4.00 instead of $2.50). And do notice that if you actually meet your own traffic projections in Figure 5, the dance club will show a very handsome profit.

Now it's time to see whether the hot dog business and your dance club really make sense together. Prepare a one-year projection, with revenues and costs allocated on a monthly basis. And you will want to do several sets of projections in which you open one business ahead of the other, change your assumptions to measure the effect on cash flow, etc. But for the sake of simplicity, let's go with all of the above assumptions and launch the two businesses simultaneously. Figure 7 summarizes the revenue and cost projections of such a plan.

As you can see from this chart, you expect your new venture to generate $20,176 in net income (before interest and taxes) during its first year of operation. All of this is really

Figure 7. Twelve Month Projections—Hot Dog Dance Club

	Mo. 1	Mo. 2	Mo. 3	Mo. 4	Mo. 5	Mo. 6	Mo. 7	Mo. 8	Mo. 9	Mo. 10	Mo. 11	Mo. 12	First Fiscal Year
Food Operations:													
Patrons	480	620	760	880	940	980	980	980	980	980	980	980	10,540
Unit Price	$3.55	$3.55	$3.55	$3.55	$3.55	$3.55	$3.55	$3.55	$3.55	$3.55	$3.55	$3.55	
Revenues	1,704	2,201	2,698	3,124	3,337	3,479	3,479	3,479	3,479	3,479	3,479	3,479	37,417
Disco Operations:													
Patrons	1,350	2,600	2,340	2,080	810	900	1,350	1,800	1,575	1,350	1,350	1,350	18,855
Unit Price	$3.50	$3.50	$3.50	$3.50	$3.50	$3.50	$3.50	$3.50	$3.50	$3.50	$3.50	$3.50	
Revenues	4,725	9,100	8,190	7,280	2,835	3,150	4,725	6,300	5,513	4,725	4,725	4,725	65,993
Total Revenues	6,429	11,301	10,888	10,404	6,172	6,629	8,204	9,779	8,992	8,204	8,204	8,204	103,410
Cost of Goods Sold:													
Food (.529)	901	1,164	1,427	1,653	1,765	1,840	1,840	1,840	1,840	1,840	1,840	1,840	19,790
Disco (.114)	539	1,037	934	830	323	359	539	718	628	539	539	539	7,524
Total Cost of Goods Sold	1,440	2,201	2,361	2,483	2,088	2,199	2,379	2,558	2,468	2,379	2,379	2,379	27,314
Gross Profits	4,989	9,100	8,527	7,921	4,084	4,430	5,825	7,221	6,524	5,825	5,825	5,825	76,096
Operating Expenses:													
Food—Salaries	1,200	1,200	1,200	1,200	1,200	1,800	1,800	2,400	2,400	2,400	2,400	2,400	21,600
Food—Other	500	500	500	500	500	500	500	500	500	500	500	500	6,000
Disco	1,760	3,160	3,160	3,160	1,760	1,760	1,760	1,760	1,760	1,760	1,760	1,760	25,320
Acting/Legal	2,000											1,000	3,000
Total Operating Expenses	5,460	4,860	4,860	4,860	3,460	4,060	4,060	4,660	4,660	4,660	4,660	5,660	55,920
Net Operating Income Before Interest and Taxes	(471)	4,240	3,667	3,061	624	370	1,765	2,561	1,864	1,165	1,165	165	20,176

from the dance club. The food operation's revenues are flat for the second half of the year and it loses money each month, particularly because of the salaries you must pay two employees (assuming you are back in school). It may be necessary to develop some promotional ideas to increase the revenues of the food operation.

With this expected cash flow, you can afford to assume the <u>mortgage</u> on the property or buy the property from the owner or the bank. Let's assume the property is worth $100,000 and you want to use no more than $5,000 of your savings. You would need to finance $95,000 or 95% of the cost over as long a period as you can negotiate.

A lender or seller will probably want you to put up more than $5,000—probably more like $20,000—so you will need to locate a $15,000 partner. You can offer a potential partner a variety of incentives, including part ownership, a short-term, interest-bearing loan secured by a <u>second mortgage</u>, a participating loan entitling the lender to share in your profits plus earn interest, or any combination of the above.

The key, however, is that you will need to increase business only slightly (increasing profits by less than $5,000) in the second year to continue paying interest ($10,000 per annum) and perhaps consider paying off the $15,000 loan entirely. (Or you can keep paying off the loan at whatever terms you've negotiated and pay yourself a higher salary.) At the end of two years, you will have achieved the following:

1. Bought a piece of real estate for $5,000, whose value is at least $100,000 (perhaps as much as $200,000, because you will have made it a destination location). After paying off all your loans, you will probably have made money on the real estate alone.
2. Created a business that is worth at least five times earnings—$100,000—that you can sell to a buyer. This is your real profit on the deal—twenty times your initial investment!

Thus, after an investment of $5,000 and two years of <u>sweat equity</u>, the Hot Dog Dance Club would return at least $100,000 to you, even more if the real estate has appreciated as well. That is an enviable rate of return under any circumstances.

Should It Work?

Let's look at the DEJ factors for the Hot Dog Dance Club opportunity:

1. & 2. Existence of a large number of qualified buyers

Teenagers must have safe, fun and inexpensive places to go for entertainment. What are their current options? Not many. Your dance club should work. And locating a hot dog stand near a high school certainly seems to be a fairly safe bet.

3. Homogeneity of buyers

Most teenagers tend to like hot dogs, french fries and rock 'n'roll.

4. Existence of competent sellers

Not much training is required to manage the Hot Dog Dance Club. Observe how the quick service restaurants operate and copy their techniques.

5. Lack of institutional barriers to entry

The neighbors may complain about noise pollution. Better check with them first. And there will be some required licenses, health department checks, etc. But nothing that a little research and paper filing can't take care of.

6. Easy promotability by word-of-mouth

The teenage grapevine moves information faster than a speeding bullet.

7. Invisibility of the inside of the company

You could be hurt by being too visible—some smart alecks may get jealous of you. Tell people you work at the club, *not* that you own it—nobody needs to know you're on a faster track then they are.

8. Optimum price/cost relationship

The dance club is a high-profit margin business, the food operation is not. The latter will require work, but it has greater stability than the dance club, which is trendy and more subject to competitive pressures.

The Hot Dog Dance Club passes the DEJ Factor test.

Look For Extra Ways To Generate Income

Are there other SDMs that you can implement to generate ancillary sources of revenue? You bet there are. The Hot Dog Dance Club is essentially a consumer product launch, but there are a myriad of other SDMs than may be spun off. Here's just a sample list of ideas:

1. Tee shirts — Consumer product
2. Birthday parties — Facilities management
3. Concert sponsorship — Celebrity endorsement
4. Game room — Leveraging with OPM
5. Rental of space — Prepaid subscription
6. Franchise to teens in other cities — Franchising

This completes the description of the discipline known as entrepreneurship. Is it everything you need to know to go out tomorrow and start the next IBM? No. No one book could pretend to cover the specific problems that occur in so many different kinds of entrepreneurial endeavors. But it should give you the basis for deciding if entrepreneurship is for you and, if so, how you should proceed.

And here's an offer you can't refuse. If you have a specific question or would like to submit some of your entrepreneurial ideas to me, write to me in care of the publisher. I will try to be helpful.

8 Individual Exercises & Projects

1. Can you come up with a better name for the Hot Dog Dance Club?

2. What if every person bought two hot dogs instead of one? Rework gross profit, break-even analysis and operating plan calculations accordingly.

3. What if half the anticipated traffic bought one hot dog, a *small* fry and a drink and the other half *two* hot dogs, a *large* fry and a drink? Rework gross profit, break-even analysis and operating plan calculations accordingly.

Section Two

Collecting & Investing

9

Alternative Roads To Wealth

It may take up to five years, sometimes longer, to create wealth by starting your own company...presuming you manage to stay in business that long. And, since some 75% of new businesses fail in their first two years, it is certainly not for sure that you will.

75% of new businesses fail in their first two years

Most people, lacking the resources, tenacity, money and/or motivation (or rightly fearing such god-awful odds), never even consider starting their own companies. For them, the road to wealth is via investing in someone or something else. While it probably takes them a little longer to achieve wealth this way, at least ten years, perhaps twenty, thirty or even a lifetime, most investors do not risk what entrepreneurs do every day—their money, their time and, sometimes, their credibility.

Good judgment is required in order to achieve wealth through investments. Some investments appreciate—add value—on their own. These are passive investments. Others require you to hire the right people to add value. These are active investments.

In the following five chapters, we will look at both active and passive opportunities to create wealth via investing in a number of areas: art, antiques and other collectibles (chapter 10); bonds (chapter 11); stocks (chapter 12); partnerships (chapter 13); real estate (chapter 14); even investing in entrepreneurs (chapter 15).

But before we can start discussing specific investments, it's necessary to spend some time on some basic definitions and concepts.

Disposable Income

In order to be able to invest in anything, your income must exceed your living expenses—the cost of food, clothing, shelter, education, entertainment, charitable contributions, and taxes, plus amounts set aside for insurance and savings. This "pile of cash" that's left over after all your expenses have been paid—your disposable income—is what you use to invest. Let's use your local family doctor as an example.

Let's presume your physician sees 4,000 patients a year at an average fee of $50 each. His or her gross income, therefore, is $200,000 per annum (4,000 X $50). "Per annum" or "p.a." means "per year".

From this amount, he or she first deducts professional expenses, which may include a receptionist, nurse, medical equipment leases, bookkeeping costs, malpractice insurance and other administrative expenses. Let's assume that these expenses total $100,000 per annum.

The physician's *personal* gross income is therefore $100,000 per annum ($200,000 — $100,000). Out of this amount, he or she must then pay *personal* living expenses— income taxes, food, clothing, shelter, tuition, vacations, charitable contributions, home repairs, etc. Let's assume these total $70,000.

In addition, there are two other kinds of living expenses—insurance for happy emergencies (savings) and insurance for tragic emergencies (insurance)—that we'll discuss later in this chapter. For now, let's estimate $5,000 for each.

Calculating the physician's disposable income, therefore, means subtracting all living expenses from his or her personal gross income:

Gross Personal Income	$100,000
Minus Amount Spent on Living Expenses	-70,000
Minus Amount For Savings	- 5,000
Minus Amount For Insurance	- 5,000
Equals Disposable Income	$ 20,000

In other words, our sample physician would have $20,000 available to invest in stocks, bonds, art, and other assets.

Savings

After you've paid your living expenses, but before you start investing, there are two other things to include in your budget: savings and insurance.

The purpose of a savings account is to meet family emergencies. Not tragic emergencies like death, fire or bad health, which are generally paid for with insurance, but those "happy emergencies"—college tuition, vacations, a swimming pool, adding a new family room to the house—that are too expensive to be paid for out of normal income.

Whatever money you can afford to save each month or each year is usually stored for safekeeping at a commercial bank or savings and loan institution in a <u>passbook savings account</u>. While earning less interest than other relatively safe places to park your money (<u>treasury bills</u>, <u>certificates of deposit</u>, savings bonds, etc.), such an account has the advantage of being highly liquid—you can generally withdraw some or all of your money from a passbook savings account anytime you need it.

Banks pay interest on savings accounts to attract deposits— the money you earn—so they can make loans to people and businesses that need money.

Banks pay interest on savings accounts to attract deposits—the money you earn—so they can make loans to people and businesses that need money. The difference between the rate of interest the bank pays you on your savings account and the rate of interest it charges borrowers is the bank's profit. For example, the bank may pay you 7% interest per annum on your savings account (i.e., $7.00 for every $100.00 that you save at the bank for one year) and then loan your $100.00 to a company that needs to buy a truck at an interest rate of 11% ($11.00 per $100.00 per year). The difference in interest rates—4% or $4.00 per hundred—is the bank's gross profit, from which it must pay salaries and other expenses each year. Doesn't sound like the bank is doing very well, does it?

What banks lack in profit margin they more than make up for in volume—even relatively small banks receive millions of dollars in savings from people whose incomes are larger than their living expenses. And there are millions of borrowers who are willing to pay them 11% interest for car loans and business loans and personal loans, so that $4.00 per year starts adding up to a very large number.

When banks fail, and they do so occasionally, it is because their borrowers are unable to pay the interest on their loans or unable to repay the loans themselves. This makes it difficult for the banks to pay their savings account customers interest; eventually, it may make it impossible for them to even return the customers' savings at all. When this happens, people lose the uninsured part of their savings.

Compound Interest

Money <u>compounds</u> when the pile of cash is left alone in a savings account or similar instrument, which means you earn interest on interest. Over a lifetime, the first $10,000 of savings will double many times. In slightly more than ten years, $1,000 will become $2,000 at an annual interest rate of 7%:

Figure 8. Compounding of Interest

Year One	$1,000.00 x 1.07	=	$1,070.00
Year Two	$1,070.00 x 1.07	=	$1,144.90
Year Three	$1,144.90 x 1.07	=	$1,225.00
Year Four	$1,225.00 x 1.07	=	$1,310.80
Year Five	$1,310.08 x 1.07	=	$1,402.60
Year Six	$1,402.60 x 1.07	=	$1,500.70
Year Seven	$1,500.70 x 1.07	=	$1,605.80
Year Eight	$1,605.80 x 1.07	=	$1,718.20
Year Nine	$1,718.20 x 1.07	=	$1,838.50
Year Ten	$1,838.50 x 1.07	=	$1,967.20
Year Eleven	$1,967.20 x 1.07	=	$2,104.90

You might want to take out your calculator and do some compound interest examples using a 5% interest rate and a 10% interest rate. You will see how much faster your savings will grow at 10% than at 5% (and, in case you haven't figured it out, it will be *more* than twice as fast.)

If a bank has lots of borrowers lined up for your savings (high demand, low supply), it will raise the interest rate that it pays for savings because it needs your money. Similarly, if it has fewer borrowers (low demand, high supply), then it will lower the interest rate that it pays you, because it needs your money less. Smart investors move their savings accounts to the banks paying the highest interest rates. Borrowers go to the banks that are most willing to loan them money at the lowest interest rates.

This is another example of economic growth—the ever-widening circle of giving. More borrowers mean that a community is growing—more people adding bedrooms to their houses, more companies adding trucks to their fleets and more workers saving their excess incomes for happy emergencies. Money has a multiplier effect—when it earns the highest rates of return, it multiplies faster, benefitting everyone in the community (although not necessarily equally).

Money multiplies when saved or invested. The higher the rate of return, the faster it multiplies.

Insurance

Tragic emergencies are generally paid for by insurance. According to insurance legend, two ships were passing each other one storm-tossed night in the fifteenth century. The first, laden with valuable cargo, was taking on a lot of water, and its captain feared it would sink. The other ship, heading for home without cargo and not in any danger, passed close by the sinking ship. The first captain frantically signalled it, "Help us. We're sinking." The second ship's captain signalled back, "How much is our help worth?" They agreed on a price, and the troubled ship was saved.

The safe ship "bought the risk"—solved the problem—of the troubled ship. Major insurance companies do today what that second captain did five centuries ago—buy the risk.

Fifteenth century ships incurred two kinds of emergencies: piracy and storms. To solve this problem, Dutch entrepreneurs began to insure the risk of piracy and storms by raising capital from investors. If the ships did not return to port or returned empty, the insurance entrepreneur would pay the investors the amount of their loss.

Insurance companies use probability analysis to determine the price they will charge for insurance. For example, they might insure a ship captain's cargo for five cents on the dollar if the probability of piracy and storms is low, but charge twenty cents on the dollar if it is high. If the insurer guesses correctly (and probability analysis is all about reducing such "guesses" to a science), its gross income from the sale of insurance policies will exceed its payouts for losses, and the remainder will be profit. Let's see how this would work:

Insurance companies buy risk.

Assume that of every 1,000 ships that sailed from Amsterdam to New York City in 1550, 43 were usually lost to pirates or high seas. Further assume that the value of each cargo is $10,000, so the total value of every 1,000 sailings is $10 million (1,000 x $10,000). The insurance company might have charged the ship captains and their investors 5% percent of the cost of their cargos—$500 per ship, $500,000 for all 1,000 ships—to insure them against loss from piracy and bad weather.

The insurance company received $500,000 *which it has the free use of for one year*. If the banks in Amsterdam were paying interest on savings accounts of 5% back then, the insurance company earned $25,000 in interest for the year.

Let's assume that 35 of the ships returned empty due to piracy and five didn't return at all, slightly less (40 ships vs. 43 expected lost) than the insurance company expected. The insurance company must pay the investors the value of the cost of their cargo, or $400,000 (40 ships x $10,000). If operating expenses—salaries and bookkeeping costs—were $20,000, the insurance company's profit would be $30,000. Plus it would have earned $25,000 on the advance payments for its insurance policies, for a total profit of $55,000. And the $25,000 would <u>compound</u> each year that it remained in the savings account. (Notice that if the anticipated number of ships—43—were actually lost, the insurance company would have broken even; that is, made no profit on the insurance business itself. *Except* that it still would have the $25,000 in interest earned on the advance payments, a nice profit anyway.)

Who would buy death insurance?

After learning how to "buy risk" in the shipping business, insurance entrepreneurs began to seek out—particularly in the risk-laden New World—other tragic emergencies that they could insure. Life insurance seemed like a good place to start, once the average life expectancy of pioneers could be calculated. While the risks of disease, weather, floods, bandits and Indians seemed a trifle high, settlers in the New World did not seek very large death benefits, merely enough for a proper burial and a few hundred dollars for their families. (The word "life," of course, should really be "death," but who would buy "death insurance?"). The life insurance industry flowered in Dutch and German communities in America, and the corporate headquarters of these early insurance companies are still concentrated there: New York City, Milwaukee, Chicago, Hartford and Des Moines.

Along with savings accounts for happy emergencies, Americans today can buy life, health, fire and casualty, personal injury, automobile and a wide variety of other insurance policies for tragic emergencies. The cost of not being properly insured if an unforeseen tragedy occurs is so high that most of us find insurance an absolute necessity. In some cases, you have no choice: If you borrow money to buy a house, the bank will insist that you have fire and flood insurance, and all automobile drivers must have insurance.

The insurance industry in America is enormous. Because it is paid in advance for a service that it *may* provide in the future (some houses never burn, some cars are never vandalized), the insurance industry has over $2 trillion to invest in start-up and expanding companies; it is one of the largest investors in new ventures and, therefore, an important component of the circle of giving.

Rates of Return

There is lots of confusion about this subject, but I will simplify things for you. Commercial banks, savings and loan associations, lotteries, mutual funds, real estate developers and brokerage firms advertise continuously to try to attract everyone's disposable income. If you open an account with *them*, they claim they'll give you the "highest yields", "high rates of return", help you "build a fortune", "start your nest egg", "get in on the ground floor," or "become a millionaire." What does all of this mean?

The way to figure out if an investment is good or bad is to calculate how much your pile of cash will grow in one year, five years or ten years. This amount is your investment's rate of return (sometimes called return on investment or yield). It should be expressed in terms of *time*—the usual time period people use in figuring rate of return is one year—so that dissimilar investments can be measured by the same yardstick. The return on any investment, therefore, should be expressed as "so-and-so percent per annum."

Rate of return: how much your pile of cash will grow in one year

As we discuss various investment opportunities in the next chapters, I will frequently refer to the return that should be expected from each. The following drawing is a simple way to compare every investment, whether it is expressed as a yield, rate of return or times factor.

Figure 9. Times Factor

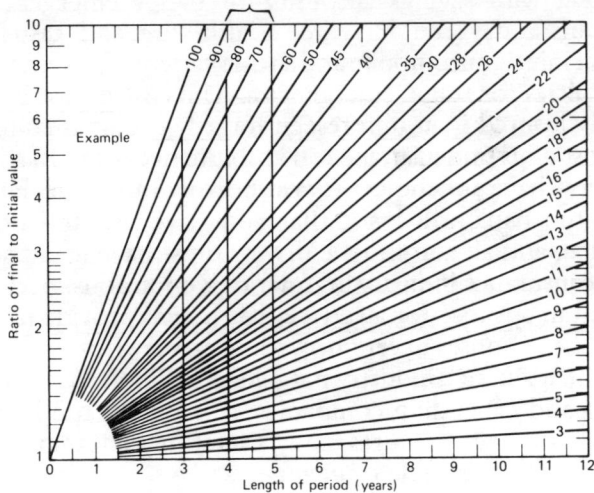

If someone says you can triple your money (make *three times your investment*) in five years, for example, find "5" on the horizontal (time) scale at the bottom of the graph and "3" on the left-hand scale. Draw a straight line up from the "5" and another over (right to left) from the "3." Make a dot where these two lines cross. This dot will be on or very close to one of the oblique lines running from the bottom left to the top right. Follow the nearest oblique line to the upper right hand corner. The numbers running in a semi-circle tell you your annual rate of return. In our example, this exercise would show that an investment that promises a three times return on your investment in five years is offering a rate of return of 26% per annum.

Note that the same rate of return—in this case, 26% per year—may be achieved in other ways: Multiplying your money ten times in ten years, doubling it in two or increasing it five times in seven years all result in the same 26% per year rate of return. Do this exercise yourself using a variety of values for the time period and times factor until you are able to consistently find the annual rate of return for a number of such combinations.

Some people express rates of return as percentages rather than "times your investment." You simply have to convert the percentage into the proper multiplier to use the chart. 350% is equal to 3.5 times, 60% equals .6 times, 100% equals 1 time. But remember that you'll still need to know the time period involved to use the chart. Whether a return on investment is expressed in percentages or times factor, there must be a time period specified in order to calculate the annual rate of return, the figure you'll use to compare all investments.

Returns on investment expressed without a time period—"Increase your money by 50%!," "Double your money!," etc.—are meaningless. Doubling your money in two to four years is terrific, in five to seven years good, in eight to ten years not so great, in eleven or more years terrible. Unless you know the time period involved, therefore, you have no way to calculate the rate of return and can't tell whether the investment is good or bad.

Returns on investment expressed without a time period are meaningless.

Setting A Target Rate of Return

Assume that a family earns enough income to pay for all living expenses, insurance and savings, and there is excess income each year of $20,000. If the $20,000 is invested each year for 10 years at a target rate of return of 20% per annum, what would be the result?

Figure 10. Growth of $20,000 Invested at 20% per annum

Year	Annual Investment	+ Previous Balance	X Rate	= Year-End Balance
One	$20,000	$ 0	120%	$ 24,000
Two	20,000	24,000	120%	52,800
Three	20,000	52,800	120%	87,360
Four	20,000	87,360	120%	128,832
Five	20,000	128,832	120%	178,598
Six	20,000	178,598	120%	238,318
Seven	20,000	238,318	120%	309,982
Eight	20,000	309,982	120%	395,978
Nine	20,000	395,978	120%	499,174
Ten	20,000	499,174	120%	623,009
Eleven	20,000	623,009	120%	771,611
Twelve	20,000	771,611	120%	949,933
Thirteen	20,000	949,933	120%	1,163,920

In twelve and one-half years, $20,000 invested each year (a total of $250,000) grows to more than $1 million.

To some people, that figure represents wealth. To others, $1 million represents a nice round number, but falls somewhat short of *real* wealth. *My own definition of wealth is that sum of money ("pile of cash") that earns enough income at 7% per annum (the lowest interest rate currently available, indicating the safest haven for my money and least risk) to pay all of my family's living expenses, insurance expenses, contributions to savings and charitable donations.*

Wealth is free to be!

If the sum of these expenses is $100,000 per annum, then wealth would be a pile of cash totalling $1,428,571.43 (the result of dividing .07 into $100,000).

If my family's needs are $200,000 per annum, then my definition of wealth is a pile of cash totalling $2,857,142.86.

If my family's needs are $300,000 per annum, then my definition of wealth is $4,285,714.29.

And so on.

(Wealth doesn't have to be such monstrous numbers; it's a function of your needs. If all you need is $10,000 per year, then wealth for you is a pile of cash of $142,857.14; if your expenses are $25,000 per year, wealth is $357,142.86; etc.)

Net Worth—Assets Minus Liabilities

A balance sheet lists what you own (your assets) and what you owe (your liabilities). Subtracting your liabilities from your assets reveals your net worth.

When your family buys a car, for example, it may choose to borrow some of the purchase price from a bank. If the car costs $15,000 and your family uses $5,000 of its savings and borrows $10,000 from a bank, the family's net worth does not increase. Although it adds a $15,000 asset to its balance sheet, it made the purchase by deducting $5,000 from one asset (savings) and borrowing $10,000 (a liability). Do the math and prove to yourself that the net effect of this adding and subtracting equals zero.

The car is a depreciable asset. That is, it will decline in value each year it is used. Depreciable assets generally do not increase their owner's net worth unless they become antiques (at which time the owner may not be alive to enjoy the addition).

If a person's net worth is made up of assets such as cars,

boats, furniture and clothing, it is <u>illiquid</u> net worth, consisting, in other words, of assets that are not immediately convertible into cash. A real definition of a millionaire, therefore, is someone who can get his or her hands on one million dollars in cash within 24 hours. That is <u>liquid</u> net worth.

A real definition of a millionaire is someone who can get his hands on one million dollars in cash within 24 hours. By this definition—people with *liquid* net worth greater than $1 million—there are fewer millionaires in America than you probably thought—only 70,000 or so. That is a very small number in a country of 240 million inhabitants.

In order to significantly increase your net worth, you should be seeking <u>appreciable assets</u>, the kind that increase in value or, at least, are supposed to.

A real definition of a millionaire is someone who can get his hands on one million dollars in cash within 24 hours.

Appreciable Assets:

The most common investments in America are art, antiques and other collectibles; common stocks and bonds; partnership interests; real estate; and entrepreneurial ventures.

To invest in these appreciable assets, you will have to convert liquid assets—cash—into illiquid assets, meaning it will be more difficult and take more time for you to actually get your money out of such investments. But remember: Cash produces a relatively low rate of return—7% per annum in a savings account, slightly more in certificates of deposit, etc.—and you cannot achieve wealth in your lifetime by leaving your disposable income in a savings account. (Remember how slowly $1,000 appreciates at 7%? See page 122). To earn more, you will have to assume greater risks.

To make the next chapters practical for you, I have assumed throughout that you have very little capital—as little as $50, no more than $1,000—but that you can come up with at least $500 from working and saving to invest each year. I will also assume that your objective is to grow that small pile of cash into as much wealth as possible in ten years.

Let's look at the plusses and minuses of investing in these six kinds of appreciable assets.

9 Individual Exercises & Projects

1. Make a list of all the types of investments you can think of, then mark each one "passive" or "active."

2. If your parents let you get involved with your family's budget process, analyze it with them. What's your family's disposable income? How much goes to savings? How much to insurance? Are there expenses you can help reduce? What should your family do with the money you save?

3. Did you research your local bank? What are the various rates they currently offer for different savings alternatives—passbook, CDs, etc.? Are there other banks in your neighborhood or city that offer better rates?

4. What insurance does your family have? What insurance do you *need*?

5. Using Figure 9, figure out the annual rate of return if you double your money in four years. Triple it in four years. Multipy it five times in eight years. Ten years.

6. Refer to Figure 10. Recalculate, presuming the same annual investment but higher and lower rates of return. How much would you have if you invested only $1,000 a year?

7. What's *your* definition of wealth? In other words, how much do you need to live on each year and how big would your "pile of cash" have to be to earn that annual amount?

8. List examples of depreciable assets.

10

In Search of the Perfect Collectible

Van Gogh, Picasso And Soho's Undiscovered Gold Mines

The best thing about investing in art is that you get more for your money than just a boring piece of paper—bond, stock certificate, etc. A piece of Art is an investment that provides visual pleasure and brightens your environment every day. In fact, art is one of the few investments that you can enjoy for its own sake while it appreciates in value.

You can begin an art collection with very little money. Most art galleries and artists will accept installment payments (monthly payments for up to six to nine months) if you are unable to pay for a work all at once, often allowing you to take the painting or sculpture home before it's completely paid for...and without charging interest. (This generous policy is not without limits: It does not extend to the work of dead artists or very expensive living artists' works, unless you have dealt with the gallery previously and they know that your payment pattern is regular and absolute.)

And here's something to look forward to: If you develop an important art collection, gallery owners, indeed the artists themselves, will fight to be represented in it; extending a collector's discount (typically 15%) and credit terms is the normal practice. Why would they do so? Because they believe that their artists' work will appreciate in value more than 15% if it is purchased by collectors and hangs or stands in the midst of other art of comparable or even greater quality.

So if you are thinking about buying a particular painting or sculpture, ask if the artist has other pieces in museums or

> Art is one of the few investments that you can enjoy for its own sake while it appreciates in value.

> You can begin an art collection with very little money.

important collections. (There is frequently a brochure that cites the names of museums and collectors that have purchased the artist's work.) This is the kind of information that's of prime importance to an investor, as it will help you identify those artists that more-knowledgeable collectors have already dubbed "promising" (read "investment worthy").

There is a collector family in New York City that has succeeded so handsomely at art investing—buying hundreds of pieces on the installment plan for less than $1,000 each, most of which are now worth more than $50,000 each—that artists whose pieces sell for over $50,000 apiece ask the collector family to buy a piece for $1,000 merely to be in its collection.

That is an extreme example of the importance to the art market of certain successful art collectors, but it points out the uniqueness of art as an investment. The collector's discount does not exist in any other market for appreciable assets. There are well-known and highly successful investors in the stock market who are never offered a collector's discount by their stockbroker when they buy a new stock!

Your ability to purchase art and pay for it in installments without paying interest is another unusual feature of the art market, but one that makes sense if you know a little of how the art world operates: Gallery owners generally pay their artists from 40-60% of the selling price for each work, but only after the piece is sold. Since the gallery owner has very little investment in such works—wall space, a few advertisements and some brochures—he or she can afford to accept installment payments. If a gallery is unwilling to extend credit for the work of a certain artist, it may be a clue that the work is not a particularly good investment.

Some artists are not represented by galleries or are "in between" galleries. In this instance, you can buy directly from the artist and should save from 40-60%—the cut the artist would have given to the gallery owner. The artist may even be willing to permit you to buy on the installment plan, especially if you express your desire to collect his or her work throughout his or her career.

Don't limit your concept of art to the Old Masters or "Latest Raves." There is a group of artists who paint and sculpt amateurishly—that is, without formal training—but in unique ways and with unusual materials. Their art is known as folk art, and it is primitive in both technique and

If a gallery is unwilling to extend credit for the work of a certain artist, it may be a clue that the work is not a particularly good investment.

subject matter. In Santa Fe, New Mexico, for example, there are primitive sculptors who carve howling coyotes out of tree stumps and make snakes out of old bottle caps. Art collectors have recently become very interested in their work and the State of New Mexico built a Museum of Folk Art to acquire and display some of it. The museum has given New Mexican folk art prestige value, increasing its worth to collectors.

But you never know where such an opportunity might present itself. A Cuban immigrant named Puchio Odio came to New York City in the early 1970s without a penny to his name. But he could carve dogs and cats out of the fallen branches of trees that he found in Central Park, selling them on the street for $20 apiece. He drew the attention of Jay Johnson, one of New York's best-known folk art gallery owners. Johnson sponsored him and advanced him money for his wood carvings. Today, some dozen years later, Odio's work is well represented in museums and important collections and fetches prices above $3,000 apiece.

From 1978 to 1987, the prices of folk art have risen more than five times (an annual rate of return of 20%).

If you go to any region of the country, you will find folk artists painting or sculpting important scenes or creatures that inhabit that particular area. Some of them may become as important as Grandma Moses, Kathy Jakobsen or Mattie Lou O'Kelley—three primitivists whose pieces (and prices) can compete with any in the art world.

Can you create wealth through art? Let's assume you are 15 years old and your budget will permit no more than two $500 purchases per year for five years (using the installment plan), then four $500 purchases per year for five years, then eight per year for the next five years, then sixteen per year for the next five years. Assuming the value of their work increases at the rate of 20% per annum, how much wealth will you create by the time you are 35 years old if you begin investing in unknown artists?

Figure 11. A 20-Year Art Investment Plan		
Period	**Cost**	**Value After 20 Years**
Years 1-5	$ 5,000	$ 50,000
Years 6-10	10,000	75,000
Years 11-15	20,000	100,000
Years 16-20	40,000	60,000
Total	$75,000	$285,000

One final point about art as an investment: Art is not liquid—it cannot be converted into cash quickly. (Complete liquidity means that there is a ready market in which to sell the asset for cash within 24 hours.) Individual pieces may be sold through galleries on a consignment basis—the gallery will display it for you at no cost and, when the piece sells, remit 70-80% of the selling price to you. Alternatively, one, several or many pieces—a whole collection—can be sold at auction. The two best known auction houses for art are Sotheby's and Christies, both in New York City and London. It will usually take several months to schedule a collection for sale at a well-known auction house.

Although much of this discussion has focused on collecting living artists, clearly there is an active market for the work of dead artists—Van Gogh, Picasso, Matisse and the like (though one that probably requires a far higher entrance fee than you can currently afford). True to the Law of Supply and Demand, prices for their works increase as the available supply decreases (and death certainly limits supply). In addition, there is a certain snob appeal that drives prices of some artists skyward—wealthy people and museums vie for certain high-priced works simply because they confirm their ability to afford multimillion dollar art. This can sometimes drive prices to pretty insane levels—Van Gogh's "Sunflowers" was sold in 1987 for $38 million. Not long afterward, his "Irises" fetched even more—$53 million!

Talkin' Mickey, Willie And The Duke

I am a pack-rat, someone who never throws anything away. The first thing that I collected was baseball cards, beautifully painted pieces of cardboard that were produced in fairly small quantities to enhance the sale of bubble gum. The year 1952 was a big baseball card collecting year for me. Fortunately, most of my collection is intact today because my mother, like me, never throws anything away.

Baseball cards have appreciated considerably in value because the supply of older cards is relatively small—many mothers were more fanatical cleaner-outers than mine. A mint condition Mickey Mantle card from 1951, his rookie season, is worth perhaps $6,500 today. That's an appreciation of 650,000 times its cost (a penny)! I have two "good condition" Mickey Mantle cards from 1952, worth only $800. See the value of good judgment—being able to figure

---

Complete liquidity means that there is a ready market in which to sell the asset for cash within 24 hours.

Baseball cards have appreciated considerably in value because the supply of older cards is relatively small.

out that the rookie card would be worth more than any other? I didn't have it at age 10, and my loss is the difference between $6,500 and $800 today.

Few assets have appreciated as much in value as certain baseball cards. And there is no reason to believe that they will not continue to be an excellent investment, because the characteristics that make the 1951 Mickey Mantle card so valuable still exist: Cards are limited in supply and in duration, are a liquid asset (there is a ready market of buyers and sellers) and you can receive cash for your baseball cards within 24 hours.

Art is not limited in supply—it is being created constantly. On the other hand, antiques (like baseball cards) are finite: Their supply is not only limited, but shrinking in quantity every year. (When an important artist dies, however, his or her work leaps in price because the supply of his or her work is suddenly limited. It then takes on some of the characteristics of antiques.)

Buffalo Heads, Roosevelts, Lincolns

After a brief concentrated period of collecting baseball cards, I became interested in coins. So, in 1953 or thereabouts, I bought the little blue coin books with circles in them that held pennies, nickels and dimes (quarters were too expensive for me to collect) and began bothering every grocer, pharmacist, bank teller and restaurant manager in Knoxville to let me look through their coins so I could fill all the empty circles in my blue books. My friend Arnold and I would go downtown to the coin counter at Woolworth's to read their numismatic books and calculate what our coins were worth.

What a magical day when we found that a merchant had traded us a valuable Buffalo head nickel, worth fifteen cents, for a new Jefferson nickel worth only five! We had discovered a mechanism for creating value out of the Law of Supply and Demand.

Coin collecting works that way: the fewer the number of coins minted in a certain year, the higher their value. Lower the supply and, assuming that demand remains constant, the price will go up. Given constant demand (that is, no snob appeal or mob appeal) for virtually the identical product, the lower the supply, the higher the price.

If coins were never circulated, but purchased directly

> The fewer the number of coins minted in a certain year, the higher their value.

from the mint, they are worth much more. Thus, a collector can continually seek to improve his collection by upgrading the quality of individual coins from those in the poorest condition to the highest.

There is one constant in antique investments: All of the investment quality pieces are man-made. Machine-made assets, as a rule, do not appreciate very rapidly in value, certainly not as rapidly as man-made assets. Coins are machine-made, but a man-made error like double-striking a date drives the value of those coins sky high. The same is true for stamps: A man-made error in the drawing on the face of the stamp significantly increases its value.

The best known example of a man-made error in American coins is the double-die error on the 1955 Lincoln head penny (1987 value: $3,000 in mint condition). The upside down airplane on the 1918 one cent stamp has driven its price to $250,000.

But errors come around too infrequently, so the thrust in coin and stamp collecting is to accumulate complete sets in mint or excellent condition. A complete set of Lincoln head pennies from 1909 to 1958 (when the "tails" side changed from shafts of wheat to the Lincoln Memorial) is worth $658.33 in good condition and $2,822.15 in extra fine condition. If the extra fine pennies were purchased for one penny apiece in 1958, or $1.50 in the aggregate, the rate of return is so high that it is off the chart. But then, the likelihood of your being able to buy those 150 old pennies in "EF" condition for one penny apiece, even in 1958, is between slim and none.

Demand may also be increased because of a particular antique's prestige value.

Demand may also be increased because of a particular antique's prestige value. To return to baseball cards for a bit, when a player is enshrined in the Hall of Fame, the price of his baseball card increases in value. The player's newly-minted prestige rubs off on his card.

The examples in Figure 12 on the next page (from Current Card Prices, PO Box 480, East Islip, NY 11730) illustrate how prestige value can inflate the price of baseball cards.

Figure 12. The Effect of Prestige Value
1988 prices for 1951 Topps baseball cards in excellent condition

Hall of Famers	
Mickey Mantle	$6,500
Eddie Matthews	1,500
Roy Campanella	1,500
Duke Snider	225
Hoyt Wilhelm	450
Jackie Robinson	800
Willie Mays	900
Pee Wee Reese	800
Bob Feller	150
Non-Hall of Famers	
Billy Goodman	60
Ted Kluszewski	75
Don Mueller	62
Preacher Roe	85
Mel Parnell	85

If you intend to collect baseball cards seriously, you might consider accumulating cards of today's outstanding rookies, the (hopefully) Mantle and Mays of tomorrow.

Baseball cards, by the way, seem to be more collectible than football or hockey cards because the players wear less equipment—hence are less machine-made, if you will. The more natural the object and the smaller its supply, the greater its value as an investment.

The Importance of Primitivity

I cannot explain why, but there seems to be a positive correlation in investments between primitivity and perceived value. The more primitive the art, the greater its value to collectors. Note, for example, that the highest price ever paid for a painting—$53 million—was paid for Vincent Van Gogh's "Irises". Van Gogh was not just primitive—amateur, natural, primal—but downright psychotic (as anyone might become if he painted, like Van Gogh, one painting every six hours...and never sold a single one in his lifetime).

The more primitive the art, the greater its value to collectors.

Why is the price for a 1951 Mickey Mantle baseball card higher than a 1952 Mickey Mantle? Because rookies are more primitive than experienced professionals. Baseball franchises, cards, memorabilia and collectibles are more valuable than their football or basketball counterparts because baseball is a more primitive sport. Which prompts me to present a hypothesis you may attempt to use in your own investment planning:

$$\text{Value} = \frac{\text{Primitivity}}{\text{Supply}}$$

Value equals Primitivity Divided by Supply

The greater the primitivity—naturalness, evoking primal feelings, not machine-made—and the lower the supply of an asset, the greater its value. Test this hypothesis on other assets that have risen in value. I can't really explain why primitivity is important, but I believe that it should be given some weight when you process information about investments.

Elvis And Girls—Buffalo Heads Lost

My simultaneous discovery of Elvis Presley and girls in 1955 pretty much ended my career as a serious coin collector. In a weak moment when I needed $2.00 for a date, I used a handful of Jefferson nickels (worth probably $4.00 then and $40.00 today). Girls obviously had greater perceived value to me at age 14 than my coin collection.

And girls certainly meant more to me than Elvis, though if I had saved all of the Presley memorabilia that flooded the market in 1955, I would have another valuable antique collection. His early death, of course, could not be predicted at that time, so very few people collected early Presleyana. Mob appeal—relentless demand—is the great driving force on memorabilia, much of which is machine-made and lacking in intrinsic value. (The relative shortness of baseball players' careers, for example, is what adds to baseball cards' value.)

Although Presley memorabilia was machine-made, and by definition not primitive, let's face it, Elvis himself was the very essence of primal man—natural, sensual, faithful to friends and fans, earthy, untrained, his music rooted in gospel, a rookie in the dog-eat-dog music industry. Even his songs were primitive, all about tenderness, jail, loneliness, rain, dogs and his mama. Elvis was so primitive that the man-made quality of Presleyana didn't matter. His untimely death, of course, also limited the supply of original product.

Elvis was so primitive that the man-made quality of Presleyana didn't matter.

If you are going to invest in Presleyana or the memorabilia of other uniquely skilled people—whether singers, baseball players or even politicians—remember that objects related to their rookie years are more valuable. Why? Smaller supply and greater primitivity ("rookieness").

Ephemera

Paper collectibles—post cards, song sheets, autograph books, calendars, comic books, etc.—are called ephemera. While generally machine-made, they offer personal value— the memory of an old friend, an interesting inscription and the like—and are very affordable for the beginning collector, frequently costing less than $5 apiece.

Autographs of famous people—man-made—are the most expensive ephemera, as well as the most difficult and time-consuming to acquire. It is very difficult to get into autograph collecting as inexpensively as art, coins, baseball cards and other antiques. The law of supply and demand and the primitivity hypothesis explain why.

There's Gold In Krypton!

Early Superman comic books in good condition (as opposed to mint or excellent) command prices in the $100 to $300 range. With Superman still very much in the media, old comic books are quite valuable, and will probably increase in value as the Man of Steel solidifies his place in American legend.

Although comic books are machine-made, the heroes they portray have primitive values. Each of them has a guilt that drives them to save the world from evil. Superman's guilt is that he lived while his parents died on Krypton. Guilt is like sin, and sin is a primitive concept. If you look through the first comics featuring Batman, Robin, the Hulk, Spiderman and other comic heroes, you will find in each some guilt that drives them.

Thus, if you want to begin a comic book collection of today's superheroes, it may be wise to obtain the first issue to make certain the superhero is driven by guilt or some other equally primal emotion

Unfortunately, my collection of early Superman's, Batman's, Archie's and Joe Palooka's...well, their importance was just not properly explained to my parents when I went off to college. They are in comic book heaven. I frequently remind my mother of the large sum of money she cost me. She reminds me of the coins and baseball cards she didn't throw out.

Furniture

Furniture is the most actively and seriously-collected antique, and, like baseball cards, coins, stamps and ephemera, it is relatively liquid. You could sell most antique furniture six days a week to a dealer who trades in the specific kind of furniture you collect.

Furniture is the most actively and seriously-collected antique, and, like baseball cards, coins, stamps and ephemera, it is relatively liquid.

If the item you wish to sell is fairly expensive (let's say over $10,000), you may not find a dealer willing to pay you for it because it would tie up too much of his or her working capital. Your alternatives would be to give the piece to the dealer on consignment and let him or her sell it for a commission (typically 15 to 30% of the selling price) or to put the piece up for auction. Auction firms generally work on smaller commissions than dealers' consignment commissions.

The major benefit to investing in antique furniture is that you can use it in your home while you're collecting it, paying for it with money you may have had to use for depreciable assets...like new furniture. Isn't it nice to have an asset that makes money for you while you sleep on it, sit on it, store things in it or serve the family dinner on it?

There are so many different periods of antique furniture to collect and so many species within those periods that the subject, if it interests you, is worth a trip to the library for some research. Clearly, if you are going to begin collecting antique furniture on a small budget, you will find it necessary to "buy American." Most European antiques are several hundred years older than American and, not surprisingly, considerably more expensive. Chinese and Greek antiquities are several thousand years older and much more expensive.

The rule of thumb in collecting antique furniture is to

buy man-made pieces that you enjoy living with in as fine a condition as you can locate and/or afford. Do not restore these pieces or they will lose their value (because it makes them less primitive). An American Indian basket with two small tears in it will always be worth less than a similar basket without a blemish. But if you attempt to repair the torn basket, it could lose its investment value altogether.

American antique furniture (including tools, wall decor, sports equipment, toys, dolls, kitchen utensils and the like) goes up in value every year. It is primitive and in short supply. While demand is not constant, it is growing each year.

You should be able to find a number of pieces that cost less than $500. Some dealers will permit you to pay on an installment basis without interest; most dealers will offer discounts of 10 to 20%, particularly in slow months or if you tell them that you are a serious collector. There is much that is still relatively undiscovered in American primitive antiques. Here's just one example—a whale of an investment idea.

Ice Fishing Decoys

Bird decoys, particularly those in excellent condition that have been signed by the carver, have recently sold for as much as $250,000 apiece. Ice fishing decoys are usually available for under $100. And if you live in Minnesota, Michigan or other states where ice fishing is popular—and ice decoys plentiful—you could probably build a handsome collection of 500 decoys at an average cost of $50 apiece. (though in 1986, my wife found a collection in an upstate New York junk store for less than $10 a decoy).

There are dozens of other still-inexpensive items that a young collector can focus on.

The ice fishing decoy is but one example of dozens of other still-inexpensive items that a young collector can begin with, including sleds, marbles, shoe shine kits, civil war books, buoys, tricycles, door stops, etc.

Wealth, as I have defined it, may not be achievable by investing in antique furniture, but you can achieve a significant appreciation on your investment, be surrounded by beautiful objects, furnish your house with functional objects that increase in value daily and meet a lot of interesting people along the way.

A good way to identify outstanding opportunities in antique collecting is to make a habit of reading the appropriate trade magazines (or journals). Among the best for American antiques is the *Maine Antique Digest*. You should also start talking to dealers, visiting antique trade fairs, attending auctions and taking careful notes about items and prices. You won't learn about antiques (or any area of investing, for that matter) overnight. It will require long hours of dedicated study.

10 Individual Exercises & Projects

1. Visit an art gallery in your town or city. Is there a painting you like? Ask the gallery owner what credit terms you could get. Would he or she accept installment payments? For how long?

2. Refigure Figure 11 at $1,000 per year. How much value would you have at the end of 20 years at 20% a year? At 10%? At 30%?

3. If you don't have a hobby, why not start a collection of something that interests you? Find out if any trade shows are coming to your city. Find and read newsletters (at your local library) of items you think you may be interested in collecting yourself.

4. Visit a local antique store and study the kinds of furniture and other items they offer for sale. Do they give you any ideas for your own budding collection?

11

Dow Jones Wants You!
Part 1

Who Has Money and What Do They Do With It?

The "renting of money" during the time that goods were on the high seas from Europe to the Far East or the New World was the origin of commercial banking. It began in Holland in the 15th century, using bookkeeping records created by the Italians. For many centuries, these banks were the primary providers of credit to businesses. Then, as we saw in chapter 9, insurance companies began to build up enormous sums of cash, becoming, by the 20th century, very large lenders on their own.

Corporate and government <u>pension funds</u> began to accumulate enormous sums of money by the middle of the 20th Century as well. Prior to the 1960s, many people spent their entire adult lives working for one corporation. When they retired, the company grandly gave them a gold watch as a thank you for all those years of dedicated service. (You can still see vestiges of this treatment in large, paternalistic corporations. Just look closely at the collars of the older employees—some of them still sport the small diamond-studded pins signifying 25, 40 or 50 years of service.)

In our mobile society, such long-term service to a single corporation is now an anachronism. As <u>social security</u> benefits are inadequate to support most retired people—especially given the periods of rapid inflation we've experienced—government and private pension funds were developed to reward employees a bit more handsomely when they retired. By the 1960s, corporations and state and local government agencies were routinely adding 3-5% to their employees' salaries and putting that money into employment retirement (commonly called pension) funds.

The amount of money currently in corporate and government pension funds is staggering. Remember how interest compounds on itself, and that money earning interest at 7% per annum doubles in slightly more than ten years? Well, corporate and government pension funds now have close to three trillion dollars available to invest.

How Secure Is Your Bond?

The form of investment pension fund managers like best is corporate bonds. A bond is an obligation of the corporation that issues it to pay the bondholder a specific sum of money on a specific date, plus interest until the bond is repaid in full. Conveniently, the way that corporations and state and local governments like to raise money for expansion is by selling bonds—that is, borrowing large sums of money—from corporate and government pension funds.

Insurance companies buy corporate and government bonds as well, but many of them prefer to make real estate development loans because these loans are very often secured. A secured loan is one backed by collateral: In the event the loan is not repaid, the lender can take possession of the collateral and sell it to try to recapture the amount of money that it has loaned. Corporate and government bonds are frequently unsecured, and the lender cannot take possession of anything if the loan is not repaid.

The higher the risk you are willing to take, usually the greater return you will be promised.

Unsecured loans pay a higher rate of interest than secured loans because they are inherently riskier. The higher the risk you are willing to take, usually the greater return you will be promised. The difference in interest rates between secured and unsecured loans is around 2-3% per annum. (Notice that the emphasis on loans—and a bond is a loan—is safety of principal. Lenders want to be sure they get their bait back each time they offer their line to a fish.)

Why do corporations and governments borrow money by selling their bonds when they could just as easily borrow from banks? In the first place, banks charge higher interest rates than a corporation would usually have to pay in the bond market. In the second place, banks do not make very long-term loans—seven years is about as long as a bank will loan money to a corporation. This is because banks have actually borrowed *their* money from depositors for a much shorter term, and banks that borrow money short and loan it long wind up in trouble. The life of corporate and government bonds is usually measured in decades!

Why do banks loan money for even a year, if not doing so would eliminate the risk of going out of business? Because of the yield curve (an example below is reproduced), which states that the longer a loan is outstanding, the higher the rate of interest or yield to the lender. If a person or corporation borrows money for 20 years, it may pay an interest rate 4-5% *higher* than if it borrows the same amount of money for only three or four years. The yield curve looks the same for secured loans as it does for unsecured loans, except that secured loans pay a lower yield than unsecured loans.

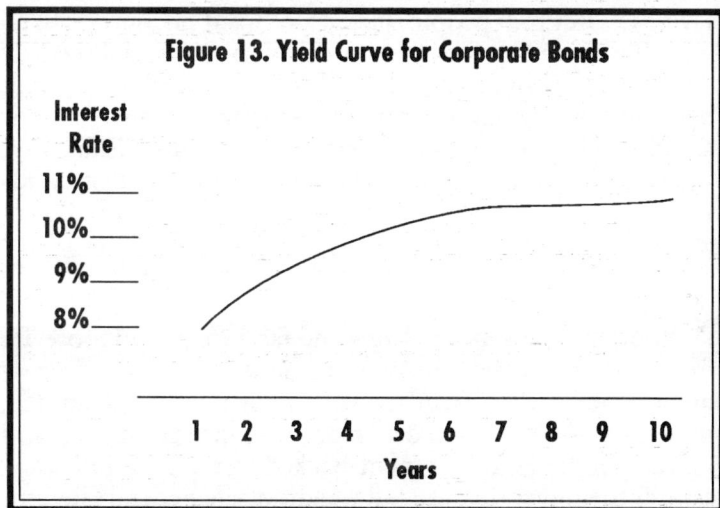

Figure 13. Yield Curve for Corporate Bonds

The prime rate—the rate of interest that banks charge their best corporate borrowers—falls around the center of the yield curve. New York City banks—Citibank, Chase Manhattan, Manufacturers Hanover Trust, Bankers Trust and Chemical Bank—usually determine the prime rate, simply because they are the largest and most influential banks in the country.

The prime rate is the interest rate banks charge their best corporate borrowers.

The prime rate is important since interest rates are frequently expressed as a function of it—"prime plus 2%," "prime plus 4%" (signifying a riskier loan), etc. A fixed rate of interest means that the interest rate that is charged for a loan is fixed for the life of the loan, regardless of what happens to the prime rate. A floating rate of interest means that if banks raise their prime rates, then the rate of interest you are paying will rise proportionately. The same will happen, but in the opposite direction, if banks lower their prime rate. You can find out what the current prime rate of interest is by reading the *Wall Street Journal*, the trade journal of the financial industry.

Tax-Free Bonds, Munis and Government Guarantees

When a local government borrows money by selling bonds, they are tax free to the buyer—that is, the bond holder does not pay taxes on the interest income. As a result, the interest rates are lower (by roughly the amount of the tax savings). Retired people living on fixed incomes—fixed monthly payments from their pension plans, social security benefits and savings accounts—like to invest in tax-exempt bonds because they do not like to pay out any of their earnings in the form of taxes. Retired people also dislike risk, so municipal governments will frequently secure their bonds with water treatment facilities or tolls from bridges. There are hundreds of billions of dollars of municipal bonds (or munis, as they are known) outstanding, all available through most stockbrokers.

Student loans, home loans and farm loans and more are frequently packaged together and sold by banks to investment bankers who, in turn, obtain a government guarantee, then resell them to pension funds, insurance companies and retired people as government-backed loans. The guarantee assures the buyer that the full weight of the Federal Government is behind the loan. Government-backed loans are known by nicknames—Ginnie Mae, Fanny Mae, etc.—and are also available through brokers.

Debentures

Debenture is another word for bond or loan, but whereas bonds can be secured or unsecured, debentures are *always* unsecured. Corporations will occasionally borrow money by making their debentures convertible into the company's common stock. They do this because their ability to pay interest on the debenture is questionable. The convertible option is a sweetener to attract lenders, kind of like your mother offering a special desert to induce you to finish your vegetables.

There are many varieties of bonds that you can buy, but most of them merely offer an interest rate somewhere along the yield curve. For a young person interested in creating wealth, bonds are not a good investment vehicle—you cannot be both risk averse and earn high rates of return.

There are three exceptions to this generalization: buying mortgage loans on distressed properties in foreclosure, buying bonds of distressed or bankrupt companies at a steep discount from <u>par</u> and buying <u>convertible debentures</u> of small, rapidly-expanding companies.

The first will require you to use personal labor in order to create a high rate of return on your investment. Although you will not have to pay the bank with cash to buy the loan, you may be at risk personally for the amount of the loan. I will discuss this more in chapter 13.

If you are able to buy the bonds of a distressed corporation at a deep discount and the company subsequently returns to financial health, you will sell the bonds for a substantial profit. This is a very specialized form of investing, quite a bit more difficult to learn than betting on which baseball cards to accumulate, and I do not recommend it for young people.

As to convertible debentures, there is an opportunity to double and perhaps triple your investment within 12 to 18 months, but to do that, you will have to carefully study a number of industries and find companies the professionals have overlooked. From this initial list, you will need to identify those with convertible debentures outstanding, where the stock and bond market has not adjusted the price of the stock for the conversion feature of the debenture. Finally, from this even shorter list, you will need to determine the direction in which the corporation's earnings are headed. This is a very time-consuming and highly analytical series of tasks and one that unsophisticated financiers should avoid.

To avoid doing all this work yourself, you can purchase shares of <u>mutual funds</u> that specialize in convertible debentures. (A mutual fund pools the money of numerous personal investors to purchase a diversified portfolio of common stocks and bonds. The logic of mutual funds is simple: in diversification there is safety. And the fund can afford to diversify with a lot of people's money far more easily and effectively than any one person could. Of course, you shouldn't plan to get rich on mutual funds, even those that tend to specialize in high-risk products. Whenever the words "diversification" or "safety" come into play, you can be fairly certain that the upside potential is relatively small.) The bottom line is that convertible debentures require good information in order to generate high rates of return.

This Little Piggy Went To Market

The stock market is where many fortunes have been made and lost. I started my own education in the market when I was 21 years old, opened my first account with a stockbroker and bought 10 shares of Data Products Corp.— a California-based manufacturer of computer printers—at $7 per share. I sold the stock a few years later at $12 per share, making a not-insignificant profit at the time.

But had I held onto those ten shares for 25 years, they would have been worth $700, a 100 times return on my investment (a rate of return of 18% per annum). Of course, I could have really scored if I had used that $70 to buy 70 1951 Mickey Mantles for $1.00 apiece. 1988 value: $455,000!

There are legendary players in the market, like Warren Buffett, who began with $10,000 or so and created a portfolio worth over $1 billion in slightly more than 30 years. There are thousands of smaller investors who buy a stock, hold it for years and collect dividends. Others, like Buffett, may be in and out of a particular stock almost daily, betting thousands or even millions of dollars on the swing of a single point.

Whichever kind of investor you become—conservative or aggressive, incredibly successful or just comfortable—the rest of this chapter and the next will help you understand the ins-and-outs enough to at least play the game to win.

Stock Market Basics

Common stocks are units of investment in corporations. Most American businesses are organized as corporations, which means they have stockholders as opposed to partners.

There are three major markets in the U.S. for stocks and bonds: the New York Stock Exchange, the American Stock

Exchange and the <u>Over-the-Counter</u> market (OTC and NASDAQ). A corporation is able to list its securities on the New York and American Stock Exchanges once they meet certain size requirements. Until then, their stocks trade over the counter. (Although many large corporations remain in the over-the-counter market because it is considered the market of rapidly-expanding companies and perhaps more exciting.)

Twenty million or more people in the U.S. have stock brokerage accounts. If that doesn't say we are a nation of optimists, I don't know what does. As we discussed, several hundred billion dollars managed by pension funds, insurance companies, investment managers and university endowment funds also buy and sell common stocks and bonds. Foreigners invest in the U.S. stock market as well; some of this money is flight capital sent over the two oceans by people in nondemocratic countries who regard the U.S. as a safe place for their money. And so it is.

The public market for common stocks and bonds deals in nearly perfect information. Stated another way, there is less uncertainty in the public market for stocks and bonds than in most other markets. Prices correct themselves quickly, just as soon as information about a corporation's results flash across the <u>Quotron</u> machines in stock brokerage offices, on pension fund and insurance company investment managers' desks, via television on the Financial News Network and in the *Wall Street Journal* and other financial journals the next morning.

Before we get into the real nitty gritty of the market, let's talk about some basic terminology. First, the unimportant things. <u>Par value</u> is unimportant, except to state treasurers who tax companies incorporated in their states based upon the number of shares of common stock created upon their formation. If a corporation is formed with an initial investment of $10,000 and issues 1,000,000 shares of common stock, its par value is $.01 per share ($10,000/1,000,000). If it is formed with $5,000 and 5,000,000 shares of common stock, its par value is $.001 per share ($5,000/5,000,000). Some states tax corporations on a per share basis and, as you might imagine, those states run new corporations away. Now that you know what par value is, you can forget about it.

The number of shares that a new corporation issues when it is formed is also unimportant. Whether it *begins* with

5,000, 50,000, 500,000 or 5,000,000 makes no difference.

Certain strategies may require the corporation to *end up* with a certain number of shares. If a company starts by issuing only 5,000 shares and then earns $500,000 after taxes, its earnings per share would be $100. If the corporation then decided to go public by selling some <u>Treasury stock</u> to the public, and if similar companies trade in the public market at a p/e ratio of 15x (see page 151 for a complete explanation of this important term), the corporation's stock would trade at $1,500 per share. That is not an affordable price to purchasers of new issues—corporations going public for the first time—many of whom are individual investors, not the big pension funds or insurance companies.

To bring the price of a share of common stock down to a more affordable level, the corporation would <u>split</u> its stock. Our hypothetical new company with 5,000 initial shares, for example, might issue its stockholders 1,000 shares for every one share that they own. This, of course, lowers the value of each share by 1000%, so that, in this instance, there would be 5,000,000 shares of common stock outstanding with an earnings per share of $.10 ($500,000 of earnings/5,000,000 shares). At the same 15x p/e ratio, the stock is very affordable at $1.50 per share.

Corporations also frequently lower the price of their common stock when it runs up to over $50 per share by issuing a stock <u>dividend</u>. Assume that a corporation has 5,000,000 shares outstanding, a stock price of $50, earnings per share of $2.50 and a p/e ratio of 20x. If it wants to bring its stock price down to $25, it might split its stock "two for one" in the manner we described, or it might issue a 50% stock dividend. (For the moment, at least, both have the same result.)

To do the latter, the company's board of directors would vote a stock dividend and issue a press release stating that all stockholders of record as of a future date (the <u>record date</u>) would receive one share of the corporation's common stock for each share that they own on that date. (The day after the record date is called the <u>ex-dividend date</u>.) Peculiarly, stock prices tend to move up 5-10% up to the record date, even though a stock dividend does not create value for the recipient. But people like to get something for nothing, so they bid up the price of a corporation's shares of common stock when a stock dividend is announced.

How the Stock Market Works

There are several closely-followed common stock in-dexes: the Dow-Jones Industrial Average of 60 industrial companies on the New York Stock Exchange and the Standard & Poor's Index of 500 industrial companies, for example. When these indexes move up, it is generally considered a <u>bullish</u> indicator—it could mean that unemployment is down, corporations' earnings are up, oil prices are moving up and inflation is under control. If the indexes move down, it is generally considered a <u>bearish</u> indicator and the above factors are probably not positive.

The price of a company's common stock moves up when more people buy it than sell it. If the opposite occurs, the price will fall. More people will buy a common stock if they believe it is undervalued relative to other common stocks— that is, if they think the company's earnings will increase, that it is about to be taken over by a corporate raider or make a breakthrough that will result in future higher earnings.

One indication of the public's confidence (or lack thereof) in a certain stock is the price/earnings ratio (p/e ratio), which states that a company's value bears a relationship to its earnings ability. The stock market is made up of investment managers of insurance companies, pension funds, bank investment departments, mutual funds, university endowment fund officers, individuals and foreign nationals. If they are optimistic about the future earnings ability of a corporation, they bid up the price of its stock and its p/e ratio moves up accordingly. If they are unenthusiastic, the p/e ratio moves down.

Let's say that both ABC Corp. and XYZ Corp. have 2 million shares of common stock outstanding and pay income taxes at a 40% tax rate. In Figure 14, we can use the concept of the p/e ratio to determine what the price of one share of common stock is worth.

In this example, I used a p/e ratio of 15x, which means that every $1.00 of earnings is worth $15.00 of market value. Had I used a p/e ratio of 30x, I would have been more optimistic about the future earnings ability of the two companies. Had I used a p/e ratio of 7x, I would have been less optimistic (i.e., unwilling to place great value on those companies' future earnings).

Figure 14 Relative Values of Two Similar Companies		
	ABC Co.	**XYZ Co.**
Net Income Before Interest and Taxes	$5,000,000	$1,000,000
Interest on $5,000,000 Loan	400,000	400,000
Net Profit Before Taxes	4,600,000	600,000
Provision for Taxes @ 40%	1,840,000	240,000
Net Profit After Taxes	(a)$2,760,000	$ 360,000
Number of Shares of Common Stock Outstanding	(b) 2,000,000	2,000,000
Earnings per Share(a/b)	(c) $1.38	$.18
P/E Ratio	(d)15x	15x
Market Price of Common Stock (c x d)	$20.70	$2.70

Locating Undervalued Stocks

If you hope to make your fortune in the stock market, you should concentrate on finding undervalued companies. Is that different from poking around junk stores in Minnesota in search of ice fishing decoys? No. The task is the same: Doing the investigative work necessary to locate publicly-held corporations whose common stocks sell at unrealistically low prices in relation to other companies in their industry or to the stock market as a whole. If you are analytical by nature and enjoy searching through printed material, the stock market may be the garden in which you want to toil. If, on the other hand, you prefer the great outdoors, dealing with all kinds of people and negotiating with them, you may be more at home investing in antiques, art, real estate or entrepreneurial ventures.

If you are looking for undervalued investment opportunities in the stock market, the indexes are not too meaningful, unless they move sharply downward and remain down. This could signal that common stocks are out of favor and the undervalued stock that you have located will have more difficulty moving up, forcing you to hold onto the stock longer than if the indexes were in an upward curve.

To find undervalued common stocks, keep your eyes open and look around you. Read newspapers that discuss the nation's problems; surely an entrepreneurial company somewhere is trying to solve one of them. Read trade journals that discuss emerging industries. For every new industry there is a trade journal, whether it is biotechnology or franchising, in which you can spot new companies offering breakthrough products and services. When you open a stock brokerage account, ask to receive the new issue prospectuses and the firm's research reports. Tell your stockbroker what you are interested in and he or she will keep you well informed.

Don't expect to make your fortune overnight. When you locate an undervalued corporation and purchase its common stock, you may have to hold it for a few years until other people come to the same realization that you did. Just because *you* determined that it was undervalued doesn't mean others will follow you.

Let's look at another way to observe outstanding common stock opportunities. If you use a personal computer at your job or at home, then you are part of a rapidly growing industry. Perhaps there is a special software product that makes your job easier or an attachment to your computer without which you'd be lost. Find the name of the manufacturer, then call your stockbroker to see if it is a publicly-held company. If so, you can call the company for annual reports, quarterly reports and two kinds of documents—10-K (for annual filings) and 10-Q (for quarterly filings)—that it files with the <u>Securities and Exchange Commission</u>.

Current issues of some of the important trade magazines that report on the personal computer industry—*PC Week, Computer Retail News* or others—will let you know about competitors, their earnings, stock prices and p/e ratios. To compare their operations with the company whose product you particularly like, order their annual reports. What you are looking for is the quality of the company's earnings and its financial strength.

11 Individual Exercises & Projects

1. What are the five biggest pension funds in the U. S.?

2. What's today's prime rate?

3. Who rates corporate bonds and what does a "AAA" bond have that a "BAA" bond doesn't? What do those ratings mean?

4. List the different kinds of bonds or bond funds you could buy today with $1,000 and the yield you would expect. Which seem to offer the best combination of reward and risk aversion?

5. Which mutual funds performed best in the last month? Last year? Last ten years? Can you find any pattern that would lead you to pick one or another if you were ready to invest *your* own pile of cash today?

6. In Figure 14, assume that ABC split its stock 2 for 1. How many shares would now be outstanding? What would be the new earnings per share? Assuming the same p/e ratio, what would be ABC's new market price per share?

7. Similarly, if XYZ managed to double its income, what would its stock be worth? What if it tripled its sales?

8. Is there a particular product or service—toy, book, ice cream brand, etc.—you think is superior? Research the company. Would you buy the stock?

12

Dow Jones Wants You!
Part 2

Analyzing Annual Reports

There is an amazing amount of information you can glean from a company's <u>annual report</u>. Although this subject is very broad, I will point out some guides to use in analyzing financial statements. The bible for this subject is called <u>Securities Analysis</u>, written by Graham and Dodd over 30 years ago. My favorite ratios for a quick analysis are the following:

Gross profit margin—Subtract the Cost of Goods Sold from Revenues and divide the remainder (called Gross Profit) by revenues to get gross profit margin. The more valuable the product and the fewer the competitors, the higher a company's gross profit margin.

A company's gross profit margin measures its manufacturing efficiency.

This ratio also measures manufacturing efficiency, because the lower the cost of goods sold, the higher a company's gross profit margin. Over several years a company's gross profit margin should rise, reflecting a long life for its older products and customer acceptance of its new products. A downward trend in gross profit margin means that the company is having to lower its prices to sell its products.

In the 1960s, Polaroid's gross profit margin rose by 1 or 2% each year—44 percent, 45.5 percent, 47.8 percent—because it was selling more film—which boasts a very high mark-up over cost—than cameras. This is known as razor blade marketing: Keep the price of the razor affordably low and charge as much as the market will bear for the blade. Then sell blades!

Some personal computer companies, such as Apple

Computer Corp., offer software that runs on their machines. Because of its razor blade marketing strategy, Apple's gross profit margin is higher than its competitors'.

Inventory turnover—Look on the balance sheet and get a figure for <u>Inventory</u>, then divide it into Cost of Goods Sold. The result will usually be a number between 6 and 9, which represents how quickly the company is <u>turning over</u> its inventory. A rapid turnover (a number from 9 to 12) means that the inventory is popular, current and hard to keep in stock. A lower inventory turnover figure, on the order of 4 to 6, means that the company's inventory is slow-moving, possibly obsolete in places and not popular in the marketplace.

If you divide the inventory turnover number into 365, you can see how many days of inventory the company has on hand. The fewer the days on hand, the more popular the product.

Total debt to net worth ratio—Take the Total Liabilities shown on the company's balance sheet and divide them by Net Worth (Total Shareholder's Equity). The resulting figure is the debt to worth ratio. The higher the number (above 1.5), the more highly-leveraged the company and the less likely its chances of riding out hard times. The lower the number (.5 to 1.5), the less leveraged the company and the better capitalized it is to survive tough times.

Leverage is wonderful when profits grow every year.

A highly-leveraged company will have less net worth, which means fewer stockholders with whom you will have to share profits. Leverage is wonderful when profits grow every year. However, if the company suffers a bad year and loses money, a high debt to worth ratio means that it may not have the cash available to pay its debts.

It is the job of management to produce a high return on stockholders' equity (net profit after taxes divided by net worth). That means maximizing stockholders' equity to generate the highest possible returns. If management borrows most of its capital to purchase raw materials, to convert them into inventory and to hire a sales force, then clearly if the company is profitable it will have produced a high return on equity. That is the plus side of leverage. It argues for borrowing as much money as people will loan you. Entrepreneurs do this all the time, because frequently they cannot get people to invest in their companies to the extent they would like.

But you would not want to buy stock in a company that

is fully leveraged, because if the market for the company's product or service turned sour, there would be little or no cash to pay the debts. Thus, you would be most interested in a company's common stock where the debt to worth ratio was prudent.

(This word, prudent, has crept into the dictionary of investments. It means simply acting wisely with money; acting as if the money you were managing was not your own but entrusted to you for safety and growth. A company manager who does not observe and respect prudent asset management may not be a person whose company's common stock you want to own.)

Sales per employee—This is another useful ratio, derived by dividing Annual Sales by the total Number of Employees. Several rapidly growing companies in innovative industries produce over $150,000 in sales for each employee. If the average employee earns $30,000 a year, the company would be very efficiently generating 500% of the cost of each of its employees.

> You would not want to buy stock in a company that is fully leveraged.

Older industries with union-negotiated labor contracts— steel, automobiles, textiles, etc.—rarely achieve sales per employee numbers over $80,000. That indicates that a lot of people are standing around the water cooler and either not doing whatever they were hired to do or not doing it particularly quickly. I like this operating ratio because it measures the excitement level at the company. The higher this number, the more employees there are putting in quality time, overtime and the greater their enthusiasm for what they are doing.

> Sales per employee measures the excitement level at the company.

Selling expenses to revenues—This ratio measures the relative difficulty of convincing the marketplace to buy the company's products.

A company that can sell its product by using a nickel out of every sales dollar (a 5% selling expenses to revenues ratio) to make its sales pitch doesn't have to work too hard to sell product. If the ratio is 20% or higher, then the product is not easy to sell. This occurs with non-proprietary products or services where delivery systems are easy to duplicate. Cigarettes are non-proprietary—there is nothing particularly unique about a cigarette—as are beverages, cars, bank loans and cosmetics. Thus, their selling and advertising expenses are quite high.

Unless there is a breakthrough product in these industries which *is* obviously unique, you can expect that 20 cents or more of every dollar you invest in them will be used for selling or advertising expenses. That gives me a reason for concern: Are non-proprietary products or non-duplicable services *really* solving problems for people or servicing a need? And if they are *not,* then are they economically valid companies? If the answers are "no" to these questions, the prices of their common stocks may not grow very rapidly.

All Information Is Not Created Equal

The preceding sections should have convinced you of the importance of obtaining detailed information on any companies whose stocks you're thinking of buying. But be careful: Not all information is created equal!

If you obtain your information by careful research and investigation, a thorough reading of industry trade journals or by observing the frequency with which people request the company's product in a local store, then you have obtained your information fairly and legally and may freely act on what you've learned.

If, however, you work at a law firm that is preparing takeover documents for ABC Corp. and you then buy the target company's common stock based on such insider information, you have committed a crime. Employees of publicly-held corporations who have insider information about their corporation's future earnings or a forthcoming favorable announcement can't act on that information. They cannot tip others about it. And they cannot have blood relatives buy the stock, either for themselves or for the tipster. They must keep their mouths shut. Period.

Unfortunately, knowing something is wrong does not necessarily stop people from doing it. Despite a whole slate of laws against trading on such insider information, it's difficult for a lot of people not to act on information that they *know* will make them lots of money. Which is why the insider trading scandals on Wall Street have been in the news so much lately.

(In the movie *The Big Chill,* the character played by Kevin Kline gives a tip to the character played by William Hurt. That was an illegal act on his part, and I have been curious since I first saw that movie whether or not anyone connected with it knew that.)

Opening a Brokerage Account

Before you can begin buying and selling stocks, bonds or any other security, you will need to choose a stockbroker and open a brokerage account with his or her firm. This broker will actually <u>execute</u> the <u>trades</u>—the buy and sell transactions—you want to make. Since a broker makes a commission on every transaction—every security you buy, every security you sell, whether or not you make or lose money on your trades—whoever you choose will be most happy to see you—a new customer—sitting across his or her desk.

To open a brokerage account, you must complete a simple account form, requiring mainly the same information a bank would ask to open an account—name, address, phone, citizenship, marital status. You will be asked to name any relatives who work at the brokerage firm, your income, whether or not you own a home and to identify your investment objectives—income or capital appreciation (growth). Since all brokerage acounts are identified by social security number, you will need your own number before you open an account. (The only exception is for corporate accounts, which utilize the corporation's Federal tax identification number.)

You will also be asked to specify the type of account that you want to open—the broker will assume that you are opening a <u>cash account</u>. If you want to open a <u>commodity account</u> or <u>option account</u>, you will have to demonstrate financial knowledge in these areas. And if you wish to open a <u>margin account</u>—which means that you will be borrowing a portion of the price of stock and bond purchases from the brokerage firm—you will have to provide enough detailed financial information to convince them you are a worthy credit risk. You will also need to instruct your broker whether dividends you earn should automatically be deposited in your account or mailed to you.

Your broker will ask for (and verify) the name of your bank and appropriate bank account numbers, unless you send in a deposit before making your first transaction. This is just reference information; your bank will not be involved in your stock transactions. (Although there is a type of brokerage account called DVP/RVP—literally "Deliver Versus Purchase" and "Receive Versus Purchase"—in which securities are held in custody for you by your bank. If you buy stock, the brokerage firm delivers the stock to the bank and receives payment directly from them. Similarly, when you sell a stock, the bank delivers the certificates to the brokerage house and receives payment for the sale. Many very large personal accounts are handled this way.)

The broker will use the back of your account form to record all of your transactions over time, entering the date of each buy and sell order, the name of the stock or bond, the number of shares and the price. Each separate acount that you open will require its own new account form and recording page.

Stock or Bond Power

Stock and bond certificates are valuable pieces of paper—if any you own are lost or stolen, you could be out a lot of money. In order to avoid dealing in stolen securities, brokerage firms decided cooperatively that they would not <u>negotiate</u>—that is, buy or sell—a stock or bond certificate unless it was accompanied by a <u>stock or bond power</u> signed by the person whose name appeared on the certificate. So even if you lose a signed stock certificate (an unsigned certificate is not a negotiable instrument—it cannot be converted into cash), the stock or bond power—if unattached from the certificate—protects you.

It's best not to tempt fate at all and simply avoid signing any stock or bond certificates until you are ready to sell them. Just bring any certificates you plan to sell to your broker's office and sign them there. If you find it inconvenient to do so, send your *unsigned* certificates to your broker by registered mail; your broker will send you a bond or stock power form to sign. If yours is the only name on the certificate, just sign your name (exactly as it appears on the front of the certificate) to the stock or bond power and send it back, again via registered mail, to your broker. If the certificate is jointly registered, make sure you and whoever else is named on the certificate signs. Your broker will fill in the rest of the information.

Once you and your broker decide to buy or sell stock, the broker must confirm the transaction to you with a trade confirmation slip. Keep these slips. You will need to reconcile your buy slips with your sell slips at tax time.

Some Specialized Investments

Brokerage houses can no longer specialize in just selling Stock A or Bond B. Because of their need to survive in a very competitive market, they have been extremely creative in conceiving new products—investment vehicles—to capture and hold their customers' attention. Additionally, as the line between stockbrokers, bankers, real estate brokers and consumer credit firms blurs, more and more firms are offering more and more financial products. Indeed, it's now possible to find over 80 different financial products at a single brokerage house. Let's review some of the more popular of these products:

Treasury Bills—The United States government has to borrow money, just like everyone else. One way it does so is by issuing Treasury bonds, notes and bills. Treasury bonds are issues of longer than ten years maturity. Treasury notes mature in from one to ten years. And Treasury bills—"T" bills for short—are issued for periods of three, six or twelve months. Treasury bills are the safest (they're guaranteed), most liquid (they may be cashed in any day) marketable securities in the financial world.

T bills are the safest, most liquid marketable securities in the financial world.

Treasury bills, whatever their maturity, are offered at a discount from face value. The difference between this discounted price—what you pay for them—and the price on the maturity date—what you get back—is the interest you earn on the T bill. If you had managed to save $10,000, for example, by September but really didn't need the money to pay your college tuition, room and board until January, you could buy a three-month T bill. If the current interest rate on a three-month bill were 3%, you would pay $9,850 for a bill with a face value of $10,000. The difference between your cost and what you receive at maturity—$150—is the interest earned on the bill, which accrues every day until maturity. You need not hold T bills until maturity—if you sell any time before the maturity date, you will receive back whatever you invested plus the interest that has accrued so far.

Money Market Mutual Funds—These funds were originally formed when interest rates soared in the mid-1970s to take advantage of these higher rates and offer investors another alternative to savings accounts. Money market mutual funds are very popular because of their high rate of return, their liquidity and the ease with which one can buy or sell them. If you wish to participate in the money market fund of your broker's firm, you simply give him or her a check for the minimum amount of purchase, as little as $1,000, and he or she will make the purchase for you the next business day.

Money market funds are similar to day-of-deposit savings accounts—interest accrues and is compounded each day, and there is no redemption penalty. Current money market funds are paying 10% and automatically reinvest your monthly interest (as opposed to savings accounts paying 6% or less). You may add to your money market fund at any time (usually a minimum of $500 at a time) and withdraw from it at any time...as much or little as you want.

There are so many of these funds out there right now you may have trouble deciding which one to choose. Your broker will be able to suggest one or more; his or her firm will usually have its own fund, which it will undoubtedly recommend. Funds are quite similar and interest rates don't vary that much from one to another. They differ primarily in terms of some of the ancillary privileges they may or may not offer, such as check writing privileges or an accompanying credit card.

Stock or Bond Mutual Funds—If diversification is your goal, you can purchase shares in a numbing variety of stock or bond mutual funds from your stockbroker or directly from the fund itself. Minimum investments in this type of fund are generally as low as $500, with additional investments accepted in $100 increments.

Most funds allow you to reinvest your dividends automatically, bettering your chances for portfolio growth. However, should you need to dip into monies you have placed in a fund, you can cash in at any time. You may also withdraw only a portion of your investment.

Virtually any (and every) type of financial instrument can make up a mutual fund (or <u>unit trust</u>) and any portfolio goal can be served. There are nearly-risk free funds that produce tax-free income and high-flying funds that invest in commodities. There are gold funds, bond funds, utility funds, and dozens more. But they have one thing in common: the goal of offering small investors a way to invest in a professionally selected and managed portfolio that meets that fund's specific objective, whether that be long-term growth, short-term income, tax savings, or some combination of all three.

Who would invest in unit trusts in the first place? The investor who is seeking diversification, professional evaluation and supervision and lacks the money and/or experi-

---

Money market funds are similar to day-of-deposit savings accounts.

Mutual funds—the small investor's way to invest in a professionally selected and managed portfolio.

ence to achieve those goals from separate investments. A mutual fund gives this investor access to securities that, if bought individually, might be beyond his or her financial reach—$1,000 invested in a mutual fund might buy participation in a diversified investment portfolio that would otherwise cost an individual $15,000, $25,000 or more.

Income funds tend to be safe and secure, investing in government-backed T bills, high grade corporate bonds and the like. Investors in a fund whose primary goal is income are not willing to accept the risk reaping potentially huge profits demand. They seek safe, secure income, money they can count on.

Growth funds were created to meet the need of investors for whom long-term growth is more important than short-term income. Money placed in one of these funds is usually left there, perhaps building up for retirement or to cover future college expenses.

Despite similar goals, managers of growth funds often take different paths to reach their long-term objectives. One fund might invest solely in the stocks of blue chip companies, another try to achieve capital growth by investing in smaller, entrepreneurial growth companies. It's important you investigate the investment strategy of the fund you're considering.

Balanced funds are dedicated to achieving a balance between income and growth, usually by investing equally in bonds, preferred stocks and common stocks.

All of the funds mentioned above meet the majority of investors' goals: safety, income, growth, liquidity. These are not risky investments and they are popular with millions of investors.

Investing in commodities—farm products like corn, wheat, orange juice, pork bellies, precious metals such as gold, silver and platinum or foreign currencies like the Japanese yen, the German mark or the Swiss franc—has become increasingly popular, though it remains one of the riskiest investments available and is not recommended for the young, faint of heart or anyone who cannot afford to lose everything in less than a day.

A stockbroker must be registered with the Chicago Board of Trade in order to execute a commodity order. Since the rapid rise in the price of gold and silver earlier in the decade, which served to introduce commodities to a larger portion of the public, most brokers are now able to execute such trades, either through their own firm or a participating Board of Trade member.

Instead of buying shares of stock or a bond with a par value, commodity investors buy <u>futures contracts</u>, which represent their commitment to buy or sell a commodity at a preset price before the contract expires several months in the future (hence, people buying "May wheat" or "July pork bellies" in January). If you assume a <u>long</u> (purchase) <u>position</u>, you are betting that the price of the commodity will rise and will make money if it does so. A <u>short</u> (sell) <u>position</u> is just the opposite—you're betting on the price to decline. Your profit in either case is the difference between your contract price and your sale price.

Since most commodity contracts require only a small down payment when they are purchased on margin (and there are completely different margin requirements than for stocks), the leverage on even a small price move is enormous. And, as you've learned, leverage cuts both ways—the more you stand to win, the more you must be prepared to lose. If the price moves against you, even just a few cents, you may face an immediate <u>margin call</u>—a "request" to put up more money. If you don't have the money to put up, your contract will be liquidated and you will lose everything.

There are many variables to consider when you are trading commodities, including the economy, domestic and international events and the weather. One commodity's fall may signal a rise in another. If you feel the dollar is particularly "weak," for example, and ripe for a fall, you would purchase another relatively strong currency like the yen or Swiss franc, both of which would rise if the dollar did indeed fall.

Obviously, the risk in commodities investing is considerable. Remember the movie *Trading Places*, when Eddie Murphy and Dan Akroyd managed to bankrupt one of the world's largest brokerage firms in just a few hours, all by buying and selling orange juice at the right time? Commodity trading is only for the very active investor, one who knows how to act quickly in the fastest-action pit of all. And for the high risk investor, too, not for one who suffers at the loss of even the smallest stake.

I have left out many details about common stock and bond investing—as well as some of the more esoteric financial instruments such as options, puts, calls, etc.—but you will pick them up as you become more actively involved.

Some final words of wisdom: Avoid investment clubs, insider information, hot tips, over-leveraged companies, tired old industries and greed. If you make 25 to 35% in a stock in one year, take some profits out of that one and look for another winner. If a stock goes down 25% from the price you paid, make a hard decision to either sell it or buy more.

You won't pick winners every time.

Last but not least, do not get discouraged if you fail to pick winners every time. No one does. And you certainly don't have to be right all the time to do very well indeed in the stock market.

12 Individual Exercises & Projects

1. Assuming you completed exercise 8 in the last chapter, write for the annual report of the company you chose and calculate all the ratios discussed at the beginning of this chapter. Did you decide to buy the stock before? Would you do so now?

2. Give other examples of "razor blade" marketing.

3. Prepare a report for school on the overall topic of insider trading or on some specific aspect of it. Specific topics could include the particular problems of Drexel Burnham Lambert (and, perhaps, a discussion of junk bonds), the woes of Ivan Boesky, a discussion of what should and shouldn't be considered insider trading, and a paper that distinguishes between profits and greed.

4. Pick five or ten mutual funds from the financial pages of your paper and write for information from each. Investigate each fund's purported goal, the strategies each's managers say they follow, and the types of companies in which they trade. Can you grade them according to potential risk? Which one would you invest your pile of cash in?

13

How To Make Money By Losing It

Not Quite A Roof Over Your Head

A large number of people involved in the investment markets earn their keep by helping investors lose money. Sound peculiar? Just remember: There's a huge difference between losing capital and losing money. No one wants to lose their capital, their investment dollars. But practically everyone would love to show losses on their income tax returns in order to lower their tax bill. That's what I mean by losing money: strategies wherein investment losses are returned to you in tax savings.

Since most of you don't have enough income to worry about taxes or ways of reducing your tax liability, I will not bore you with detailed explanations of <u>tax shelters</u> and tax advantaged investments. However, it's important that you understand this important area of investments, so this chapter will provide you with a brief overview.

The playing field for good investment ideas seeking capital was tilted throughout the 1970s and until 1985 in favor of investments that lost money for their investors. Most of these investment opportunities were structured as <u>limited partnerships</u>, with a <u>general partner</u> whose responsibility it was to manage the investors' dollars and <u>limited partners</u> who put up over 90% of the money. The general partner's liabilities were not limited—if the partnership borrowed $1 million from a bank to finance its activities, the general partner owed the bank the $1 million, just as if he borrowed it personally. General partners take on quite a lot of responsibility and personal liability. Limited partners have no

> There's a huge difference between losing capital and losing money.

responsibility and their liability is limited to the amount of money they invest.

For many years, the U.S. Congress passed laws that treated tax shelter investments more favorably than investments that lacked tax features and were completely capital gain-oriented. They did so by permitting investors in limited partnerships to invest a small amount of dollars, sign notes or loan guarantees for much larger amounts (without, usually, having to ever actually come up with the latter), then permitting rapid depreciation of the project that the partnership was formed to finance. The limited partners received the lion's share of the depreciation.

The Federal government went even further, cutting the deck in favor of limited partners who invested in oil and gas exploration, real estate projects and equipment financing— the areas that offered the greatest amount of paper losses through depreciation, depletion allowances and investment tax credits.

The result: They were often able to deduct (or "write off") far more than they ever actually invested.

As you know, depreciation is a deduction from income, a loss item. But it is an invisible expense, not an out-of-pocket expense. When you buy a new car from a dealer, it depreciates by 20% in market value one minute after you sign the papers and buy it. Why? Because it is no longer a new car. But what does "20% depreciation" mean? You lose the 20% on paper, but you don't have to pay it to anyone.

Money is attracted to the highest rate of return

Money is attracted to the highest rate of return. And tax shelter limited partnerships were offering investors higher rates of return than non-tax sheltered investments because one could "lose" ten times or more of one's investment in one year. An investment of $10,000 would lose $100,000, and for a person with a $100,000 income tax obligation, writing a check to a tax shelter partnership for $10,000 is tantamount to a 1000% or 10x rate of return in one year ($100,000/$10,000), because it wipes out the income tax of $100,000. Would you rather pay $100,000 to Uncle Sam or $10,000 to a tax shelter? You see the point.

In calculating rates of return on investments in art, antiques and common stocks and bonds, we never found a single one that yielded 100% per annum. So as you might imagine, tax sheltered investments were very popular. (Despite the fact that the projects they financed were frequently designed exclusively to lose money and were completely devoid of economic validity. In other words, if there hadn't been such favorable tax treatment, no businessperson in his or her right mind would have ever undertaken many of these projects! Lots of ugly buildings and real estate developments—all of them empty—exist today solely because they were excellent tax shelters. Perhaps their debts can be assumed by renovation-oriented entrepreneurs, who can transform such vacant real estate into something more useful to the community.)

To his credit, President Reagan did not like the way the Federal government had tampered with the investment playing field; to even everything out, he rammed the Tax Reform Act of 1986 through Congress. Now it is virtually impossible to raise money based solely on the tax shelter features of an investment—it must be an economically viable project as well.

Now it is virtually impossible to raise money based solely on the tax shelter features of an investment

Today's available partnerships are useful investment vehicles designed to generate losses for the investors in the early years and capital gains in the later years. While the 1986 Tax Reform Act has made losses of 10 to 1 a long-forgotten dream, losses in the 20-30% range are still available. When such losses are added to the income or capital gains to be generated from the investment, partnership interests are still among the more attractive investments.

Sub-Chapter S Corporations

In addition to limited partnerships, there is another form of organization that permits its investors to transfer losses and income directly to their personal income tax returns—the sub-chapter S corporation. (The "other" kind of corporation—the form utilized by all publicly-traded companies, for example—is the C Corporation).

What else is different about a sub-chapter S corporation? It is severely restricted in terms of the number and type of shareholders it is allowed. While a C corporation can sell its stock to virtually anyone and in whatever quantities the market will bear, a sub-chapter S corporation is limited to only 25 shareholders. And they must be individual U. S. citizens—no institutional investors, pension funds, other corporations, etc.

If each of these 25 investors bought $5,000 worth of stock in a sub-chapter S corporation that posted a loss of $100,000 in its first year of operations, then each investor would have lost $4,000 (1/25 of $100,000). The Tax Reform Act of 1986 states that losses on investments may be deducted only from investment-generated income, not income from one's job. So if a typical investor had income from other investments of $4,000—on which he would normally pay taxes—this $4,000 loss would offset it, a significant tax savings and an 80% return on investment in one year.

When sub-chapter S corporations begin generating income, the stockholders usually elect to change their status to a C corporation so that the income earned by the corporation does not have to be immediately declared on the investors' income tax returns. (The investors probably wouldn't mind reporting their proportionate share of such income to the IRS and paying taxes on it if they actually received it. But in most cases, the corporation reinvests this income in order to expand its activities. If the company were still a sub-chapter S corporation, the investors would have to report the income and pay taxes on it even though they didn't receive a dime. Which is why they usually elect to flip into C corporation status. The government permits this to occur one time only.)

Research And Development Limited Partnerships

The Tax Reform Act of 1986 did not eliminate the write-off of expenditures on research and development against an investor's income. So you can still become a limited partner in a partnership (or stockholder in a sub-chapter S corporation) that is attempting to find new pharmaceuticals to fight disease, new electronic equipment to detect terrorists in airports or new microchip implants to help the hearing impaired, and deduct your proportionate share of the company's losses from your income tax return. If the research leads to a breakthrough new product, you will receive a proportionate share of the income as well.

The combination of losses in the early years and income in the later years have made Research and Development Limited Partnerships ("R&D LPs" for short) very popular investment vehicles. Several stock brokerage firms design R&D LPs and offer them to their clients each year.

If the results of the research and development produce a product around which a company could be built to produce and market it, then the investors in the R&D LP get rolled-up—that is, they exchange their partnership interests for shares of common stock in the newly formed corporation.

Roll-ups are new, because the R&D LP itself is a fairly recent investment vehicle, having marched out onto Wall Street at about the time that most high-flying tax shelters were quietly put to sleep. As a result, it is particularly difficult for an investor to value a roll-up. After all, he is giving up his share of an income stream from sales of the breakthrough product that his money developed, receiving in return shares of stock in the corporation formed to produce and market that product. Those shares may or may not become valuable and liquid in the future.

Genentech, Inc., one of the more successful biotechnology companies, was publicly-held at the time that it raised $150 million from investors in an R&D LP to develop new genetically-engineered drugs. This R&D LP contracted with Genentech to perform the research, but held on to the rights to the products thus developed. The products that were developed a few years later had significant implications in the battle against cancer. Investors in Genentech's R&D LP, who had already recouped most of their $150 million in five years, could see themselves earning three times that amount or more over the next five years. But Genentech wanted the income from the products to show up on its own bottom line and benefit its stockholders, not its R&D LP investors. It offered the R&D LP investors a roll-up: $300 million in Genentech common stock. Following some quibbling and negotiating, the R&D LP investors went along and accepted the roll-up terms.

We've Got to Get Out of This Place

I've stressed the roll-up possibilities in limited partnership investments to make a point: Figure out your exit route from each investment before you make it. At the time you invest, everyone is happy and optimistic. It doesn't always last. As time passes and the honeymoon ends, the promoters and managers of the company may find fewer things they like about the investors, and the investors may start getting impatient, wanting to get some money out of the deal already so they can move on to another deal. That's when the difficulties start. So when someone asks you to invest in his or her limited partnership, make sure to ask, "What is the exit route? How do I get out of this investment if I want to?"

Limited partnership investments are illiquid. You cannot

At the time you invest, everyone is happy and optimistic. It doesn't always last.

sell them in a market place and generate cash in 24 hours. However, they are generally established with an <u>end date</u>, usually ten years or so. At that time the assets (net of liabilities) are distributed among the partners according to their proportionate shares of the partnership. But what if the purpose of the partnership was to develop, publish and market a new magazine? You cannot very well divide the interests in a magazine—something that must be prepared each month—between the partners. So agreeing in advance to terminate the partnership after ten years may sound like a plausible exit route, but, as in this example, it may not be.

A better exit route is to make sure you have the right to seek a buyer for your investment. Most general partners will agree to buy your interest before the termination date, though you will usually have to first offer it to the other partners before seeking buyers outside the group. Again it is up to the investor in a limited partnership to ask the general partner: "How do I get my money out of this deal?" In order to raise the money from you and others, the general partner may have to commit to buy you out or locate a buyer, even to do so at a predetermined price.

The final exit route, and one that I am certain will become frequently used in the future, is the roll-up. It offers the advantage of converting the investor from an income to a capital gain position after the company stops losing money. But be forewarned: Roll-ups do not guarantee you'll get your money back from a limited partnership, particularly if the project lacked economic validity in the first place.

There seems no end to the kind of investments partnerships can become involved in: equipment leasing, investing in entrepreneurial ventures, purchasing and renovating distressed property, building shopping malls, producing Broadway plays, breeding and racing thoroughbreds, staging a celebration or major event such as the 1984 Olympic Games in Los Angeles, producing a concert or tour, publishing a magazine, launching a new apparel line, and many more. Partnerships are the preferred vehicle for new companies and projects where a loss is certain and the amount of the loss fairly predictable. Because that loss is valuable to any investor who has other investment income to offset.

Major legal firms and accounting firms have staffs of experienced tax counselors who dream up creative ways to reduce clients' income taxes. While the 1986 Tax Reform Act caused such radical changes that many of the previous

Figure out your exit route from each investment before you make it

Partnerships are the preferred vehicle for new companies and projects where a loss is certain and the amount of the loss fairly predictable.

techniques developed by tax attorneys had to be tossed out, there always will be someone somewhere coming up with new tax advantaged investment vehicles. I hope that your income is soon sufficiently high to seek their services and utilize these new investment tools.

13 Individual Exercises & Projects

1. Explain how losing money could be a desirable goal.

2. Visit a brokerage house and ask for prospectuses or brochures on currently available tax shelters. Which one would you invest in?

3. What tax shelters have been created *since* the 1986 Tax Reform Act?

4. Find the names of two other biotechnology firms that have been formed in the last five years and compare their marketing strategy with Genentech's.

14

A Home To Call Your Own

Real estate investments frequently provide some of the highest rates of return of all investments. Some of the richest people in America have made their fortunes in real estate, including Donald Trump in New York City, mall developer Al Taubman of Detroit and Craig Hall, who became a millionaire before the age of 20 by renovating properties near the University of Michigan campus and renting them to students.

Some of the richest people in America have made their fortunes in real estate.

But as in baseball cards or common stock investments, the key to success in real estate is identifying undervalued assets, improving them by adding value inexpensively, then selling them at a price substantially above your cost. OK, I know you've learned that lesson. So how do you find such properties?

Finding Undervalued Retail Sites

There is a story, probably at least half legend, that a German brewer who immigrated to America in the middle of the 19th century figured out where to locate his saloons by selecting corner locations near the curbs most worn down by foot traffic. It was, apparently, a good idea (and the forerunner of traffic counts)—his name, Joseph Schlitz, is on a lot of beer.

Identifying undervalued real estate investments requires the kind of time, energy and creativity that Joseph Schlitz spent. Some investors do traffic counts with quick eyes and stop watches, painstakingly counting the number of people who pass by a particular location in an hour or a day, even analyzing the hours traffic is heaviest. Such analysis can spell the difference between a successful business and a dismal failure.

One location, for example, may be passed by numerous automobiles in the morning. Directly across the street, a second location may be passed by people on their way home. A traffic light may even stop the morning and evening rush hour traffic in front of both locations. The first location might be a gold mine for a Dunkin' Donuts franchisee, while the second would probably do better as a Kentucky Fried Chicken outlet. Reverse the two stores and they'd both probably fail for lack of customers.

Location, location, location.

Ask any real estate salesperson about the three most important factors in his or her business and you'll get the same answer every time: Location, location, location. This is your first key to finding properties for yourself. Just look around your own community. Are the retail businesses located to conveniently serve the greatest number of customers? Is the office supply store located near offices? Are the florists mingled in with other shops so passersby can be drawn in by the beautiful window displays? Which retailers do best in malls, which on busy side streets, which ones downtown, which in the suburbs?

How will such analysis help you? It will give you the information you need to spot "obvious" opportunities. For example, Federal post offices in most cities are so poorly situated that entrepreneurs have been doing very well opening mail and package handling centers in suburban shopping centers. While charging a premium for postage and handling, they save the person who needs daily postal service or a PO box the trouble and cost of driving downtown to the post office. Retail service companies are extremely location-sensitive.

Who shops at a particular store is often as important as how many people shop there. Retail businesses that men visit more than women—computer, home improvement, hardware and athletic equipment stores—are usually located *near* enclosed malls, but rarely *within* them. Why? Because men don't like to shop in enclosed malls as much as women. Which is why shops more heavily frequented by women— apparel, shoe, fabric, craft and toy stores—*are* in malls.

How they shop is also a factor. People on foot like to shop on the sunny side of streets and avoid the cooler, shady sides.

If a retail establishment caters to automobile traffic, it must offer parking.

In your search for undervalued real estate, look for retail establishments that are poorly situated and going out of business because they are inconveniently located, lack parking, are on the wrong side of the street, whatever. The current owner of such a property may be having trouble finding tenants that stick around and be ready to throw up his hands and sell the location to you. Assuming that you don't have very much money, you may be able to negotiate a small-scale leveraged buy-out—borrowing the money to buy the property from a bank, secured lender or even the seller, then repaying it from the cash flow of the tenant(s) that you locate. (If you haven't located a tenant before you have to sign the <u>Purchase and Sales Agreement</u> and loan papers, you may even be able to get a <u>grace period</u>—90 to 100 days in which you do not have to make payments on the loan.)

Buying Distressed Properties

If you like and have the ability to renovate houses, consider buying a house on which the bank is about to <u>foreclose</u>.You can often buy such properties at a substantial discount from the principal amount of the loan—say, 20 cents on the dollar—fix them up yourself and resell them, paying off the loan and keeping the difference as your profit. Many real estate fortunes have been made by entrepreneurs who started just that way. Since this is a road to wealth you can consider traveling *right now*—over summer vacation or even after school—let's discuss it in more detail.

If you like and have the ability to renovate houses, consider buying a house on which the bank is about to foreclose.

When homeowners get into financial difficulty and cannot meet their mortgage payments for five or six months in a row, the bank that holds the mortgage, after several warnings, will normally foreclose on the loan. After all, a mortgage loan is a secured loan and the real estate—the home and land around it—is the collateral.

Banks normally contact a real estate broker to sell the foreclosed real estate for them in an attempt to recoup the principal amount of their loan. (By the way, real estate taxes are frequently owing on the property as well and taxes represent a <u>priority lien</u> on the property, which means they must be paid first. Real estate taxes are assessed by the county to pay for schools, roads, street lights, the sheriff department and so forth. You can visit the county clerk's office and get a list of addresses of properties on which taxes are owing, then visit them to see which ones you may wish to purchase when they are sold at the local courthouse.)

If there are several properties in a run-down section of town near the main street, you may want to purchase the bank's mortgage loan and agree to pay the county its taxes, both on a <u>work-out</u> or <u>stretch-out</u> basis. This means that you will make regular payments to the bank and to the county, but in smaller monthly payments than the original loan called for. In the case of taxes, which are normally due all at once, you may be ablle to pay them over 6 to 12 months. You can then use the cash you have now to renovate the property, perhaps creating commercial space—art galleries, restaurants, etc.— on the first floor and residences on the upper floors, rent the property to tenants (whose <u>credit references</u> you carefully check, of course with TRW or Dun & Bradstreet), and create perceived value for the property.

As a result of your hard work, other attractive shops, perhaps antique stores, an ice cream parlor and/or a clothing store, will move into the area. Within several years you can sell the property for a price two or three times more than the principal amount of the mortgage.

The great thing about buying and renovating distressed property is that *you do not have to use much capital to begin with*. You substitute labor for capital, and with a paint stripper, wallpaper steamer, paint brush, paint, hammer, nails and a saw, you can turn a blighted neighborhood into a beautiful, valuable section of town. The use of your personal labor to create value is called sweat equity. Not only will you benefit financially, but you will have given a gift to your community.

The use of your personal labor to create value is called sweat equity

How to get started in real estate

Because it is <u>fungible</u>—readily transferable to another owner and, therefore, near-liquid—real estate is perhaps the most acceptable collateral to banks, insurance companies, savings and loan institutions and other lenders. Since it is an appreciating asset, rather than a depreciating one, a lender will usually loan as much as 80% of the appraised value of real estate. Real estate appraisers visit the property and examine it, then visit comparable properties in the neighborhood to ascertain what prices they have recently sold for. After that, they prepare their <u>appraisal</u> for the person or bank who requested it and the financing moves forward from that point. The lender indicates how much money it will advance to the buyer and secures this advance with a <u>first mortgage</u> loan, a security interest in the property that is recorded in the county clerk's office.

Let's see how these numbers work out. Assume the appraised value of your new property is $100,000 and the lender tells you that it will loan you 80%—or $80,000— against the property. That means you still need $20,000 to buy the property, plus whatever is necessary to renovate it— let's presume that's another $75,000—a total of $95,000 in all.

After renovating the property with sweat equity or hired labor and getting one or more tenants to occupy the property, it is fairly certain that the property will increase in value. The lender knows that and it will, in most circumstances, provide a <u>construction loan</u> to enable the property to be renovated by a skilled contractor. So you've got your $75,000. When the renovation is completed, the appraiser is called back to reappraise the property. Most likely, it is worth twice its original value and the lender will <u>roll</u> the construction loan, which is a short-term loan, into the first mortgage loan. This will make the first mortgage loan worth $155,000 ($80,000 plus $75,000).

If the new appraised value is $200,000, your equity in the property has increased from the $20,000 (the only money you had to put up for this whole deal) to $45,000 ($200,000 minus $155,000). Your capital gain is $25,000—more than 100% in just a few months. Based on the other kinds of investments we have been discussing, very few are both fungible (almost liquid) and capable of doubling your investment in a couple of months.

But you're a cash-poor student. And you're still short $20,000. Where is that downpayment supposed to come from? That is an excellent question. There are three sources for the $20,000:

(1) You can find partners who have the $20,000 or part of it to co-invest in the property with you.

(2) The seller of the property may provide <u>seller financing</u>—that is, he will hold onto a security interest that is subordinated to the bank's first mortgage and permit you to repay him over time, say five years, out

of cash flow (rental payments) from the property. This is known as a second mortgage. Or

(3) There are second mortgage lenders who are willing to provide most of the $20,000 in consideration for a high interest rate—perhaps 2% higher than the interest rate paid to the bank for the first mortgage—over a short period of time (three to five years).

You might be able to buy a $100,000 property for only $2,000 of your own capital.

In other words, you might be able to buy the $100,000 property for only $2,000 of your own capital. The $18,000 you borrow for your downpayment (from one of the three sources above) reduces your capital gain to $27,000 ($45,000 minus $18,000), but that means you have multiplied the money you actually invested yourself—only $2,000, remember—13.5 times in just a few months. That is a remarkable rate of return!

Before you rush out and sell your baseball cards, Presley-ana and the savings bonds that Uncle Herman gave you for your sixth birthday, and buy the first rundown building you can find for $2,000, let's review the subject of leverage. Remember what we said about managers of publicly-held companies who borrow more debt than they have equity? They were taking high levels of risk, perhaps more risk than necessary. The same applies to leveraging $98,000 on top of your $2,000 investment. If the value of the property suddenly declines or if your tenants leave and you cannot replace them, then it is quite possible that you will be unable to make the payments on your first and second mortgage loans. Then the lenders will foreclose on your property and you will lose your $2,000 investment.

Leverage works well when values are rising, but can burn a big hole in your billfold when they fall.

Leverage, in other words, cuts two ways: It works well when values are rising, but it can cut a big hole in your billfold when values are falling. (Which is why real estate investors love inflation, a time when prices of goods and services—and real estate is a good—increase without an increase in their inherent value.)

As silly as this may seem to you, there was a time in the late 1970s in California when inflation was driving up the prices of real estate to such outrageous values that real estate investors were borrowing additional money on their properties and securing these loans with third mortgages and even, are your ready for this, *fourth* mortgages. Who was sillier, the borrowers or the lenders?

The answer is both.

The borrowers invested their loan proceeds in new properties at inflated values, which violates what we have learned to this point—that investment wealth is created by buying undervalued assets, adding value and selling them at higher prices.

The lenders were equally silly for trying to earn one or two more points of interest by making loans that were subordinated to two other loans and relying on inflation—an <u>exogenous variable</u> beyond their control—to keep driving up the values of their underlying collateral. The house of cards tumbled down when the Reagan Administration began fiddling with the economy in order to halt inflation.

Clearly, real estate investors were not thrilled that the Reagan Administration was so successful in its fight against inflation. They were caught with their pants down. If that was not bad enough, the Administration designed a change in the income tax laws, known as the Tax Reform Act of 1986, that radically altered the playing field for investors, corporate managers and entrepreneurs.

For many years the playing field had been tilted in favor of real estate investors and developers. The principal <u>loopholes</u> in their favor were the investment tax credit and <u>accelerated depreciation</u>.

The investment tax credit permitted taxpayers to deduct from their income tax obligation approximately 10% of the cost of renovating or equipping a building. In our example, you hypothetically borrowed $75,000 in the form of a construction loan to renovate the property. Prior to the Tax Reform Act of 1986, you could have deducted $7,500 as an investment tax credit from your tax obligation that year.

Accelerated depreciation permitted real estate developers and any businessperson buying equipment or buildings to depreciate the cost twice as fast.

Under Reagan, the investment tax credit and accelerated depreciation were repealed, and investors lost their Federal subsidies for investing in real estate. Now real estate investments must have economic validity, just like any other investment, not merely tax credits and tax saving features.

The Tax Reform Act of 1986 kicked real estate investors in the shins one more time. The Act says that if you are a passive investor in a real estate partnership, the deductions that you can take to lower your personal income taxes cannot exceed your <u>passive income</u>. Thus, if you invest $10,000 in your friend's real estate renovation deal, you expect that losses in the first year will exceed income because there will be more outgo—interest, construction, renovation—than inflow. However, you can no longer deduct your share of these passive expenses from your ordinary income—salary, commissions, fees—only from your passive income—that is, from investments in which you are not actively involved.

I have suggested that if you're starting with a modest pile of cash, your real estate investments should be geared to distressed properties, the substitution of sweat equity for capital, the assumption of debt and a relatively fast sale at a higher price. If you have only a few thousand dollars and are handy with carpentry tools and a paint brush, the purchase and renovation of distressed property should be one of the roads to wealth that you seriously consider.

14 Individual Exercises & Projects

1. Research Joseph Schlitz. Are there other lessons that can be learned from his career and life?

2. Visit the local shopping mall or district on a Saturday morning. Keep a count of everyone entering as many stores as you can (or get a couple of friends to help you). Which stores attract the most people? Which the least?

3. Based on your research in (2), can you spot a retailer that may be in the wrong location? Or a location that would be much better if it featured a different type of product or service?

4. How do you find distressed properties, those on which the banks or the Government are foreclosing? What's required to buy one?

5. Write to TRW, Dun & Bradstreet or other credit reporting agencies. Ask to see your credit file. (If you've never had any credit in your own name, ask your parents if you can get a copy of their files.)

15

Investing In Entrepreneurs

There are five questions you will want to ask any entrepreneur who approaches you for an investment:

(1) How much can I make?
(2) How much can I lose?
(3) How do I get my money back?
(4) Who says you're good, honest and hardworking?
(5) Who else is in the deal?

In asking these questions, you are attempting to maximize your time—to accept or turn down each investment opportunity quickly. It is in your interest, as much as that of the entrepreneur, to avoid 30 days of investigation that results in a turndown. Thus, your mind-set should be to turn down a deal quickly if the answers to these five questions are not what you are looking for. A fast "no" helps both the entrepreneur and the investor.

(It's unlikely you could consider such an investment with the $500 pile of cash we've assumed you've started with, but entrepreneurial investments offer such potentially phenomenal rates of return that it's important to cover the basics, just in case you can scrape up enough cash to do so. Don't worry if you can't—just save this chapter for when your pile of cash is a little larger.)

How Much Can I Make?

In other words, what's your projected rate of return? This number, as we've seen, is your means of comparing what different investments can (or promise to) do for you—how high and how fast your pile of cash will grow. If it is substantially lower than the rate of return you want, you've discovered a good reason to pass on the deal. If a great deal higher, the main question is why? The answer is usually because the risk is equally high.

How Much Can I Lose?

How will the entrepreneur use the money you're investing? What sales or income are projected as a result? How risky is the investment—will the worst case scenario cost you just a portion of your investment or would you wind up losing every penny?

If the rate of return is absurdly high and you can afford to lose all of the money you're going to invest, you may consider the investment even if its relatively risky. On the other hand, if you really can't afford to lose your pile of cash, perhaps an investment in something a bit more certain is best for you.

How Do I Get My Money Out?

You are wondering if this company can be taken public or sold to a larger company—the conventional means of capitalizing on an investment—or if it will be a cash cow.

Who Says You're Good, Honest, And Hardworking?

This is a question about management's track record. You would like the answer to be that the entrepreneurs were involved in the founding of Hewlett-Packard or Weight Watchers International or a similar sterling success story and that they are blessing you with the opportunity to finance their second company.

This does not happen on a daily basis. In fact, investors are usually faced with "lesser of evil" choices most of the time—most entrepreneurs have track records ranging from none to poor. What you should expect to see at minimum, however, is that the entrepreneur exhibits the judgment to hire skilled managers, especially in the areas of marketing, manufacturing, finance and engineering.

Who Else Is In The Deal?

Who has endorsed the company by agreeing to provide products, credit, contracts, or purchases? The bigger the names, the more respected their judgement, the better you should feel. But don't overemphasize this point—it's only one question out of five. No matter how illustrious the backers, if you don't feel comfortable with the answers to the other questions on your list, don't make the plunge.

The Risks

Remember Silver's Third Rule of Entrepreneurship: Be risk averse. That's why we're trying to find the answers to these five questions—to judge the degree of risk associated with each potential investment. The greater the risk you take, the greater should be the potential profit.

To reduce *your* exposure to risk, therefore, you'll want to make certain that the entrepreneur has taken some of the risks himself at the appropriate stages of developing the new company. In other words, there are some risks you may be willing to assume, but some that you should expect the entrepreneur to assume.

As we saw in chapter 3, there are five primary categories of risks in a start-up or early stage company. It is up to the lender or investor to accept no more than two of these risks. The two that you can control most effectively are marketing and management. The development and production risks should be borne by the entrepreneur prior to his seeking capital. The growth risk is typically borne by public investors after the lender or investor has gotten a return on his money.

How To Avoid The Slaughterhouse

Although entrepreneurial investments (sometimes called venture capital investments) can produce very high rates of return in five to seven years, they are not liquid—it is difficult to sell them to another investor, and the entrepreneur is usually not in a strong enough financial position to buy your interest. But to remain an investor in a company after nursing it through its start-up and initial public offering, is to assume the non-controllable risk of the company's stock price declining, ensuring that you wind up giving back much of your hard-earned profit. There is an old saying from the Wall

Street district, whose winding streets were laid out in the 17th Century by farmers walking behind their pigs on the way to market: Bulls win, bears win and pigs go to the slaughterhouse.

Unless you have made sure of a way out (see question 3), you will have to hold onto your investment until the entrepreneurial company is acquired or goes public, after which time you can sell your investment, or part of it, much as you would sell any common stock. In fact, the best way to achieve liquidity in an entrepreneurial investment is to sell your investment when the entrepreneur sells his or her shares to a large company. The buyer usually pays cash or a security convertible into cash, such as the buyer's common stock.

You Can't Always Do What You Want

Entrepreneurial investments are also regulated—The Securities and Exchange Commission has a number of rules that restrict the means by which entrepreneurs can raise venture capital and the time during which venture capital investors can sell their investments.

When the Federal government determines that a group of people practicing a certain skill cannot self-govern, Congress investigates the practices of that industry and imposes rules or laws. People who are permitted to self-govern are called professionals; those who are not self-governing are practitioners. Lawyers and physicians are self-governing; commercial or investment bankers are not. (Don't try to figure out why some industries are self-governing and others are not. There's no rule you can apply.) Of the six generic types of investments we have been discussing, the sellers of art and antiques are self-governing; the sellers of common stocks and bonds, real estate investments, partnerships and entrepreneurial opportunities are not.

The SEC governs the raising of capital from the public for entrepreneurial opportunities and the selling of such opportunities to the public. If the entrepreneur sells his or her investment opportunity to more than 35 individual investors, and if any single one of those investors is not sophisticated (that is, has at least $1 million in assets or $250,000 in annual income), the SEC could determine that a public offering has been made and should have been registered with the state securities commissioner and possibly the SEC. The penalty for not registering is criminal, not civil.

Thus, if an entrepreneur approaches you to make an investment in his or her company—and I assume you are not sophisticated—you must be certain the entrepreneur has obtained an exemption from registration. An attorney can assist the entrepreneur. (Each time that Congress, made up largely of lawyers, decides to regulate an industry, it creates more work for lawyers. This is called "job security," or creating work for ex-Congressmen.)

Then, if your investment grows in value and five to seven years later you wish to sell it, once again a lawyer who understands the SEC laws will have to advise you on the legal way to make the sale. Normally this will require registering the securities that you own with the SEC and finding an underwriter to make a public offering of the securities. This is a complex two-step selling transaction, but without doing it you cannot make an entrepreneurial investment liquid. And, as you know, if you cannot make an investment liquid, then you cannot realize a capital gain from it and add to your pile of cash.

The Rewards

Why bother with an investment that is so difficult to make liquid? After all, there is a ready market in most of the other investment opportunities we have discussed. Why not just stick with art, antiques (coins, stamps, baseball cards, furniture, ephemera, Presleyana), real estate and common stocks and bonds?

The answer is that some entrepreneurial opportunities have big pay-offs. Just look around you at the products you've purchased recently—the clothing you're wearing, the items in your desk, the appliances in your kitchen, the magazines that come in the mail. All of these products were conceived, developed, produced and marketed by entrepreneurs.

Drive through your community and look around all of the retail stores and restaurants. Except for the small businesspeople who open service companies—bankers, tailors, pest controllers, frame shops, gasoline stations—all of the retail stores and restaurants were started by entrepreneurs. McDonald's, Burger King, Pizza Hut, Wal-Mart, Baskin-Robbins, General Cinema, Hertz Rent-a-Car and many more are the result of an entrepreneur with a dream.

(For the biographies of 100 of America's most successful

entrepreneurs of the last 25 years, you may want to read one of my other books—Entrepreneurial Megabucks, John Wiley & Sons, 1986. I am particularly proud of this book because the New York Public Library gave it to the valedictorians of New York City's 115 high schools in 1986 along with Goethe's Faust and a Bible. As an entrepreneur, I was thrilled to see the circle of giving widened with my book.)

When you are presented with an entrepreneurial opportunity to invest in, remember what we have discussed about information and how you process it. Keep your target rate of return in mind. Most venture capital investors use the target of 60% per annum as their target rate of return. That works out to approximately five times your investment in three years and ten times in five years. The entrepreneurs profiled in Entrepreneurial Megabucks achieved rates of return vastly greater—more like *600%* per annum.

Hundreds of entrepreneurs have achieved big pay-offs—over 20 times their investors' cost in five years—and that is what makes entrepreneurial opportunities popular investments.

From The Entrepreneur's Standpoint

If an entrepreneur has the right answers to the five questions posed at the beginning of this chapter, it's easy for him or her to find investors, even if numerous other factors seem to be lacking. If he doesn't, it could be very difficult indeed to find the kind of dollars needed. Some small companies have trouble paying for postage, while others have to send back offers to invest because they are oversubscribed.

Apple Computer Corporation raised more venture capital in 1978-1980 than the rest of the personal computer industry combined. Its founders were two unseasoned engineers under age 26, but the manager they hired to run Apple, Mike Markulla, was considered one of the marketing stars at Intel Corporation and he attracted venture capital from Arthur Rock, a well-known venture capitalist, and others.

Fred Smith, age 29, raised $96 million from Prudential Insurance, General Dynamics and twenty-six venture capital funds to launch Federal Express Corporation in the pit of the 1973 recession...on the basis of a college term paper and without any substantive previous business experience.

Peter Farley, the molecular biologist who founded Cetus

Corporation, raised over $36 million from industrial corporations and venture capitalists in the mid-1970s and then $125 million from the public in early 1981 without a product or more than a few million dollars in contracts.

Meanwhile, it took Chester Carlson, a patent lawyer, twelve years to raise capital to finance the development of his product. Perhaps it had something to do with the fact that there was no business plan, merely a demonstration by a tall, cragged man in a wrinkled raincoat with a small piece of stainless steel, a rabbit's foot, some dark powder, and a piece of paper. He did eventually raise the money—and the early investors did quite well with Carlson's company...Xerox.

And in the shadow of these success stories lies the wreckage of thousands of economically viable, socially useful businesses that have been unable to attract financing. Their entrepreneurs did not have correct answers to the five questions. Make sure any entrepreneur in whom you consider investing *does*.

15 Individual Exercises & Projects

1. Look in the classified section of your local newspaper. Are there entrepreneurs looking for financing? Call or write some of them and ask them the five key questions in this chapter. Based on their responses, decide if you would invest in their companies.

2. Are there other questions to which you'd want answers before you committed your own money?

3. What exactly does the Securities and Exchange Commission regulate?

4. Apple, Federal Express, Cetus, Xerox—all major entrepreneurial success stories cited in this chapter. Where are the founders of those four companies now? Can you spot any new start-ups you think might match these success stories over the next decade?

Section Three

Appendices & Index

Appendix 1

Class Trips & Projects

Dear Teacher:

Your First Book of Wealth is a primary resource you can use to teach your students the basics of business, entrepreneurship, collecting and investing. And it was designed so that you can add it to any curriculum attempting to introduce these topics.

Each chapter has a series of exercises at the end. While purportedly "individual" exercises, many of these problems, projects and recalculations can be adapted to an entire class. So look through each chapter and, as you prepare your lesson plan, see which of these exercises you wish to incorporate as homework assignments, class or team projects, etc.

There are also numerous topics for class discussion, book reports and research projects that can be gleaned from each chapter. Whatever actual experience you can give your students through such assignments will, I am convinced, help them learn the specific lessons covered in each chapter. So in the first section of this appendix, I have suggested a variety of class trips you may be able to undertake to introduce your students to the people already doing what you're trying to teach your class.

But there are some larger lessons to be learned from this book that require more preparation and research than any individual student could probably manage. In order to maximize the use of this book, therefore, I have separately included in this Appendix four projects that can be undertaken by your whole *class* .

Each of these projects can be readily adapted to your own students, school and class size. The larger the class size, for example, the more feasible it would be to create two or more teams to work simultaneously on the same project. A class on entrepreneurship or one with many gifted students may choose to create smaller-sized teams, increasing the level of "real-world" competition and work required of each student accordingly.

Whatever your particular situation, I hope you will be able to utilize these more extensive projects to help your students learn the major tenets in this book *by actually doing the necessary tasks*—starting their own business, forming their own investment club, etc.

Since I offered in the Introduction to answer any of your students' questions, I certainly want to extend the same invitation to you. Just write me in care of the publisher.

Whatever your students' eventual career plans, I feel strongly that a basic grounding in the principles of business and finance are essential. I feel certain this book will enable all of us to give these young people this framework for their lives.

A. David Silver

SUGGESTED CLASS TRIPS

1. If you are situated near one of the U. S. stock exchanges, call their public relations office and arrange a class trip.

2. Arrange with a local bank for a tour of its various departments, including meetings with some of the key officers.

3. Arrange with a local brokerage firm for a tour of their offices, including meetings with the heads of various departments/functions (stocks & bonds, commodities, currency, etc.).

4. Plan a trip to a local service company and a local manufacturing company. In each case, arrange with their public relations department for a complete tour of the plant but, more importantly, for sessions with the heads of each major department—administration, marketing, sales, production, etc.—with an emphasis on "what we do here."

5. Visit an industry trade show being held somewhere in your area, whether open to the public or not. Contact the trade show office and ask for guest passes for your whole class.

6. Visit a specific collectible show being held somewhere in your area, featuring stamps and coins, comic books, baseball memorabilia, etc.

7. Is there an entrepreneurial success story right in your own backyard? Arrange a visit at the company and, especially, with its founder.

8. Identify twelve local companies, each of which utilizes a different SDM. Visit each and give your students the chance to understand the

types of products and services that would use each Solution Delivery Method.

9. Find the closest "Big P" company—a major pharmaceutical house, biotechnology firm, high technology firm, etc. Can your students see any differences between the operation and employees at such a company and those at some of the "small P" companies you've also visited?

10. Take your students to a sheriff's or bank's auction on foreclosed (or seized) properties.

11. Is there a venture capital firm (or large insurance company, pension fund or similar group that invests a lot of venture capital) anywhere in your area? See if you can arrange a visit to their offices and spend some time with the decision makers.

MAJOR CLASS PROJECTS

Project #1: Student Business(es)

There are undoubtedly products or services that your school or local community need that no one is providing. Why not encourage your class to start a business that will solve one or more of these problems? (If your class is large or talented enough, you may even consider letting two or more groups compete with different businesses.)

Every step of a normal new business launch should be part of this project, from a detailed explanation of the problem and formulation of the solution to the DEJ Test, selection of solution delivery methods and raising capital, to development of a launch plan, creation of the operations team and actual full-scale production. (See chapters 3 through 8 for the necessary lists of steps, plans, charts, etc. that should be included.)

Presuming that the entire class will be part of one project, start with each student researching what problem he or she thinks needs to be solved and how he or she would solve it. Each suggestion should be accompanied by enough research, including a complete DEJ Test, to sell both you and the rest of the class on the idea.

By majority vote (or administrative fiat!), pick just one of the many excellent choices your students will probably give you.

Once a product or service has been chosen, you may proceed in whatever manner and at whatever speed you feel best works for your particular class. Various research projects could be assigned to different "teams." Likewise, as your project develops, teams could be assigned to be in charge of key functions—advertising, public relations, production, marketing, sales, etc.—with the entire class acting as the "entrepreneurial team."

(Alternatively, you could divide your class into two or more teams and have all teams work on each aspect of the launch, submitting their own plans and assignments for each step. If one team can convince the others to accept its plan, ad campaign, etc., then you'd go with it. If not, you could pick the one you feel has the best chance for success.)

If at all possible, your class's business plan should actually be put into practice—after all, there's no better teacher than experience. And who knows, you may start a student business that actually makes money for the school! If this is difficult (or even impossible due to school or school board policy), you could still "pretend" that the business was actually being launched. Whenever a decision has to be made based on particular results, give your class the numbers, research or feedback necessary to make that decision. For example, if your hypothetical retail store has just launched an ad campaign in the local newspaper, tell your class how many people showed up at the store during the next week and what they bought. From this, they should be able to make decisions on future advertising campaigns, media placement, etc. If everything is going along smoothly, throw a monkey wrench in the production process or "raise" the price of a key raw material to see how they handle the kinds of everyday problems every entrepreneur faces.

Project #2: Student Investment Club

Divide your class into teams of three to five students each. Give each team a hypothetical pile of cash of $5,000.00 and one simple assignment: to grow that pile of cash as much as possible in one term. (The project, of course, can be extended to one year). Teams should be told they are allowed to do whatever having $5,000 would actually enable them to do in the real world but be given no other specific ground rules. (In other words, don't limit their creative strategies before they even get started. If a team, for example, is able to prove to your satisfaction that they could borrow $10,000 from a local bank, friend, parent, etc. if they actually had $5000 in cash, or that they could leverage that cash into a $50,000 house, let them proceed on that basis. But don't suggest such methods for increasing their initial capital before the project even begins!)

Each team should submit a weekly or monthly report (depending on your curriculum and your own ability to oversee such a project). The first report should include a one paragraph summary of the team's overall investment strategy, then detail the various accounts each felt it necessary to open (savings, brokerage, etc.) and the initial allocation of their money. This and all subsequent reports should also include a detailed explanation of all of the steps necessary to execute every strategic decision. If a brokerage account was "opened," for example, the team should include with its report the forms the brokerage house had it fill out. Likewise, with checking, savings, commodity and any other accounts.

All subsequent monthly reports should include the results of the previous period's investments, a detailed plan for the next period, and an explanation of all steps necessary to achieve that plan. Lastly, each report should end with a current "net worth" of each team, based on the results of their previous period's investments. It would be helpful to assign one day of the week or month as "buy and sell" day, the one time changes in investments can be made. This will make it easier for students to have enough time to calculate how they are doing and to plan for the next "buy and sell" day.

I hope you will try to make this experience as real as possible for your students. The only difference between the students' experience and "reality" should be the lack of actual money to invest. Even if they aren't actually opening a brokerage account, for example, they should have gone through every step with a broker, just as *if* they were.

Teams should be judged not only on the ending pile of cash, although that should be a significant factor, but on the creativity and judgement exercised throughout the project. One team, for example, might elect to keep its money in a tax-free municipal bond for the entire year and, in fact, may end up with more cash than other teams taking more creative, but also riskier, investment approaches. Should such a team be rewarded for doing little work—each report will be virtually interchangeable!—and learning less? Alternately, should a team that made a variety of questionable investment decisions and lost all their cash get a top grade for creativity and work? My suggestion is that you do whatever you can to make your students experience a variety of investment possibilities and, at the same time, teach them the most important lesson of all: yes, Virginia, results really do count.

Project #3: Working With A Local Business

Your school may not allow you to pursue any sort of student business and you may decide that doing it as merely a hypothetical exercise isn't good enough. One alternative is to contact a local business, especially an entrepreneurial one in the start-up phase. Offer to involve your class in the new business. Volunteer to be (or organize) a focus group, do research, create an advertising campaign, help with clerical chores, etc.

While you want to stop short, of course, from simply supplying a company with free manual labor, there's nothing wrong with encouraging your class to get its hand dirty and learn first-hand some of the chores necessary to virtually any operation. Whatever duties your class is able to perform, the entrepreneur should be required to spend time involving the class in some or all of the planning phases, including product development, writing the launch plan, etc. (even if the class itself does little or none of the actual work in some of these specific areas).

Most entrepreneurs are short of two important items, money and help (time). Your class can certainly help with the latter problem, which may give the entrepreneur the time to go out and raise needed capital!

Project #4: Industry or Collectible Newsletter

There are emerging industries or industry segments that lack a professional communications vehicle—a newsletter. Likewise, there are small groups of people involved with less popular collectibles who would probably welcome a newsletter giving them access to others interested in their objects.

Your class can work on one or both of these areas. In both cases, the first step is to find a market or market segment that requires a newsletter (the problem) and then create one for them (the solution). You should assume you will utilize the newsletter/seminar SDM, though the exact timing and detailed plan of the launch are, of course, up to you. Likewise, you can consider all or some of the SDM sub-sets discussed in chapter 6 and even, hopefully, discover or create some new ones.

It is not necessary to actually launch either or both newsletters, though you can certainly consider doing so. What is more important is involving your students in all the research and planning necessary to arrive at the launch phase, including the actual production of the first "mock" issue and, of course, a detailed business plan of how the newsletter would actually be launched, printed, promoted, paid for, etc.

While a hypothetical market or collectible could be created for this project, I believe there are identifiable market segments that really *need* a newsletter. So why not give your class a chance to deal with a real problem involving real people?

Glossary

Accelerated Depreciation Prior to the Tax Reform Act of 1986, owners of buildings and equipment could elect to depreciate the cost of these assets on their income tax returns (thus lowering their income tax obligations) over a shortened period of time. Real estate developers utilized accelerated depreciation to minimize their income taxes for many years, which means they were able to raise capital more easily than many other businesspeople.

Acquire (see **Mergers and Acquisitions**)

Active Investment When an investor must spend time working for or advising the company in which he or she has invested, it is an **active investment**. Venture capitalists typically make such investments; investors in publicly-held companies do not.

Alpha Test (see **Beta Test**)

Ancillary Capital A corporation's financial safety cushion, **ancillary** (meaning subordinate, subsidiary) **capital** is that raised over and above **primary capital**—perhaps in the form of a commercial bank line of credit.

Annual Report A summary of a company's operating results produced once a year by its managers and distributed to its shareholders. While detailed financial statements and, perhaps, a page or two summarizing those results in prose are the only essential ingredients, many companies view their annual reports as high-profile promotion pieces. The resulting four-color extravaganza may resemble a glitzy sales brochure more than a boring financial document, with high-quality photographs, reams of promotional prose and professionally-executed design.

Appraisal (see **Real Estate Appraisal**)

Appreciable Asset (see **Assets**)

Assets Things that you own—cash, clothing, books, furniture and food in the cupboard. Some assets are **appreciable**–they rise in value. But most are **depreciable**—they decline in value. Some assets are **liquid**, such as cash or money in savings accounts; some are **near-liquid**, like common stocks or antiques; others are **illiquid**—it will take several months to convert them to cash.

If one's liquid assets exceed all of one's liabilities by $1 million, that person is said to be a millionaire. But if one's illiquid assets exceed all of one's liabilities by $1 million, that person is said to be **asset rich**. Back in the days when Texans were oil rich (but not liquid), they used to brag that wealth was a measure of how much you could borrow based solely on your financial statement. Now that oil-invested Texans are poor, the stories out of that region show that they at least haven't lost their senses of humor: How can you tell the difference between a Texan and a pigeon? A pigeon can still make a deposit on a Mercedes.

Assumable Mortgage (see **Mortgage**)

Balance Sheet A listing of all of your assets and all of your **liabilities** (obligations to pay). Subtracting your liabilities from your assets results in your **net worth**.

Balanced Fund An investment fund whose portfolio contains a relatively even mix of investments that produce income (such as bonds) and those that produce capital gains (such as stocks).

Bankable An asset is deemed bankable if its earning power is so strong that a commercial bank will loan money to the company (like a movie producer) that has a contract with the asset (a movie star with the box office appeal of a Tom Hanks or Barbra Streisand).

Bankruptcy A condition that exists when your liabilities far exceed your assets and you cannot pay your obligations as they come due. A bankrupt person or company files a petition for protection from creditors in a Federal bankruptcy court. The judge determines if the bankrupt person or company has a suitable plan of reorganization to repay his or her creditors over time (**Chapter XI bankruptcy**) or if his or its assets should be sold and the proceeds distributed among the creditors (**Chapter VII bankruptcy**).

Banks There are two principal kinds: **Commercial banks** accept deposits (store cash) from people and companies and make loans to people and companies at interest rates in excess of the rate they pay for deposits. **Investment banks** raise money for companies by selling their stocks or bonds to public and private investors and by assisting them with acquisitions and refinancings of their liabilities. Both types of banks also operate trust or investment departments that manage the investments of pension funds, endowment funds and wealthy families.

Barter Trading one asset for another, usually to obtain an asset that can be converted readily into cash.

Baseball The game loved by entrepreneurs because it is not played against a clock, but continues until the last batter makes an out. The words of baseball are the words of entrepreneurship: sacrifice, home run, run home, strikes, balls and errors.

Bear Market (see Bulls and Bears)

Beta Test When a group of engineers produce an innovative new product, they initially test it in their own laboratory. This is the **Alpha** (the first letter of the Greek alphabet) test. They then ask a potential customer to test their product at its facility—the **Beta** (second letter of the Greek alphabet) test. You'd be surprised at how many modifications the potential customer will come up with in such a test.

Black Market When a product is in great demand but cannot be bought or sold openly in a free market—like U. S.-made blue jeans in Russia—a clandestine or black market generally develops, in which sellers smuggle in the sought-after product and secretly inform buyers of its availability.

Blue Chip Top drawer, head of the class, first among equals—a term generally applied to the best-managed, publicly-held companies.

Bond An obligation by a company or municipality (state or local government entity), the Federal government or the governments of other countries to repay indebtedness, plus appropriate interest, to their lenders over a prescribed period of time. Bonds can be secured—that is, backed up by assets (**collateral**)—or unsecured. Bonds of companies can also be convertible, which gives the lender the opportunity to exchange the bond and future interest payments for the company's common stock. Corporate bonds can also be accompanied by **warrants** to buy the companies' common stocks, and the bondholder can both hold the bond until it is repaid in full and exercise the warrant to buy common stock. Conversion and warrant features that accompany bonds are sweeteners used to attract lenders to provide loans to companies whose ability to make interest payments and repay the indebtedness in a timely manner is questionable.

Bottom Line The bottom line of an operating statement—sales less all expenses—is the company's, government's or person's income or loss. If the bottom line is positive, the entity is demonstrating economic viability and prudent management. If the bottom line is negative, then the opposite is true. One cannot operate very long with a negative bottom line because the losses must be replaced with capital, which means borrowing money, selling partnership interests or selling off assets to raise cash.

Break-Even When a company, government or person spends exactly what it earns—its *sources* of cash are exactly equal to its *uses* of cash—it breaks even. Its bottom line is zero.

Break-Up Value The amount of cash that could be generated by breaking up a company and selling its various parts. If a corporate raider, for example, determines that a company's break-up value exceeds its market value, it means that he can buy the company, sell off its parts—break it up—and realize more cash than he'd have to pay to buy the company.

Such a move is rarely in the interest of management and employees, who may well find themselves out on the street. To thwart such a raid, management fights back or pays **greenmail**—using the corporations' cash to buy back the raiders' ownership of their companies. (Paying greenmail is an advertisement to raiders that the entrenched management *knows* the company's break-up value exceeds its market value but doesn't itself know how to take advantage of the opportunity. So more corporate raids will probably follow.)

A family also has break-up value. Charitable institutions frequently court wealthy families whose patriarch or matriarch does not wish to pass along the wealth to the heirs, competing among themselves for the assets.

Bribes Sellers give bribes to buyers to induce them to buy the sellers' products. Bribes go by different names in different countries and markets: "baksheesh" in the Middle East, "vigorish" in the underworld and "discounts" by companies selling their products in America.

The American press usually reports bribes incorrectly. When a government official asks a company to pay him a bribe in order to sell a product or service to the agency that he manages, the press says that he "took a bribe," which implies that the seller has "given a bribe." In fact, sellers are *asked* for bribes by "bribees;" rarely do they *offer* bribes, because to offer a bribe does not make economic sense. But then, the press knows very little about business.

The entire area of bribes, inducements, discounts, gifts to customers, baksheesh and vigorish needs to be thoroughly understood by people entering business so that they may maintain high ethical standards while remaining competitive. For instance, is it ethical for an American businessperson to give baksheesh to a Middle Eastern customer if he or she needs to do so to compete with companies in other countries who have no ethical problem doing so? Should elected officials be permitted to receive campaign contributions from real estate developers who then hire the elected official's law firm to provide legal services? The area of bribes needs some serious intellectual investigation; it is probably as important a subject for our schools as algebra or history, but for some reason it has been neglected.

Brokerage Account A contract between an investor and a stockbroker that sets forth, in writing, the terms and conditions of their relationship so that each party knows what to expect of the other. Most such accounts are **cash accounts**, which require the investor to deposit a pile of cash which will be used to purchase and sell the stocks, bonds, mutual funds, etc. that he or she orders. A **margin account** will allow the investor to borrow funds from the brokerage firm, enabling him or her to purchase more securities than the cash in his or her account would normally allow. If the investor intends to deal only in commodities, options or other more esoteric financial instruments, separate accounts (with differing requirements in terms of cash and expertise) will be opened.

Budget A plan in which you list all of your expenses over time (a month, a year) and figure out how you will go about paying them or, in some cases, reducing them.

Bulls and Bears One is said to be bullish if he or she thinks an asset is undervalued and will appreciate, and bearish if the opposite opinion is firmly held. A **bull market** is one in which the prices of most stocks are on the rise; a **bear market** one in which most are falling.

Business Plan The plan that an entrepreneur or small businessperson constructs (and later implements), in which he or she describes in great detail how he or she will convey the developed solution (new product or service) to the people who have the problem.

Cacophony Lots of noise created by many voices shouting at the same time. A cacophonous din is created by large corporations shouting that their products or services are superior to the competition's. When a cacophony exists in a marketplace, the product or service is missing several DEJ Factors (it is neither unique, non-duplicable nor elegant), but there is sufficient profit margin in the product or service to permit a large advertising budget.

Products or services in cacophonous markets—automobiles, savings & loans, real estate, breakfast cereals, beverages, laundry detergents, clothing, investment instruments—are things that all of us need from time to time. Unfortunately, we must put up with noise pollution from the sellers who want us to fill our needs with their products or services.

Capital A word with many meanings. Its general meaning is the money that pays for the assets that generate the sales that pay for the labor, inventory, equipment rental and other expenses which make a business operate.

Karl Marx, the philosopher whom Lenin studied to lay the groundwork for Communism, regarded labor as capital and demanded a greater voice for labor in management. While Marx's philosophy has not been implemented in the Communist countries that purport to follow it, it *has* been implemented by cash-starved entrepreneurs, who must use their own labor—100 hours a week or more—as a substitute for money.

Capital Equipment The bricks and mortar of a manufacturing facility, the walls of a racquetball court, the sewing machines of an apparel factory, the presses that stamp roofs, hoods and fenders from sheets of steel in an auto plant—these and similar assets are capital equipment.

Capital Gain A positive return on invested capital. If you buy an asset for $100 and sell it for $150 you have earned a capital gain of $50, on which the Federal government applies a capital gains tax.

Taxes are the price we pay for living in a free country, and America's tax rates are much lower than those in almost every other country. The Tax Reform Act of 1986 set the capital gains tax rate at the same level as the Federal income tax rate for upper bracket income earners. In doing so, it is discouraging investment, which is vital to the circle of giving, by not offering a premium (a lower capital gains tax rate) to people who invest their disposable income in the solutions that entrepreneurs develop. The Tax Reform Act of 1986 discourages investment and entrepreneurship and encourages spending on depreciable assets and saving.

Since our legislators feel an uncommon need to continuously redesign the economic canvas on which entrepreneurs and managers paint, the capital gains tax rate will probably drop under the income tax rate in a few years (Five state governments, for example, have already offered tax credits-deductions from state income taxes—to people who invest in entrepreneurial companies in their states.)

Capital-Intensive Describes a company whose energy is derived from its ownership of large and expensive assets, such as the power plants owned by public utility companies or the washers and dryers owned by Laundromats.

Cash Account (see Brokerage Account)

Cash Cow A business that generates cash as regularly, quickly and easily as a cow produces milk.

Cash Flow The cash that remains at the end of each month after a company has paid all expenses. Achieving positive cash flow—actually having something left at the end of each month—is one of the key objectives of both rapidly-growing and troubled businesses. Smart businesspeople continually and tenaciously manage their business so as to maximize cash flow. Those who don't take this goal seriously are the equivalent of a basketball player attempting the game-winning shot while staring at the crowd. It doesn't happen too often, even for Larry Bird.

C Corporation (See Corporations)

Ceiling (see **Floating Rate**)

Certificate of Deposit (CD) A short-term loan made by an individual or company to a bank, similar, in fact, to a savings account, except that the money in a savings account can be easily withdrawn at any time and a "CD" must be sold in the marketplace to a buyer.

Channel of Distribution (see **Marketing Channel**)

Collateral An asset or assets provided to a lender as auxiliary means of repayment for a loan, the primary means being cash flow.

Collectibles Assets that appeal to groups of people in a very positive way, leading them to gather and assemble them, then meet with others of a like mind to trade both information and assets. The late Andy Warhol considered cookie jars and Mickey Mouse watches collectible. Bill Cosby collects antique American furniture. Department store entrepreneur Stanley Marcus (as in Nieman and...) collects miniature antique books.

Collectibles can appreciate in value if a large number of people perceive that they have significant value. Baseball cards are a perfect example of a collectible item that has "crossed over" to the investment arena.

Collector's Discount It has been demonstrated that the works of artists tend to increase in value if they are hung alongside the works of other respected artists. Knowing this, gallery owners are frequently willing to charge a person with many works of art in his or her collection less for a specific artist's work than a "wanna be" collector would pay. This difference in price is often referred to as the "collector's discount."

Commercial Bank (see **Banks**)

Commodity Account (see **Brokerage Account**)

Compound Interest Interest paid to the holder of a loan on the principal as well as on previously accrued interest. Compounding grows one's initial pile of cash faster.

Consumer Product Everything that a person buys that is not a service, from soft drinks and tennis rackets to shoes and automobiles. Consumer products that are supposed to be used up quickly—food, diapers, stationery, etc.—are termed non-**durable products (or goods)**; those expected to last several years—autos, furniture, appliances, etc.—are termed **durable products (or goods)**.

Construction Loan (see **Mortgage**)

Contrarian An investor who consistently acts directly opposite the consensus of others. For example, assume that a hurricane has just torn through a section of Louisiana. Conventional investors might absorb this information and then buy the common stocks of furniture retailers and construction firms servicing the area. A contrarian hearing the same information might sell the stock of Louisiana power companies, reasoning that they will need to buy and construct new power poles and lines, reducing profits.

Without contrarians, there would be only one or two ice cream flavors. They're different.

Convertible Bond (see **Bonds**)

Convertible Debenture (see **Bonds**)

Copyright The exclusive right, granted by law for a certain number of years, to make, use and sell copies of a literary work, song, work of art or computer software program.

Corporations The usual conveyance mechanism by which an entrepreneur delivers a solution to people with a problem is via a **corporation**. A corporation is a legal entity whose existence is recorded with a state and which is allowed to issue stock to its founders, investors and employees (investors of time and skill, if you will).

In the early years of a corporation's life, it may incur start-up losses which do it no good. However, if it incorporates as a Sub-chapter S Corporation, the company's losses can be passed through to the stockholders, who can deduct them, to a certain extent regulated by law, from their individual income taxes. (If a Subchapter S corporation has income, it must be *added* to the stockholders' personal income, on which, of course, they must then *pay* taxes.) Sub-chapter S corporations are restricted in some ways, however—they can only sell stock to U. S. citizens, for example, and they must have no more than 25 stockholders. A regular (**Class C**) **corporation** has no such restrictions, though its income and losses are not directly passed through to its stockholders.

Cost of Goods Sold The expenses that a company incurs—usually inventory and labor—to manufacture the product or perform the service it sells to its customers or clients.

Credit To obtain credit (or **credit terms**) is to receive trust. A lender of money or a supplier of goods or services will extend you credit—the option to pay for money, a product or service over time—if you are trustworthy. To gain their trust you must have **credit references**—an already-established history of trustworthiness. (One relatively easy way to obtain a good credit reference is to borrow money from a bank...and repay it in 30 days.)

There are companies that check on the credit worthiness of people—TRW, Dun & Bradstreet and others—and sell this information to lenders—credit card companies, banks, etc. You can (and should) obtain a copy of your personal credit files from such companies to make sure they are accurate.

Bad credit is surprisingly easy to obtain. Frequent check bounces, for example, will appear on your credit file and will destroy your reputation for trustworthiness or credibility. In some instances, insurance companies will deny you their services if your credit references are negative, which could prevent your borrowing money to buy a home or car or insuring these major assets.

Credit References (see **Credit**)

Customer-Financed Those businesses who receive payment for their goods or services before they have to deliver them are said to be customer-financed, since it is actually the customers who pay the cost of producing and selling the goods or services, not the businesses themselves. Insurance companies and magazine publishers are just two examples of customer-financed businesses.

Debenture A promissory note issued by a company that is not secured by any asset, but relies strictly on the borrower's ability to repay.

Debt Financing Money provided to a company by means of a loan; the money must be repaid on a certain date and a rental cost—interest—paid for its use.

Debug To "take the bugs" (mistakes) out of a new product or service. This is usually done by testing the product on potential customers. Whatever doesn't work is called a "bug." Fixing the bugs "debugs" it.

Deficit The amount by which a sum of money falls short of the required amount. (*Also see* **Shortfall**)

Demand (see **Supply & Demand**)

Depletion (see **Depreciation**)

Depreciable Assets (see **Assets** and/or **Depreciation**)

Depreciation Assets are depreciable or appreciable—lose or gain value every day—depending on a number of factors, the most important of which is their naturalness or **primitivity**.

If you buy a baseball card, for example, it will appreciate in value more if it is the rookie card of an outstanding player who eventually is voted into the Hall of Fame. Any other baseball card may depreciate with use and handling and become valuable only if it is part of a collection. Machine-made objects almost always depreciate in value unless they have an underlying naturalness or primitivity, such as an early, well-maintained Mercedes-Benz, an Elvis Presley concert announcement or the first edition of a book. Collecting assets once regarded as depreciable but suddenly regarded as having investment value—such as antique watches, ice fishing decoys, old license plates, etc.—can reward you with a handsome return on investment.

Depletion is a concept similar to depreciation, but it applies to resources such as oil and coal, which, though natural, are limited in their supply.

Depression A period during which the economy, employment and the value of investments declines sharply. While the vast majority of products and services (understandably) don't do well during such a period, some do—like greeting cards, psychotherapy and books on how to make money in a depression.

Direct Response A form of advertising in which immediate response—via a mail-in coupon or toll-free telephone number—is expected and encouraged.

Disposable Income The "pile of cash" that's left over after all of your expenses, including funds set aside for savings and insurance, have been paid. Disposable income is what you use to invest, unless you're unwise enough to use the rent money in an attempt to make a quick killing in the stock market. Don't.

Dividends Payments by corporations to their stockholders to keep them happy with their investment. A company that does not pay dividends is stating that it can invest the money better than its stockholders can. When they do so, the stock goes up in value and the stockholders frequently receive stock dividends as their reward for keeping the faith and remaining illiquid.

Downside Planning Managing a business with an eye on all the things that could go wrong and planning accordingly. This kind of management style is also known as readiness.

Durable Products or Goods (see Consumer Product)

Earnings Profits; money earned; the amount by which revenues exceed expenses.

Elegance (of solution) A product is an elegant solution if it is unique; a service is an elegant solution if it has a non-duplicable delivery system. Cadillac's newest model is not elegant—there are lots of cars on the road; a revolutionary engine that produces 50 miles per gallon in a Cadillac *is* an elegant solution to an obvious problem..

Entrepreneur Society's gift giver and principal wealth creator who uncovers a problem that affects a large number of people, conceives a solution to the problem, then forms a company to convey the solution to the people with the problem. The personality characteristics of successful entrepreneurs include heart, patience, insight, courage, a willingness to cooperate and an understanding of leverage.

Based on my own experience with hundreds of entrepreneurs, I would say they generally dress simply, wear little jewelry, talk rapidly, prefer European cars, live in cities, suffer from a high divorce rate, abstain from chemicals and alcohol, are rarely overweight, never ill and always optimistic, and tilt to the liberal side of the political scale (though they move to the right as they accumulate wealth).

Ephemera The plural of *ephemeron* (from the Greek): Items designed to be useful or important for only a short time—pamphlets, tickets, notices, etc.

Equity The value of an asset or a business less its liabilities; net worth.

Ex-dividend Date (see Record Date)

Execute (a transaction) To carry out the buy or sell order given to a stockbroker by a customer.

Exemption An exception to a rule, usually having to do with the payment of a tax or fee. The interest paid on municipal bonds, for example, is tax exempt to the receiver. If such tax exemptions could be applied to bonds of entrepreneurial companies whose goals are to conquer disease, reduce food shortages, etc., these major problems might be solved more quickly.

Exit Routes The planned means by which investors in illiquid assets intend to become liquid.

Exogenous Variables Random events beyond anyone's control that knock the best laid plans askew.

Exporter One who sells his or her products to customers in foreign countries. An **importer** buys products from foreign countries and resells them in his or her own country. America, for example, exports Country & Western music and imports British rock 'n' roll. In their prime, the Beatles' music was Britain's largest export product.

Facilities Management A customer-financed business whereby an entrepreneur manages a customer's facility, using its building, equipment, personnel and budget. H. Ross Perot created this entrepreneurial solution with Electronic Data Systems Corp. in 1964.

Fasttrack(er) Someone in a hurry to reach his or her goals is on a **fast track** or termed a **fasttracker**. Fasttrackers think three promotions in a single year are the minimum they should receive; chairperson of the board in less than a decade is not out of *their* realm of possibility.

FICA Deductions from an employee's paycheck that are put in the social security trust fund (administered by the Federal government), to be paid back to the employee in equal monthly installments when he or she retires at age 65.

Financial Instruments Stocks, bonds, leases and other vehicles used to inject money into a company.

First Mortgage (see **Mortgage**)

Fiscal The year end a company or government uses, mainly for tax reasons, which may or may not be the calendar year.

A "fiscally responsible person" is generally regarded to have a serious concern for "bottom line results." However, the use of two idioms in the same sentence is usually indicative of BS.

Fixed Costs (see **Overhead**)

Fixed Income Money received by people who no longer earn an income from their skills or time, but rather receive it from pension funds, social security benefits and interest on bonds.

Fixed Rate (see **Floating Rate**)

Flat Sales, earnings, profits, etc. are said to be flat if over a period of time—six months, a year, etc.—they neither go up nor down. A mature product—one that is no longer growing in sales but isn't declining either—is, for example, said to have **flat sales**. This should signal management that an upgraded model or new product is needed.

Float A check drawn on a bank is a promise to pay. If a car manufacturer mails a check to its steel supplier, the money it promises is, for a few days at least, neither in the manufacturer's nor the supplier's bank accounts. It is floating in space.

Floating Rate An interest rate that is tied to the **prime rate** and goes up or down as the prime goes up or down. Should a lender offer you money at a floating rate, be sure to ask in return for a **ceiling** (a cap on how *high* the interest rate can float). If the lender agrees, he may only do so if you agree to a **floor** (a limit on how *low* the rate can sink). An interest rate that does not float is a **fixed rate**.

Floor (see **Floating Rate**)

Focus Group Prior to introducing a new product into the marketplace, a group of potential customers are called together (and usually paid a small amount of money) to test it. Their comments on its shape, size, feel, look, packaging, etc. are solicited and then analyzed.

One of my college jobs was in market research. I was fortunate to observe a focus group made up of male beer drinkers who were testing Miller High Life beer. One of the group said, "Because the glass is clear, it seems like this is a light beer; not filling." That was in 1963. Could that comment have led to the new product that was soon to take over America—Lite Beer? I wonder.

Foreclose If the owner of property defaults on the mortgage loan on the property, the bank (or other lender) may foreclose on it—taking back the title, selling it at auction, recouping the money owed on the loan and, if anything is left, remitting it to the previous owner.

Foundation A not-for-profit corporation set up by wealthy families or charitable organizations to dispense the income from its assets to causes that it considers worthy and to invest the **principal** of the assets in attractive investments. The Ford Foundation exists, for example, to reinvest the fruits of Henry Ford's entrepreneurial achievements in future generations of problem-solving ideas.

Franchise In the broadest sense, a franchise is an asset that is replicable in a multitude of regional locations and that will generate revenues for the **franchisee**—the person who buys the rights to make, use and sell the asset in each location. The person selling those rights and also making money on each location is the **franchisor**. Frequently the franchise is a formula for providing a service, such as Arthur Murray Dance Studios or H & R Block Tax Centers. In other instances, it is a restaurant concept, like McDonald's, Roy Rogers, etc., complete with design, menu and staff training manuals.

One of the keys to successfully selling and managing a franchise is to make the formula goof-proof at the franchisees' locations. The staff training manual and the franchisee's operations manual must be carefully written. Further, the asset/formula that is franchised must be something that people want and need locally, something they cannot otherwise purchase save for the existence of the franchise in their community.

Free Market Have you noticed that in any conversation involving two or more people, one person is usually "selling" (describing, persuading, informing) and the other "buying" (listening, commenting, requesting clarification)? This is a market, albeit one of ideas. And it is free as long as both parties are able to speak freely and without fear of government censure.

The same concept applies to goods and services. As long as a person can open a store or booth to sell a product to other people without having to hurdle regulation, licensing or other barriers, then that market is free. The opposite of a free market is a **regulated market**, such as that which exists for pharmaceutical products, stocks and bonds, health care, insurance and similar goods and services. Although the United States has fewer regulated markets than most other countries, many U. S. goods and services are still heavily regulated by Federal, state and local governments.

Fungible Exchangeable, liquifiable, tradeable or having a propinquity for liquidity.

Futures Contract That which is bought or sold in commodity trading, a futures contract gives its holder the right to receive a quantity of a commodity—gold, silver, pork bellies, orange juice, etc.—at an agreed-upon price on a specific future date.

General Partner (see **Partnership**)

Gift A solution to a problem that an entrepreneur conceives, creates and conveys...if he or she believes it will be reciprocated. If a society has an operating Law of Reciprocity, gift giving will be encouraged and enhanced. Free societies operate with this Law in operation; totalitarian societies do not. Many gift givers in free societies have escaped the tyranny of totalitarian societies where their gifts would not have been reciprocated. As a consequence, it is probably true that the need to give gifts is biological.

GNP (See **Gross National Product**)

Go Public When a new or rapidly-emerging company begins to achieve success in marketing its innovative product or service, its founder(s) frequently raise expansion capital by selling a portion of the ownership of the company to the public. In so doing, the ownership that remains in the entrepreneur's hands and those of his or her early investors has a value placed on it—the price paid by public investors. This price per share of ownership, when multiplied by the number of shares of common stock held by the founders, frequently represents a considerable amount of wealth. As a result, "going public" is frequently synonymous with achieving wealth.

Bill Gates, founder of Microsoft, which licenses IBM, Apple and other personal computer manufactures to use its software, is a perfect example. Bill was just 29 years old when, in 1986, he decided to take his very successful company public; when the dust cleared, his remaining shares of Microsoft were worth $1 billion. In 1988, Gates sold a few thousand shares for $23 million in cash to diversify his estate, but his remaining shares were still worth over $1 billion.

Grace Period A period of time during

which a lender will forego interest payments.

Greenmail (see **Break-up Value**)

Gross National Product (GNP) The sum of all the revenues of all the businesses in a country, this is clearly a difficult number to measure, since the revenues of so many separate businesses—not all of whom may even wish to provide their true revenues—need to be calculated.

Nevertheless, GNP is a determining factor in analyzing whether a particular country's economy is growing. As such, it is a number that is heavily relied on, particularly changes that occur in its month-to-month calculation.

(If California were a country rather than a state, it would have the ninth-largest GNP of any country in the world—greater than Belgium, for example, and fast approaching that of the United Kingdom!)

Gross Profit Margin The ratio derived by dividing total revenues into the **gross profit** (revenues less **cost of goods sold**). The higher a product's gross profit margin, the greater the value perceived for the product by the receivers. Unique, non-duplicable and elegant solutions have high gross profit margins. Standard, non-unique products have low gross profit margins. Polaroid film, for example, has a much higher gross profit margin than does film for non-instant photography.

Growth Fund A mutual fund whose managers invest in stocks of companies whose earnings growth has exceeded the rate of other companies'.

Guarantee A promise to pay the obligation of a borrower when it comes due.

Hero Someone who has intentionally taken a large step—one far beyond the capacities of most people—in solving a problem that affects a large number of people. America's hero is the entrepreneur.

High Technology Company A company whose products are designed to exert control over matter, energy or information. These include, for example, products spun off of the three most important inventions of the past 25 years—the microchip, the satellite and recombinant DNA—such as the personal computer, cable television and numerous life-saving pharmaceuticals.

Hypothesis An idea that sounds good on paper but requires scientific research to make it a theory or law, an event that repeats itself every time in the same way. Although my Three Rules of Entrepreneurship, for example, sound good, they require serious research to make them as strong and reliable as the Law of Gravity.

Illiquid Assets (see **Assets**)

Importer (see **Exporter**)

Income The fee, commission, royalty, bonus or salary that one is paid for his or her time or skill. A person's income is greater if his or her skill is unique and the audience for it is large. For example, Bill Cosby earns income in the neighborhood of $100 million per annum. Jack Nicholson comes in at about 10% of that amount and Oprah Winfrey at a reputed $8 million per annum. The yearly income of the average American worker is $22,000—.022% of Mr. Cosby's annual haul

Income Fund A mutual fund whose objective is to maintain the safety of its investors' money while attempting to deliver to them the highest possible income from dividends and interest.

Income Tax A fee charged by Federal and state governments that is used to provide us with a variety of services, such as defense, street lights, highways, water treatment, etc. Excessively high income taxes remove from society the disposable income needed to encourage investments. England and France produce very few entrepreneurial successes because their income taxes are excessively high. The Italian government collects less income taxes and, as a result, entrepreneurship thrives there.

Indexes Statistical measurements of investment vehicles wherein price is charted over time, minute-by-minute or day-by-day, to enable an investor to compare how the performance of his or her portfolio compares with the norm. Well-known indexes include the Dow Jones Industrial Average and Standard and Poors 500.

Investors can now "bet" on the rise or fall of a variety of security indexes, much as they "bet" on individual stocks, by buying and selling portfolios made up of the stocks in a variety of indexes.

Inflation The result of too much money chasing too few goods and services. When the government pays farmers not to produce and poor people not to work, it pumps money into the marketplace without corresponding productivity and the result is the bidding up of prices for goods and services.

Initial Public Offering (IPO) (see Public Offering)

Innovation Something new and different that, when introduced into a marketplace, causes changes in thinking, replacement of the old with the new and economic growth.

Insider Information Information obtained about a company—such as knowledge about a major contract award—which, if used as the basis for a decision to buy or sell the stock prior to the company announcing it to the general public, is considered an ethical violation. Similarly, paying someone to obtain privileged information about a company in order to profit on its stock price is illegal.

Installment Payment A loan may be structured so that the principal and appropriate interest are paid back in fixed intervals (installments) over time. Auto loans and other high-ticket (high-priced) items are frequently sold on this basis.

Insurance The purchase of risk. Any risk can be insured at a price, but the most common are the tragic emergencies such as untimely death or accident. Insurance companies receive payment in advance for a service they may or may not have to provide later. As a result, they amass huge piles of cash. This cash is then invested in or loaned to companies seeking to expand. Trends or laws that restrict insurance companies—such as litigation to obtain huge rewards from juries who like to sock it to the "rich" insurance companies—restrict the circle of giving.

Inventory A merchant's or company's store of goods available for sale.

Investment The conversion of disposable income into appreciable assets, which provides growth or start-up capital for entrepreneurs and owners of assets seeking to gain liquidity. Having disposable income to invest is the result of developing a marketable skill or creating wealth or partial wealth through entrepreneurship, previous investments, savings or inheritance.

Investment Bank (see Banks)

Investment Tax Credit A deduction from one's income taxes that the Federal government permits from time to time to encourage the purchase of equipment or the construction of buildings. It has never been used by legislators to spur the creation of life-saving technologies, for example, which is part of the reason why real estate development companies outnumber microbiology firms.

IPO (see Public Offering)

Joint Venture A business combination in which two or more parties each contribute an asset that the other(s) needs and which benefits the combined businesses. For example, if you developed a "solar car"—one that would be powered by the sun (free energy) and, therefore, never needed gasoline—you would require a substantial amount of capital just to produce the cars in quantity. While you may be prepared to give up a certain portion of the ownership in your new company to raise that capital, you may not want to also incur the expense of setting up a dealership organization to sell and service your new cars, since that would require raising even more capital and further dilute your stock ownership. Instead, you may consider setting up a joint venture with a truck or motorcycle company that already has such a national dealership network in place—they agree to sell and service your cars, you agree to provide them with the cars and service training manuals.

Junk Bond A bond featuring an unusually high interest rate, frequently unsecured, sometimes convertible or with warrants attached, all of which reflect the corporation's uncertain means of repayment. Junk bonds are primarily used by raiders to buy large corporations—rich in assets but undervalued in the market due to nonaggressive management—in a take-over technique called a **leveraged buy-out** (or **LBO**). Insurance companies and pension funds may buy junk bonds when they feel the higher interest rates warrant the greater risk.

Junk Mail (see **List Rental**)

Launch The "lift off" of a new business; the moment in time when an entrepreneur begins to build his or her prototype or design his or her new service.

Launch Plan The written statement by an entrepreneur of how he or she intends to get the new business off the ground. This includes details on the people that need to be involved, the physical location and description of the company's offices or space, the components needed to produce the product, the method of marketing it and delivering it to customers, etc.

LBO (see **Leveraged Buy-Out**)

Leverage Derived from "lever," a crowbar-like stick which, when positioned on one stone can lift a much larger stone out of the ground. Thus leverage is the activity of moving something big by using something small. For example, you may have only $20,000 in the bank, but with that amount, you can buy a $100,000 house by borrowing (leveraging) on the asset (the house) that you are buying.

You can use "communications leverage" similarly. Your new store on Main Street, for example, may not be able to afford paid newspaper advertising. But if you are able to convince one of the paper's reporters or editors to print an article about your store, you may well wind up attracting as many or more customers than an ad would have pulled in—at zero cost. Restaurants are only one prime example of businesses that rely heavily on (free) newspaper reviews and (free) word-of-mouth advertising as primary marketing tools.

Leveraged Buy-Out (LBO) The buy-out of a corporation in which the purchase price is raised by obtaining loans (frequently

junk bonds) using the corporation's own assets as collateral. Once the buy-out is effected (by paying the selling stockholders cash raised from the junk bond sale), the take-over entrepreneurs break up the corporation and repay the bonds immediately or run the corporation more aggressively to generate the cash to repay the bonds.

Liabilities Obligations to pay for goods or services delivered or for money loaned.

Lien An evidence of indebtedness similar to a mortgage. If you try to sell an asset that has a lien on it, the proceeds of the sale must first go to pay the lienholder. Liens are recorded in the County Clerk's office in the county where the asset is located.

Liquid Assets (see **Assets**)

Limited Partner An investor in a partnership whose liability is limited to the amount of his investment. A limited partner is similar to a stockholder: Both investors have very little to say about the day-to-day running of the company in which they have invested.

List Rental Catalogues and other **junk mail** that pile up in your mailbox are the result of your name being rented to direct marketing firms. How does your name get on a list in the first place? All too easily. If you order products through the mail, have a credit card, write anyone for information on anything, or even have a driver's license, your name is on somebody's list. And that person can make money renting that list to others interested in reaching you and consumers like you. The meteoric rise of shop-by-phone and shop-at-home services have made mailing lists more valuable than ever. When you start your own business, guard your customer lists carefully—they could be worth significant income to your business through list rental.

Long Position To own an investment, in contrast with a **short position**, which is to have sold an investment.

Loopholes Favors in the tax laws written into legislation by Congressmen to support industries in their states.

Margin The ratios derived when revenues are divided into a variety of other numbers on a company's operating statement. **Gross profit margin**, for example, is the ratio of Revenues less Cost of Goods Sold (Gross Profit) divided by Revenues. For example, if your gross revenues are $500,000 and cost of goods sold is $200,000, your gross profit margin is 60% ($300,000 or $500,000 - $200,000)/$500,000). Pretax margin is Net Profits Before Taxes divided by Revenues. (In the above example, expenses may result in a net profit of $50,000, making the pre-tax (or *net* profit) margin 10% ($50,000/$500,000).

These and similar ratios measure a company's efficiency.

Margin (buying on) The percentage of the investor's own funds needed to purchase securities or commodities, set by law though different depending on the particular type of item being purchased. The remainder of the purchase price is borrowed from a broker and the investor pays interest on it.

Margin Account A brokerage account in which the stockbroker allows an investor to deposit only a percentage of the funds needed to purchase securities, with the remainder borrowed from the brokerage house.

Margin Call If the price of a stock an investor has "bought on margin" drops sharply, the broker may require him or her to deposit more cash into the brokerage account. If that is not possible, the brokerage firm will sell the stock and repay itself the money it lent the investor before depositing anything left from the sale's proceeds to the investor's account.

Market That arena in which the business game is played. Entrepreneurs try to win by selling a product or service for more than it costs to produce and deliver. The buyer tries to find and purchase those products and services that mitigate or reduce the costs incurred by certain problems.

Marketing Channel The "highway" down which your company drives to convey its solution to the market. If you have a retail store, then the marketing channel is walk-in or drive-up customers. But if you wish to

begin selling the store's inventory to people who live too far away to walk or drive to your store, you might prepare a catalog, rent appropriate mailing lists and start mailing catalogs to potential customers, thus entering an alternative "highway"—direct mail marketing.

Market Driven A product or service that needs very little advertising or promotion to encourage people to buy it is driven by the unequivocal need for it. A baseball pennant race makes seats in the contenders' stadium market driven. But a losing team must use hat days, glove days and other promotions to drive people into the ballpark.

Marketplace An open-air market, the counter of a fast-food restaurant, the coin slot in a washing machine, a theater box office or a touch-tone phone used to place a credit card order—in short, a place in time and space where a buyer and seller come together to exchange a product or service for cash (or a promise to pay an agreed price, in cash, sometime in the future).

Market Share Anything worth doing is worth duplicating. This basic business axiom means that all innovative products and services (not introduced or controlled by a monopolist) will be copied, imitated or, as they say in the garment industry, "knocked off." As a result, many competitors will enter the field and compete vigorously for a larger percentage or share of the total market. In a large consumer market, like that for bottled soft drinks, Coke's gain of even a single percentage point over Pepsi's market share may be worth tens of millions of dollars.

Mergers and Acquisitions It is frequently quicker—and almost always less expensive—to acquire (buy) an existing company than to start one from scratch. The difference between a merger and an acquisition is that the former requires that you already own a company (with which to merge your newly purchased one).

Mob Appeal (see **Supply and Demand**)

Model Another word for prototype, draft,

first version of or early rendering.

Mortgage Evidence of security, such as a lien, that a lender receives when it provides a loan for the purchase of real property—land, buildings or homes. A **second mortgage** is a second lien on real property and it ranks behind a **first mortgage.** When the owner of real property sells property that has mortgages on it filed with the County Clerk, they must generally be satisfied before the seller receives his cash. The exception: If a mortgage is **assumable,** a buyer may purchase real property, leave the mortgage in place and simply continue paying it off. A **construction loan** is provided by a lender to someone who is building a house, building or warehouse. When such construction is completed, the construction loan converts into a mortgage loan.

Municipal Bonds ("Munis") Evidences of indebtedness issued by municipalities to build sewers, streets, water treatment plants and the like. They can be secured or unsecured; interest payments are tax exempt to the lender. Retired individuals are frequent investors in "munis."

Murphy's Law "Anything that can go wrong *will* go wrong."

Murphy's Second Law "When things go wrong, they will always do so at the worst possible time." Entrepreneurs heed both the first and second laws.

Mutual Fund A pile of cash entrusted to an experienced investment manager (or managers) by millions of individual investors for the purpose of careful and intelligent selection of stocks and bonds that meet the individuals' investment objectives.

Near-Liquid (see **Assets**)

Negotiate To bargain with another person in order to arrive at terms and conditions satisfactory to both sides.

Net Worth A figure derived by subtracting all of one's liabilities from all of one's assets.

New Issues When companies sell their common stock to the public for the first time, the offering is known as a **new issue.** Many new issues are from entrepreneurial

companies with exciting futures, and their stock prices go up rapidly. Some, however, are shares in terribly small companies that would go broke except for the emergency capital the new issue generates.

Non-Durable Products or Goods (see **Consumer Products**)

Options Account (see **Brokerage Account**)

Overdraft A condition in your bank account wherein the amount of checks presented at your bank exceeds the cash on hand to honor them.

Overhead The fixed costs of doing business; the amount of money a business will spend each month whether or not it produces any product, delivers any services or generates any revenues. These costs—utilities, insurance, salaries for clerical people, telephone, postage, couriers and the like—usually do not increase or decrease very much from one month to the next (which is why they are also called **fixed costs**).

Override The commission or royalty paid to an agent who generates a sale, brings an actor into a film or introduces a lender or investor to a borrower. In the Middle East, "baksheesh" is the word for override. In certain less-than-legal circles, it is called "juice" or "vigorish" (abbreviated to "vig").

Over-the-Counter Common stocks of new issues and other small companies are traded over-the-counter. Brokers can see the prices offered to buy or sell the stock by punching in the stock's symbol on their Quotron machines and phoning the market maker in the stock to place their order at or near the price thus indicated.

Par The face value of a bond.

Par Value The price one derives when the number of shares authorized by a new corporation are divided into the initial capital investment. It has almost no practical value.

Partnership An entity created to develop property or a new technology or to carry out a project in a proscribed number of years. Whereas corporations do not have a fixed term, partnerships do: They are meant to end when the project is over. The manager of a partnership is the **general**

partner who is personally liable for all obligations that the partnership incurs. The investors in a partnership are known as limited partners. If a project expects to incur losses in its early years, the partnership structure is frequently preferred, because the investors can take the losses personally, thereby reducing their individual income taxes.

Passbook Savings Account An interest-bearing bank account in which deposits, withdrawals and interest are entered in the customer's record-keeping journal (**passbook**).

Passive Income (see **Passive Investment**)

Passive Investment When an investor assumes absolutely no role in the company or project in which he or she has invested, the investment is **passive**. This has important income tax connotations, because losses derived from passive investments may only be deducted, in most cases, from income derived from passive investments (i.e., not salaries or other compensation).

Patent A government grant to an inventor for a stated period of time conferring to him or her the exclusive right to make, use and sell the invention during that period. Protecting your invention with a patent requires expert legal advice, as may your attempt to protect an invention after its conception but prior to receipt of a patent. (*See also* **Copyright**)

Payroll The list of persons that a company employs with the amount of payment due each, along with payments for taxes, social security benefits and health insurance withheld (**deductions**).

PBX The central nervous system of a large telephone system.

Pension Funds Large corporations, unions and government agencies set aside a small percentage of their employees' or members' salaries or dues and invest this pile of cash in order to provide retirement benefits to these people. **Pension funds** presently have more than $3 trillion in their coffers, making them a very important force in the securities markets. Pension funds have provided over $9 billion to venture capital funds that invest in entrepreneurial companies and over $120 billion to help takeover entrepreneurs buy control of large corporations using leveraged buy-out financing techniques. Pension fund managers are governed by rules established by the U.S. Department of Labor.

Perceived Value If people with a problem or need are offered a solution and are willing to pay a price for that solution, then they perceive value in it. If they do not perceive value, then they will not buy it at any price. If many people perceive value in the solution, their payment for it will lead to entrepreneurial wealth.

PERT Chart <u>P</u>lanning, <u>E</u>valuation and <u>R</u>esearch <u>T</u>ool is the technical meaning of "PERT." It is used by different kinds of people, from missile designers to entrepreneurs, to plot against time all of the steps necessary to get from the conception of the idea to a working model, then to assign these steps to whomever will be responsible to complete them in the time period indicated on the chart.

Point-of-Sale A form of advertising that occurs at the cash register or in front of the buyer when he or she is selecting products, such as advertisements on shopping carts, large end-of-aisle product displays or the magazine and candy racks right at the cash register.

Pork Barrel A government appropriation or policy that provides money for local needs, invariably designed to ingratiate legislators with their voters. The space centers in Houston, Texas, and Huntsville, Alabama, for example, did not simply land there randomly. Alabama and Texas legislators undoubtedly swapped favors with other Senators and Congressmen to garner these cash cows for their states. Federal grants for dams and bridges are other notorious pork barrel appropriations.

Portfolio The securities owned by a person or company for investment purposes.

Preferred Stock Stock issued by a corporation that has a claim superior to that of common stock to dividends of the corporation and on the assets of the corporation in the event of its liquidation.

Pretax Margin (see **Margin**)

Price/Earnings (P/E) Ratio A method used by common stock investors to measure the public's expectation for growth for a company's earnings. The higher the price/earnings ratio, the greater the public's expectation of future earnings. Two companies, each with $1.00 per share of earnings, might sell at $40 and $15 per share respectively. The market perceives greater value for the future results of the 40x p/e company than for the 15x company. As you know, I believe that a high stock price (p) reflects the size of the problem that the high p/e company's management says they can solve. In fact, for companies devoted to solving large problems ("Big P" companies), there are frequently no earnings (e) at all. P/e ratios are key tools in making common stock investment decisions.

Price Sensitive Readily or acutely affected by minute changes in price, such that sales of the product rise or fall sharply if the price changes even very slightly.

Prime Rate The rate of interest that large money center banks charge their best customers. Despite this definition, if the prime rate is 9.5% and IBM Corp., with $100 million on deposit at a New York City bank, asked to borrow $150 million at 8.75%, the bank would say, "How soon do you want it?" So although the prime rate is a stated rate and changes in it send ripples through financial markets, some borrowers can pay less than prime at a bank. And many borrowers can pay less than prime by selling bonds to the public or placing them privately with insurance companies or pension funds.

Primitive Naturalness, man-made, earthy. The more primitive a work of art or antique and the less available its supply, the greater its value. This is my hypothesis which I express as:

Value = $\frac{\text{Primitivity}}{\text{Supply}}$

Someday I will test this hypothesis and then know which art or antiques to buy

today to achieve maximum future capital appreciation.

Priority Lien A secured position on an asset that is senior to (has "priority" over) all other liens.

Problem A need which in the eyes of an entrepreneur represents an opportunity. The larger the problem that the entrepreneur determines that he can solve, the greater the value of the company. This is Silver's Rule of the Big P.

Product Something produced by labor and/or money.

Product Line A series of functionally similar items produced by labor and/or money that relate to each other but come in different sizes, models, price ranges, speeds, materials and/or colors.

Productivity Continuous activity that causes the creation of products and services that have perceived value to a large group of people. The greater the productivity in a community, the greater its circle of giving.

Professional Someone who provides a service that is not regulated by the government.

Profit The surplus money left to a producer of goods or services after all expenditures are deducted from income. A company unable to earn a profit will not long survive. Profitability is achieved by companies whose products or services have perceived value, that is, solve problems for people at a price below the receiver's cost of the problem.

Profit Margin (see **Margin**)

Progress Payment A form of paying for a product or service over the time period in which it is produced, installed and tested, frequently required when selling new and untried products and services. A typical progress payment arrangement would require payment of one third of the agreed price when production begins, one third upon delivery and the final third after 60 days of testing on the customer's premises.

Proprietary Unique, non-duplicable, *sui generis*. A solution to a problem must either be proprietary or non-duplicable to have a perceived value in excess of the receiver's cost of the problem. Patent, trademark or copyright protection makes a product proprietary.

Prospectus The offering circular prepared by the entrepreneur's lawyer to enable him or her to sell stocks, bonds or partnership interests in his or her company. The prospectus is a protective document that enables the company to comply with Federal and state securities regulations.

Protection According to a certain group of sub-legal businessmen, the name for weekly or monthly bribes solicited from other businesses to ensure their "protection" from vandalism, organized theft, union agitation, etc.

Prototype A model from which a final product can be made.

Prudent Many investors and lenders attempt to act in this manner at all times by obtaining as much information as they possibly can about a candidate for investment *before* they invest. To do less than act prudently with one's pile of cash, no matter what its size, is to eventually lose it.

Publicly-Held A company is generally publicly-held if it is owned by at least 500 owners (individuals, other corporations, pension funds, etc.) who can exchange their evidence of ownership—their common stock certificates—for cash. Such companies are regulated by both Federal and state securities laws.

Public Offering To sell shares in one's company to public investors. This is normally done through an investment bank, but there are several instances of self-underwritten **initial public offerings (IPOs)**. Control Data Corp. began by underwriting its own public offering. Its value today is approximately $1 billion. The first shares were sold at Mrs. Strandy's Coffee Shop in St. Paul, Minnesota and at the Parker House Coffee Shop in Mendota, Minnesota. Those investors made several million dollars on their investment.

Purchase and Sale Agreement A legal document prepared by one's attorney when one purchases a company or a significant asset. It sets forth the price, the terms and every known fact—most particularly the liabilities—about the asset you are buying.

Quotron A CRT terminal that sits on a stockbroker's desk and enables him or her to see the bid and asked prices of all publicly-traded stocks. Bond traders use **Telerate terminals** for the same purpose.

Raider A person who takes control of a company by unfriendly acquisition, fires the old top management team and sells some of the company's assets to repay the debt that he incurred to take over the company in the first place.

Rate of Return The most common way of comparing one investment to another—calculating its yield or annual percentage return of cash over the period of time during which the investor has no control over the money. Some collectibles and investments boast rates of return in excess of 100% per year; savings accounts generally yield from 5% to 8% per year.

Real Estate Appraisal An estimate of the value of real estate prepared by a licensed appraiser. Lenders rely heavily on real estate appraisals prior to making a real estate loan. Appraisals are fairly inexpensive and one should be obtained before you purchase any property or assume any mortgage.

Realized Gain What you get is what it's worth: Although an asset may appreciate in value "on paper," you only make a profit on its purchase when you sell it and receive cash. If you cannot sell it, your gain is unrealized and its value may decline considerably.

Recession As one humorist put it, a recession is when your friend's father is out of work; a depression is when *your* father is out of work. A national or regional recession is a period of high unemployment and low productivity, marked by numerous failing companies, stepped-up bank foreclosures and steep price drops on expensive consumer products like cars, airplane seats and designer fashions.

Reciprocity The law of reciprocity governs human behavior. People will solve problems for one another if they believe that, in so doing, they will receive rewards of sufficient value to offset the costs of producing the solution. A society that lacks a mechanism for rewarding problem solvers will eventually erode economically, because solutions are innovations and innovations create an ever-expanding circle of giving.

Record Date When a company announces its intent to pay a dividend, the recipients of those dividends are the investors who owned the stock as of a certain date. The date after this **record date** generally sees a decline in the price of the company's stock, because the stock is trading **"ex-dividend,"** which means that stockholders who buy the stock from that day forth will *not* receive the previously-announced dividend.

Regulated Market (see **Free Market**)

Research and Development Limited Partnership An investment in a partnership to conduct research and development on a new technological innovation that may have commercial value in the future. The losses incurred in doing the research may be applied against your passive income—that is, income from passive investments such as bond interest or rental income on a property that you do not live in full-time.

Return on Investment The measurement of comparative worth between two or more investment choices. *(See also* **Yield***)*

Revenue Payment received in exchange for delivering a product or service; sale.

Risk Averse Attempting to avoid risks as much as you can by insuring against them or assigning them to those who specialize in handling them. Risk aversion or risk management is central to being both a good investor and a competent entrepreneur.

Roll (a loan) A borrower who persuades his or her lender to extend or renew a loan beyond its due date is said to roll the loan.

Roll-Up When a partnership succeeds at developing a commercializable product or project and the general partner can foresee a very large future stream of earnings, he will announce to the limited partners that their partnership interests will be exchanged for stock or notes in the parent corporation or an affiliated corporation. This allows the partners to realize a capital gain (from the sale of this stock) greater than the projected income stream.

Royalty A payment expressed as "percentage of revenues" made by a licensee to a licensor—inventor, playwright, author, musician—over time for assigning the rights to his or her invention, play, book or song.

Rule 144 A regulation established by the Securities and Exchange Commission (SEC) that prohibits entrepreneurs and their investors from selling their stock to the public until they have owned it for at least two full years and only then if it is registered with the SEC.

Salary A periodic payment made to employees in consideration for their time and/or skill.

Sales Curve When sales figures are displayed on a monthly or yearly graph, they tend to flow upward in the early stage of a company's existence, level off as the market for the product becomes saturated, and eventually decline. Over time, this forms a curved line.

Savings Account (see **Passbook Savings Account**)

Savings Bond To convince people to loan it money, the United States Government sells savings bonds to individuals in denominations as small as $25.00. The interest rate is lower than other investment vehicles, because savings bonds are generally given as gifts to children who (until this book got into their hands) didn't know the difference between various savings and investment vehicles.

SDM (see **Solution Delivery Method**)

SDM Sub-Set The twelve standard SDMs (Solution Delivery Methods) are the means by which a solution is conveyed to people who need it. SDM sub-sets are ancillary (additional) cash flow-generating methods that "feed" customers back into the primary SDM. Let me explain that mouthful: Newsletter publishing (prepaid subscription SDM) entrepreneurial companies, for example, generally hold seminars for their subscribers. Such seminars not only generate cash themselves, they also give the company additional opportunities for the sale of even more products and services (books, consulting, audio and/or video tapes of seminar speakers and presentations, etc.). The seminar and other marketing channels that emerge from it are SDM sub-sets.

Seasonality A product or service that sells better in certain seasons or months than others.

Second Mortgage (see **Mortgage**)

Secured Bond (see **Bonds**)

Secured Loan An indebtedness backed up by a lien or mortgage on a tangible asset.

Securities Investment instruments—common stocks, bonds, debentures, partnership interests, mutual fund units and other such evidences of trust. When an entrepreneur issues a **security** to an investor in exchange for his or her money, he pledges that he will act in good faith to make that security valuable.

Securities and Exchange Commission (**SEC**) An agency of the Federal government that regulates the sale of securities to the public. The SEC was formed in 1933 to protect public investors from egregious promoters.

Seller Financing When the person or company selling an asset provides money to the buyer in the form of an installment loan, effectively funding its own sale.

Share A unit of common or preferred stock, expressed as one or more **shares of stock.**

Shortfall A condition of not having as much as you'd planned, such as that which exists when Monday's cash receipts can't cover the overdraft in your checking account created when you mailed out checks to pay bills due Monday.

Short Position To sell one's ownership of stocks, bonds, options, commodities, etc.

Snob Appeal (see **Supply and Demand**)

Social Security A form of retirement payment made by the Federal Government to people who have been employed. Such payments are administered by the Social Security Administration which, unlike well-run insurance companies, does not have enough money in reserve to meet its monthly payments to beneficiaries.

Solution A product or service that mitigates a problem. If the problem is big—that is, shared by many people—and exists in a society where the Law of Reciprocity operates, the solution, if conveyed to the marketplace by an entrepreneurial company, is wealth producing.

Solution Delivery Method (**SDM**) One of the twelve means by which an entrepreneurial company can convey its solution to people with a problem. A company will frequently use more than one SDM, plus a variety of SDM sub-sets, to maximize cash flow and minimize the need for venture capital.

Sophisticated A definition created by the SEC (Securities and Exchange Commission) to describe a person they deem capable of making entrepreneurial investments based on his or her income, net worth and previous experience in similar investments. No other market for investments is regulated in this manner.

Split (stock) When the price of a company's stock rises to a point where the cost of 100 of its shares is prohibitive to individual investors, the company's board of directors will frequently vote to issue every stockholder "x" number of additional shares for every one share of stock he or she presently owns. If x equals 1, for example, the effect is to double the number of shares that people own and cut the price of a single share in half. Stocks splits need not be "1 for 1;" they can be 3 to 1, 3 to 2, 10 to 1, 100 to 1 or even reverse ratios, where the goal is to *raise* the price of the company's stock.

Sponsorship To answer the question frequently asked by investors in the affirmative: "Who says you're any good?"

Start-Up The stage of evolution in the life

of a young company *after* its product or service has been developed but *before* the company has achieved sales.

Start-Up Money Cash required at the start-up stage to produce the product or package the service so that customers can determine if they need it.

Stockbroker A person who is trained to buy and sell stocks, bonds and other instruments for investors. Stockbrokers are licensed by their trade association, the National Association of Securities Dealers, and regulated by a Federal agency, the Securities and Exchange Commission (SEC).

Stock Certificate An engraved piece of paper—high fiber content, difficult to counterfeit—that evidences one's ownership of shares of a company's common or preferred stock.

Stock Exchange The physical place where the business of buying and selling securities takes place. There are stock exchanges in major countries throughout the world. The two best known are probably the New York and American Stock Exchanges.

Stock Market The place where the buying and selling of stocks takes place. Prior to the invention of the telephone, the market was a physical site where buyers and sellers came together physically to buy and sell stocks.

Stock Option The privilege of buying a company's stock at a price far below market value, generally awarded to employees for dedicated and competent service.

Stock or Bond Power A means of protecting lost or stolen stock or bond certificates, in that such certificates cannot be sold for the holder unless he or she has also executed a **stock or bond power.**

Stock Tables The financial pages of the daily newspapers list information about stock, bond, option, commodity and other prices (as well as a variety of indexes and interest rates) so that investors can make buy, hold or sell decisions. Baseball managers use box scores in much the same fashion, though there is far less data to consider in selecting the best nine players

for tomorrow's game than that needed to maximize the rate of return of one's portfolio.

Strategic Plan A series of maneuvers that a company expects will help it reach its goals or objectives.

Stretch-Out To own or assume an obligation to pay (or a loan) and convince the holder of the obligation to permit you more time to repay it. To do this two or more times is to "stretch the stretch-out."

Subchapter S Corporation (see **Corporations**)

Supply & Demand Demand is need—the evidence in a marketplace of a problem in search of a solution. Needs are fulfilled by sellers who are, if the demand is large enough, entrepreneurs. So Supply is the solution to the need. The Law of Supply and Demand governs the marketplace and determines the price of the product that is demanded. **Snob appeal** and mob appeal are two forms of demand that drive up the price of a product or service, particularly if its supply is limited.

Sweat Equity The substitution of labor for capital. Karl Marx had lots to say about sweat equity.

Takeover To buy a company by raising long-term loans which are secured by the assets of the company, such loans to be repaid by selling off the company's assets or by the company's cash flow. *(See also Leveraged Buy-Out)*

Target Market The primary consumer group at which a company aims its products or services.

Tax Exempt A bond or investment instrument on which the interest is tax free to the lender or investor. Legislators have made laws identifying one or another form of investment as tax exempt in order to stimulate money to move in that direction, such as municipal projects. It's called making the playing field uneven. The same result could be achieved by letting the marketplace set interest rates or yields higher or lower depending on the attractiveness of the loan or investment.

Tax Shelter A form of investment, typically a partnership, that generates losses for the investors, "sheltering" from taxes all or a significant portion of the money invested.

Telerate Terminal (see **Quotron**)

Tip A rumor or suggestion given by one investor to another that a certain investment is going to appreciate in value in a short period of time.

Trade (securities) A buy or sell transaction, followed by the physical delivery of the money and securities.

Trade Journals Newspapers or magazines that report information about an industry and run advertisements placed by members of the industry or by companies that sell products or services to its members. The first entrepreneur to create wealth in a new marketplace is usually the trade journal publisher, because of the enormous need that people in a market have for specific, industry-related information.

Trade Show Most industries hold an annual meeting at which vendors display products, particularly their latest innovations, that would be of interest to the attendees, perhaps their only regular opportunity to meet the manufacturers face-to-face. Computer manufacturers, for example, exhibit all the latest hardware and software at the COMDEX show, among others. A detailed program of seminars, discussions and lectures on industry-related topics—as well as more informal and unscheduled job hunting, investment seeking and partying—is usually part of such shows.

Treasury Bill A loan from a person or company to the Federal government that is due in three, six or nine months.

Treasury Stock The unissued stock in a corporation that is held in abeyance for possible future use in stock splits, for stock options or to make acquisitions.

Trust Reliance on another. Business is based on trust—even a check written out and signed in lieu of cash is a promise to pay. If trust is violated in a marketplace, every buyer would have to use cash and every seller would have to wait an interminable period of time—until the buyer in-

spected his product—to receive payment. The markets for illegal drugs and weapons operate in this manner because criminals do not trust one another. Workers in small, entrepreneurial companies seem to trust each other more than those in large corporations, because everyone in the small company has a "piece of the action" and is working toward a common goal. That is one reason that entrepreneurial companies seem to always beat large corporations at creating innovations, solutions to big problems and significant change.

Turn Over In the United Kingdom, the phrase is used for the word "sales." It literally means the selling of one's inventory in order to buy more goods to sell.

Undercapitalization To have less cash (capital) than a company needs to conduct its business as its management would like.

Unit Trust Another word for mutual fund.

Universe The total number of potential consumers for a product or service.

Unsecured Bond (see **Bonds**)

Usury The practice of charging an illegally high rate of return to unsuspecting or unknowing borrowers. Loan sharks are known for such insane interest rates, sometimes on the order of 10-20%…a week!

Variable Costs Expenses that rise when sales rise and fall when they fall, such as the cost of inventory.

Vendor A merchant or seller.

Venture Capital Investment money that seeks unusually high rates of return by investing in early-stage, innovative companies.

Volume Discount The deduction from the "regular" price that a vendor is willing to give to a consumer who buys a very large quantity of goods or services.

Wall Street Journal The principal trade journal of the securities industry.

Warrants (see **Bonds**)

Working Capital The cash, accounts receivable and inventory, less all current liabilities, that turn over rapidly in a business. Inventory is sold and becomes accounts receivable; accounts receivable are collected and become cash; some of the cash is used to pay for more inventory, some of it for investment in more production capacity.

Work-Out An opportunity to create value where there appears to be an unsalvageable business. Many entrepreneurs have created wealth by **working out** the problems of a tired old company left for dead by its officers and stockholders. A work-out expert has the eye of a painting restorer or a house renovator.

Worst-Case Scenario As Scottish poet Robert Browning put it, "The best-laid plans of mice and men gain aft agley." Planning for the **worst-case scenario** involves the forecasting of the myriad things that can go wrong and upset one's plans. Careful (prudent) managers ask their teammates to plan for the downside so that if chaos and mayhem do indeed occur, the business will be prepared for them.

Yield The return on a loan or investment, usually expressed as a percentage of the amount of the loan or investment per annum.

Yield Curve Interest rates are higher the longer the period of time for which one borrows money. Thus, the Federal government pays perhaps 2% per annum *less* interest on a Treasury bill than it does on a 10-year bond.

Index